IMAGES
of America

MONROE COUNTY

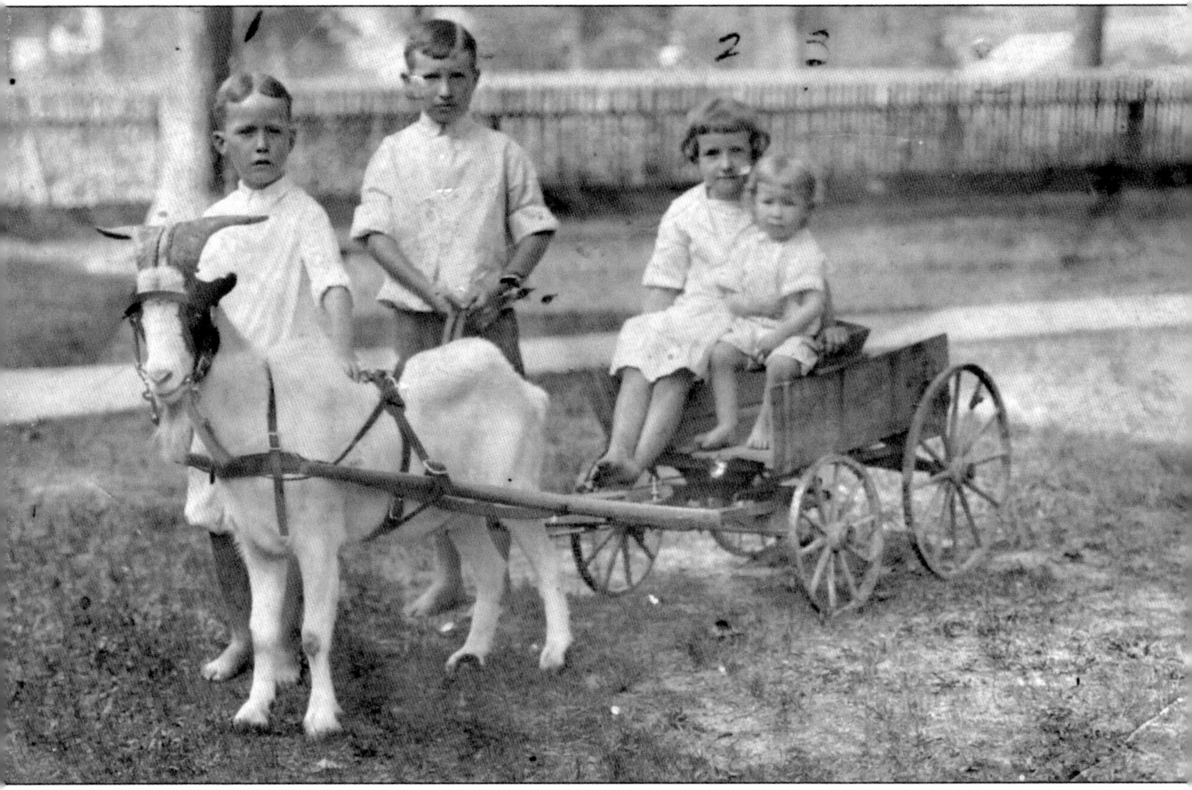

From left to right, James I. Matthews Jr., LeRoy Renfro, Bessie Mae Matthews, and Annie Elliott "Snooks" Matthews pose with LeRoy's goat and cart that he received as a gift from his parents. James Matthews Jr. later became the president of the Bank of Holly Grove, and LeRoy Renfro owned and operated Holly Grove's only theater, the Grove Theater, which began in the silent movie era and continued operation until 1959. (Courtesy of Danyelle McNeill Fletcher.)

On the Cover: The 20-millionth Ford to roll off the assembly line was a 1931 Model A. The Ford Motor Company sent it on a publicity tour during the summer and winter of 1931 with "Twenty Millionth Ford" proudly displayed on both sides of the automobile. When it arrived in Brinkley on November 6, 1931, it was accompanied by a caravan of Model As, radio cars, and a group of movie film artists who shot the reception in the streets of the city of Brinkley. It is pictured here obscured by the large crowd in front of the Brinkley Motor Company on Cypress Street. (Courtesy of the Central Delta Depot Museum.)

IMAGES
of America

MONROE COUNTY

Terri L. Kuczynski on behalf of
the Central Delta Historical Society

ARCADIA
PUBLISHING

ISBN 978-0-7385-6821-8

Published by Arcadia Publishing
Charleston SC, Chicago IL, Portsmouth NH, San Francisco CA

Printed in the United States of America

Library of Congress Control Number: 2008942612

For all general information contact Arcadia Publishing at:
Telephone 843-853-2070
Fax 843-853-0044
E-mail sales@arcadiapublishing.com
For customer service and orders:
Toll-Free 1-888-313-2665

Visit us on the Internet at www.arcadiapublishing.com

To my daughter, Jessica Lynne Clark,
who is my joy, inspiration, and closest friend.

Contents

ACKNOWLEDGMENTS

I would like to thank the members of the Central Delta Historical Society for their contributions, encouragement, and support during this project. Thanks also go out to all of the people who graciously provided me with pictures and information from their personal collections.

A very special thank-you goes out to Steve Hinton, Sarah McKnight, Ken Ziegenbein, Albert Rusher, and Laura Beth Bussell for all of their support and encouragement. A heartfelt thank-you also goes to my editor, Lindsay Harris, who has inspired and motivated me from the very beginning of this project, and to the Central Delta Depot Museum director Bill Sayger for his help in acquiring photographs and proofing this book.

My deepest appreciation goes to my husband, C. P. Kuczynski, for his loving patience and unwavering support, and to my daughter, Jessica Smith Clark, for her gentle prodding and invaluable assistance. I could not have done this without you guys.

Unless otherwise noted, all images appearing in this book were provided by the Central Delta Depot Museum.

INTRODUCTION

Courage, it would seem, is nothing less than the power to overcome danger, misfortune, fear, injustice, while continuing to affirm inwardly that life with all its sorrows is good; that everything is meaningful even if in a sense beyond our understanding; and that there is always tomorrow.

—Dorothy Thompson

These words embody what lies between the covers of this book. This is a story neither of industry nor great fortune, but rather a much more interesting tale of a people with a great love of family, friends, and community. Through the greatest of hardships, their only thoughts were of each other and how fortunate they were considering the circumstances. Monroe County consists of a two-century-old agrarian society whose fate has always been determined by the size of the harvest and whether it would sustain them until the next one. They have suffered floods, tornadoes, droughts, and nickel cotton, yet they go on undaunted, building a new tomorrow as if the disaster they had faced was just a fact of life and could not stop them. And it did not; they persevered despite what nature had to dish out at them.

In terms of national importance, the baseline of the Louisiana Purchase lies in a black-water swamp near Blackton in Monroe County and opened the way for the American expansion west of the mighty Mississippi River. From the initial point of survey came the origin of every township boundary, subdivision, and property line in all or part of 15 states.

In a land termed by the Union soldiers of the Civil War as wild and uninhabitable, the settlers of Monroe County proved different through perseverance and determination. Thus is the history of Monroe County, and so their story unfolds in the pages that follow.

The author's profits from the sale of this book will go to the Central Delta Depot Museum in Brinkley.

One

Taming the Wild Land

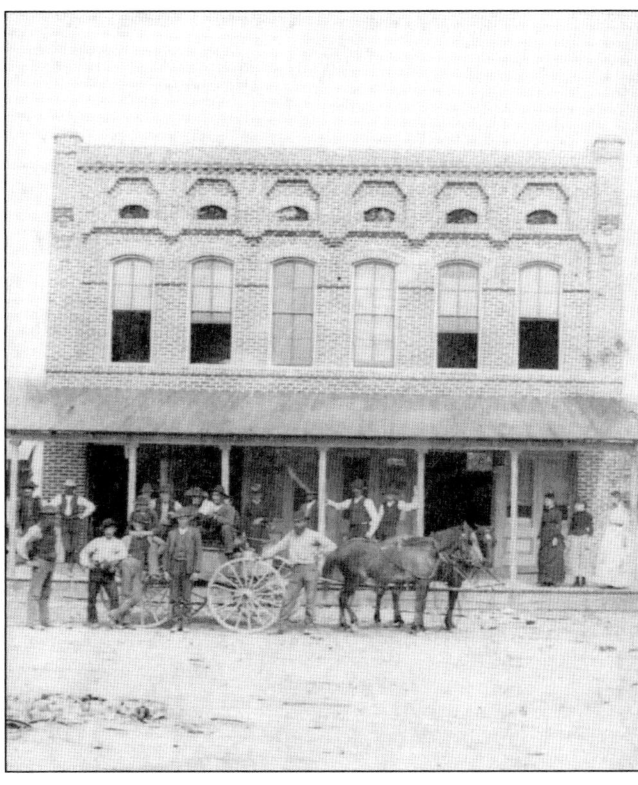

The western expansion in America was achieved through the advent of the railroads. It was through them that a young nation had the means to transport agricultural and manufactured goods beyond the Eastern Seaboard and opened up the Wild West. In 1852, a land grant was given to the Memphis and Little Rock Railroad to construct a railroad line from the Mississippi River at Memphis, Tennessee, to Little Rock, Arkansas. Railroad crews made settlements along the route, and what is Brinkley was known then by the mostly immigrant crews as "Lick Skillet." This early photograph was taken in front of the C. B. Harris store in Brinkley.

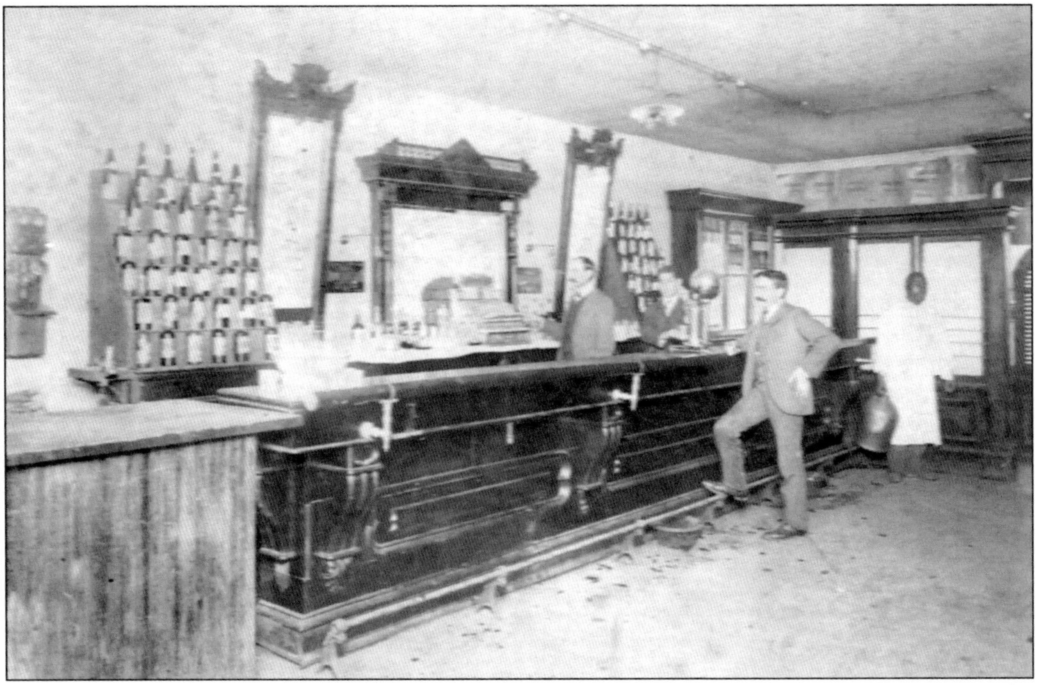

Above and below are early photographs of unidentified settlers in Brinkley in the late 1800s. The construction of the Memphis and Little Rock Railroad brought the city of Brinkley into being and established the first railroad completed in Arkansas. Brinkley is situated in the northern part of Monroe County and was laid out in 1869–1870 on lands belonging to the Memphis and Little Rock Railroad. Brinkley was incorporated on August 6, 1872, at which time the town had 50 qualified voters. Before the turn of the 20th century, Brinkley had better shipping facilities than any other city or town in the state of Arkansas. In the early 1890s, Brinkley's business district, where these photographs were taken, then located west of Main Street on Cypress Street, was destroyed by fire.

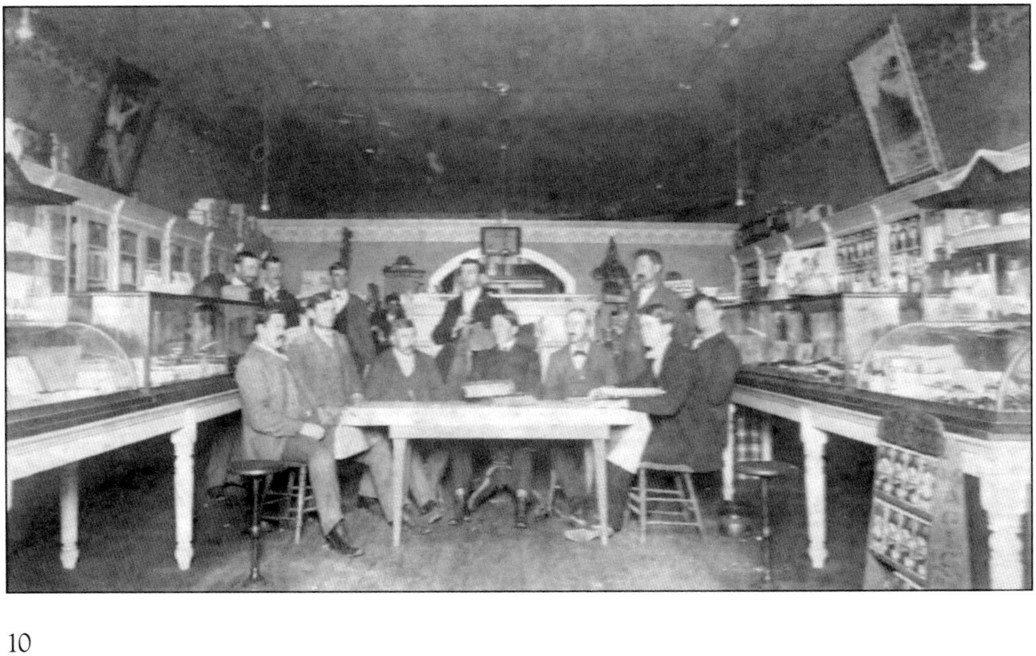

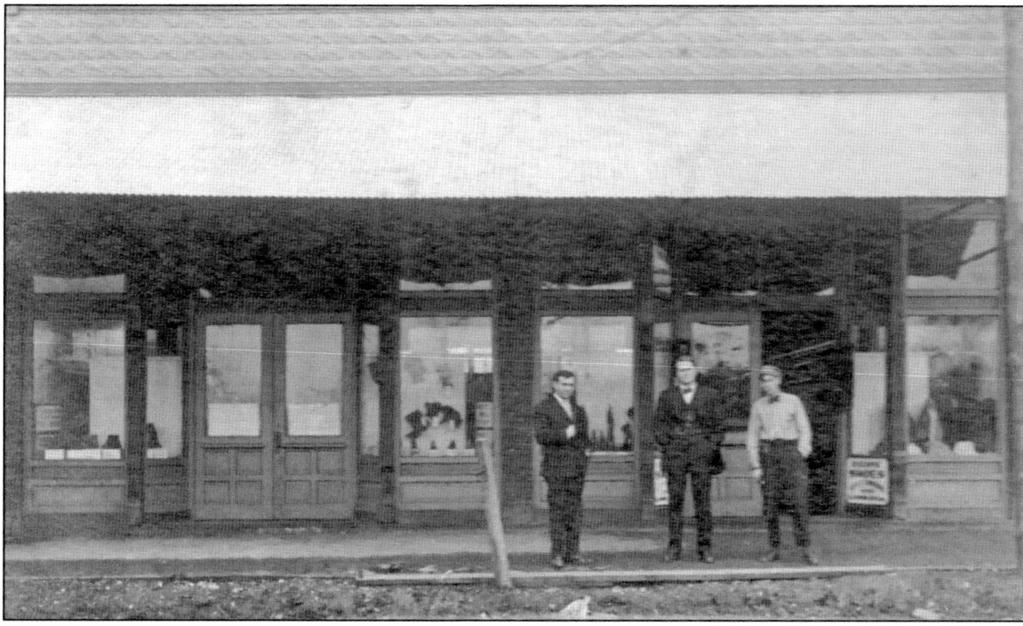

This *c.* 1910 photograph was taken in the Brinkley business district in front of the Lamb Store. In 1869, Lick Skillet was renamed Brinkley after the president of the Memphis and Little Rock Railroad, Robert Campbell Brinkley. The land surrounding Brinkley was table land and not subject to overflow, being 23 feet above the high-water mark. It was considered a healthier locality than towns situated along the rivers and thus was more rapidly settled.

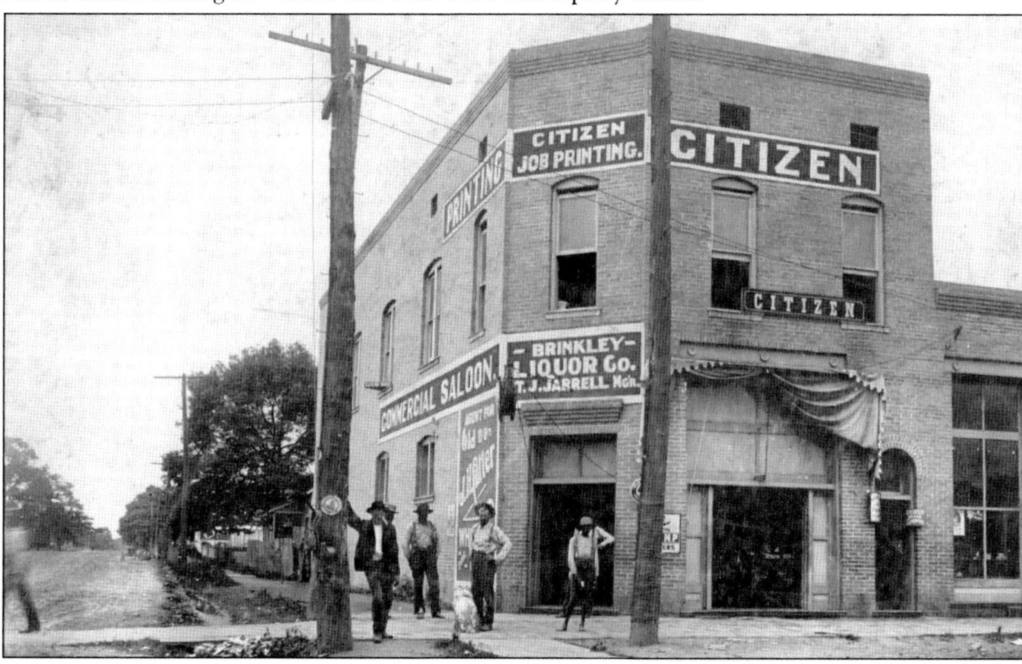

E. H. Converse came to Brinkley by train in the 1890s and accidently met Brinkley's forefathers at the depot. When they learned he was a druggist, they persuaded him to stay. At that time, his only possession was 50¢ and a gold watch. Eventually, he bought his own drugstore, which he owned and operated for over 50 years. Pictured above is what was known as Converse Corner.

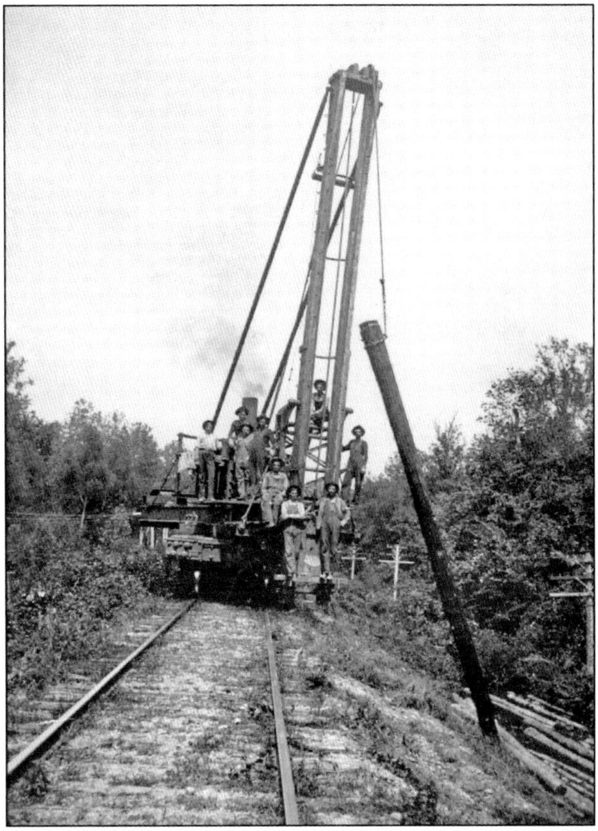

These railroad work crews are believed to be working on the Batesville and Brinkley rail line, one of the best equipped and managed short lines in the Southwest during its heyday. Brinkley was at one time the junction of the Little Rock and Memphis and the St. Louis, Arkansas, and Texas Railroads. It was also the terminal of the Batesville and Brinkley and the Brinkley, Helena, and Indian Bay Railroads. The concentration of these several lines made Brinkley a railroad center of more importance than any other in the state. The Brinkley, Helena, and Indian Bay was built by John Gunn and William Black, fore-founders of Brinkley, for the main purpose of supplying their immense sawmill with timber.

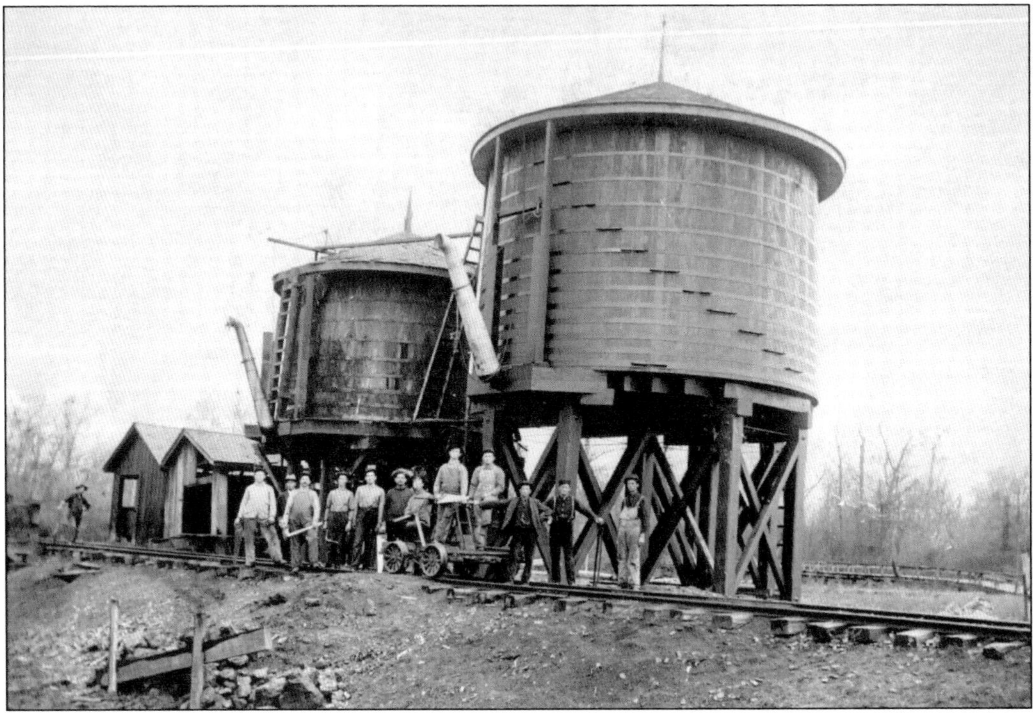

Pictured at right is William S. McCullough, who was owner and operator of the Brinkley House Hotel, pictured below. The *Arkansas Gazette* reported on the hotel in its September 12, 1891, edition, stating, "Captain W. S. McCullough, proprietor of the Brinkley House, keeps one of the most popular hostelries in Eastern Arkansas. His house is situated near the junction of the railroads, and is the popular home for traveling men. It has 25 well appointed lodging rooms, besides parlors, dining-room, office, etc. Broad verandas encircle the building its entire length and breadth, giving it a comfortable and homelike appearance." The Brinkley House was destroyed by fire in 1914. The Rusher Hotel was built in its place shortly afterward and still stands today, now known as Low's Bridal Shop.

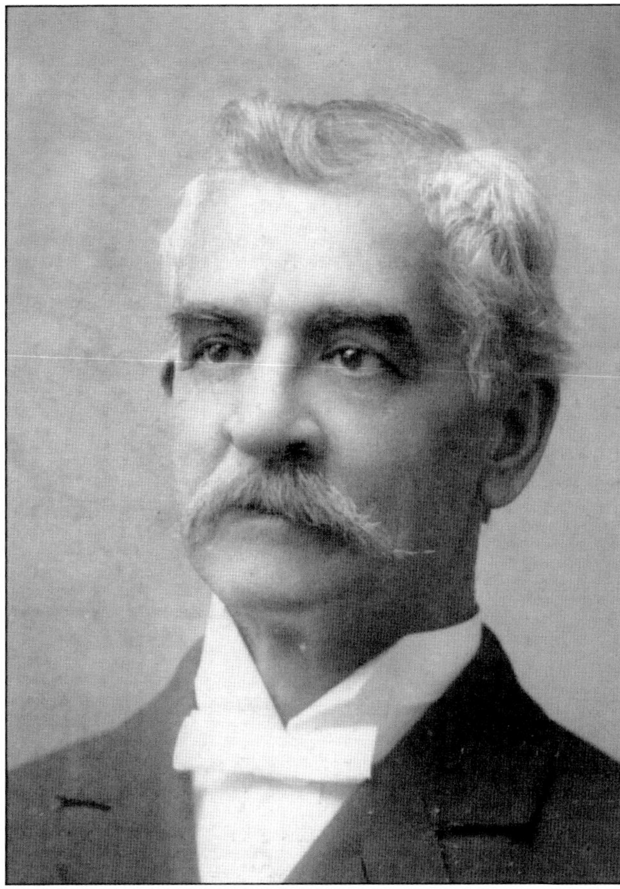

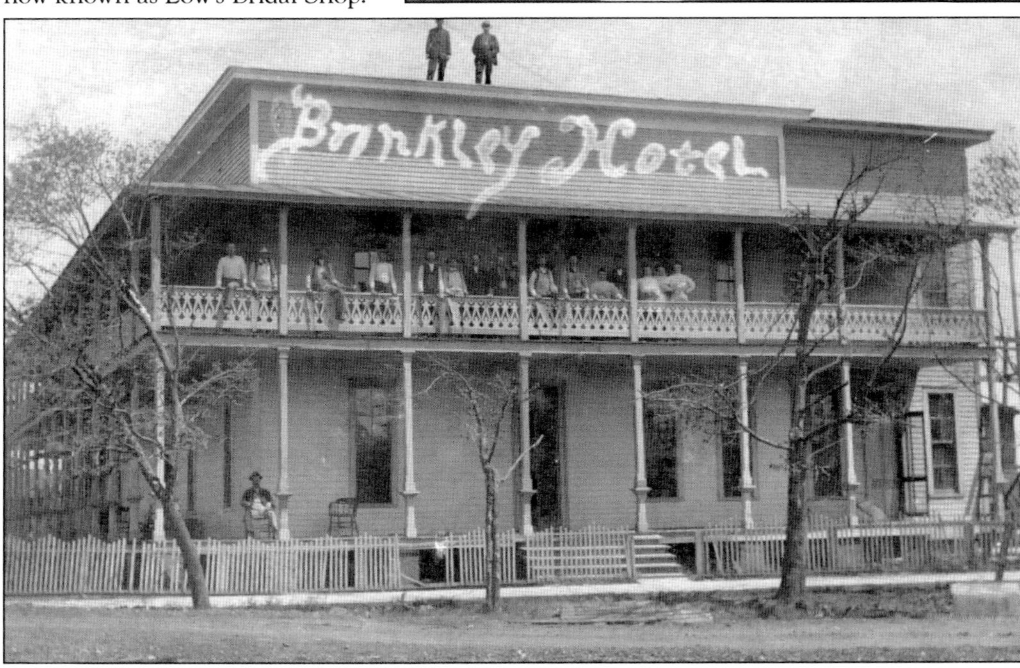

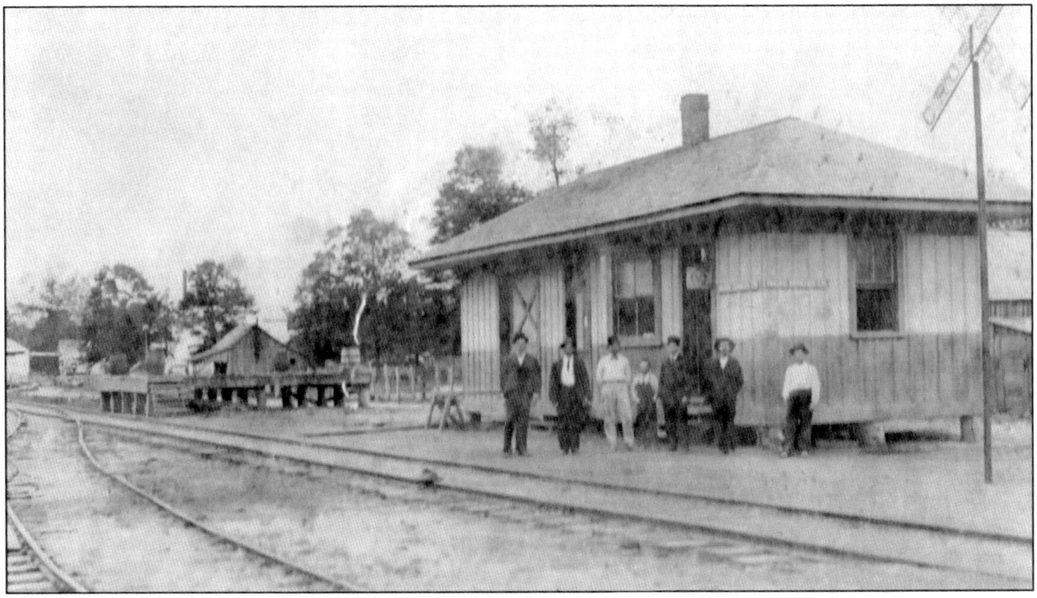

In 1890, a town site was offered by the Brinkley, Helena, and Indian Bay Railway. The offer was accepted, and Monroe, Arkansas, came into existence. The town was named after Monroe Norman, a stockholder of the railroad and associate of the Brinkley Car Works and Manufacturing Company. In its heyday, there was a train depot (pictured above), a cattle-guard company, a lumber mill, five general merchandise stores, a telephone company, a cotton gin, a blacksmith shop, and a public school.

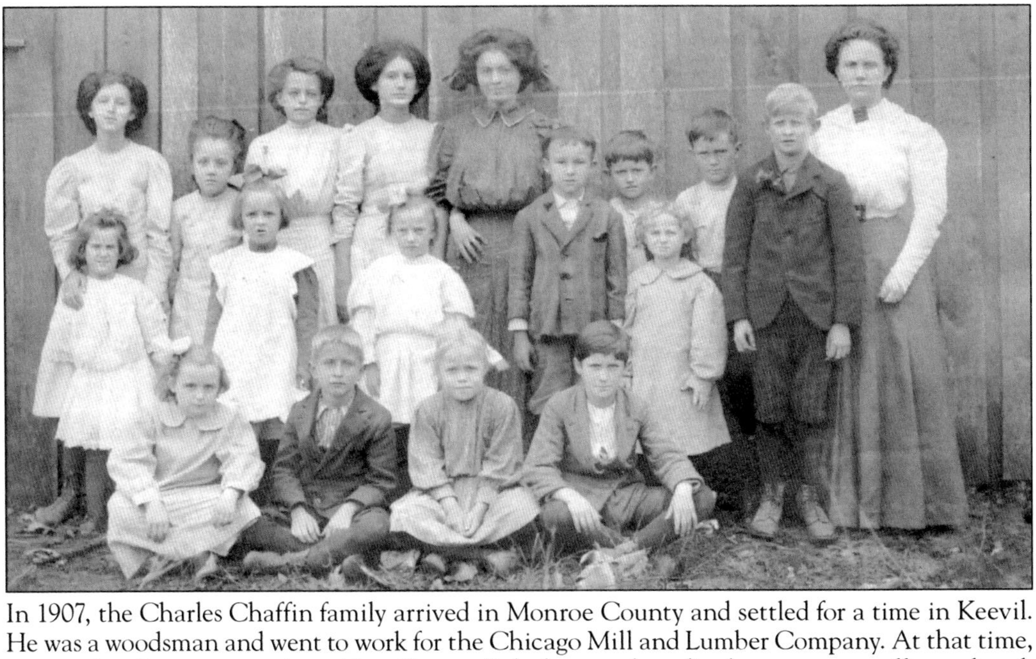

In 1907, the Charles Chaffin family arrived in Monroe County and settled for a time in Keevil. He was a woodsman and went to work for the Chicago Mill and Lumber Company. At that time, it was a bustling community, with a Cotton Belt depot, a boardinghouse, a post office, a hotel, a candy house, and a school. Keevil, like many other small lumber towns, disappeared after the timber was cleared. This early-1900s Keevil school class photograph is from the memory album of the late Flora Chaffin Moorehead.

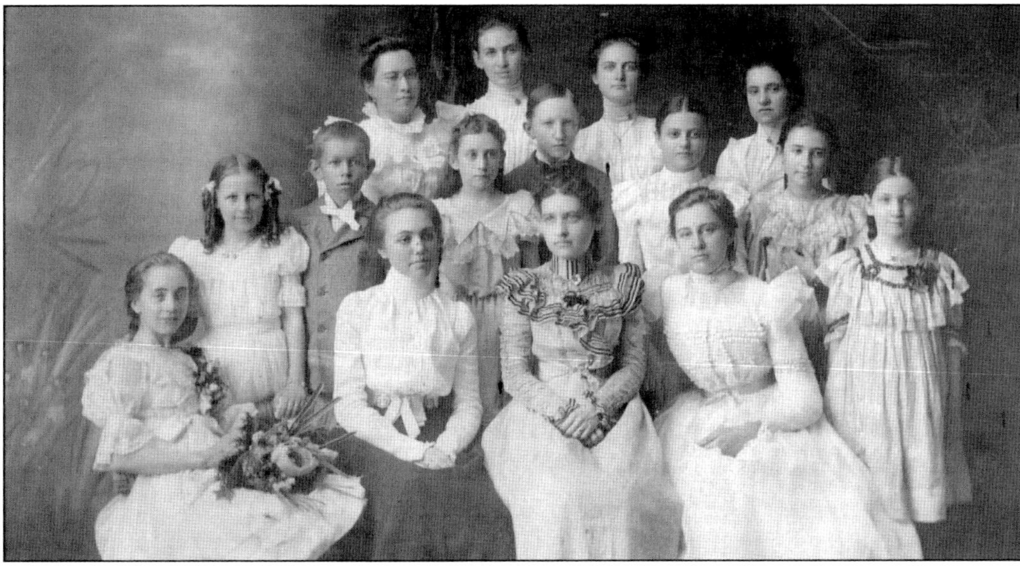

Harriet M. Folsom (first row, third from the left) is pictured here with her music students in the late 1800s. Her husband, William B. Folsom, was owner and operator of the *Brinkley Argus*, a local newspaper, and visionary of Arkansas on Wheels. The *Argus* was established by his father, W. W. Folsom, who had left Holly Springs, Mississippi, in 1875 with his wife, son, and daughter after his large mercantile and crop furnishing business had gone bankrupt. W. W. Folsom installed a printing shop in February 1876 and was so successful he paid off all of his indebtedness in Holly Springs even though he was cleared through bankruptcy. Harriet and William B. Folsom were childless and upon their passing left the family home, pictured below, and $100,000 cash to the City of Brinkley for a library. The William B. Folsom Library was dedicated on April 1, 1956, and is still in operation.

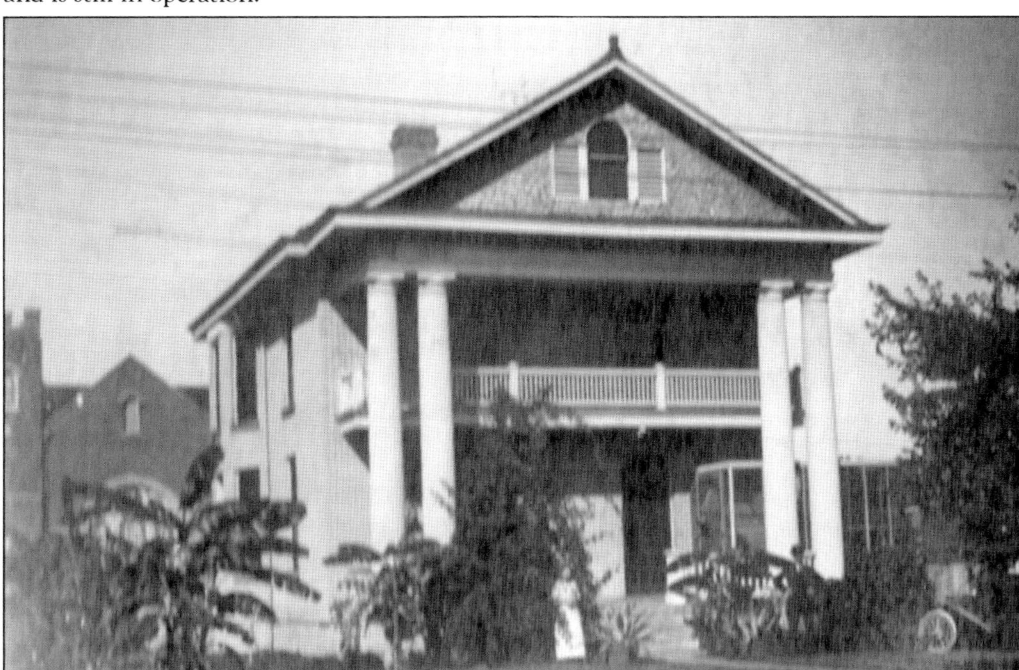

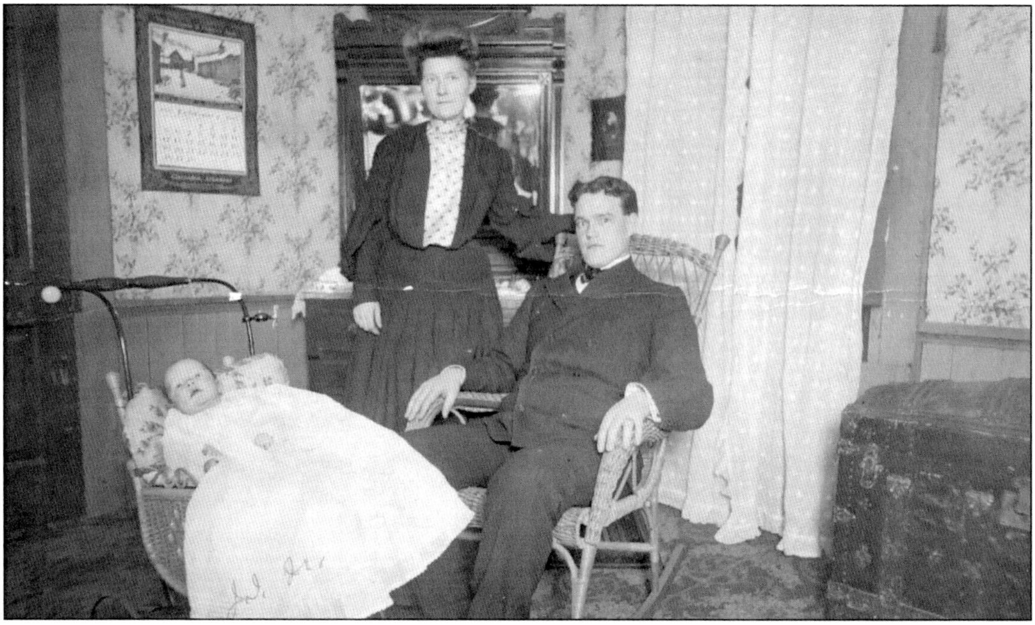

James I. Matthews Sr. (seated), Virginia Matthews (standing), and James I. Matthews Jr. are pictured in 1905 at their Holly Grove home, built in 1875 by D. B. Renfro. Renfro had five children and built a house for each one as they reached adulthood. He was a veteran of the Civil War, fighting with the 32nd Tennessee Infantry for the Confederacy. After the war, he returned home to Tennessee to discover his parents had passed away. His siblings had thought him dead and divided the estate among them; upon his return, they refused to give him his inheritance. He then came to Holly Grove with a friend, Will T. Smith, who told him his family had plenty of land and it would be a good place to start over. Below is LeRoy Renfro with his cousin Annie Elliott "Snooks" Matthews. (Both courtesy of Danyelle McNeill Fletcher.)

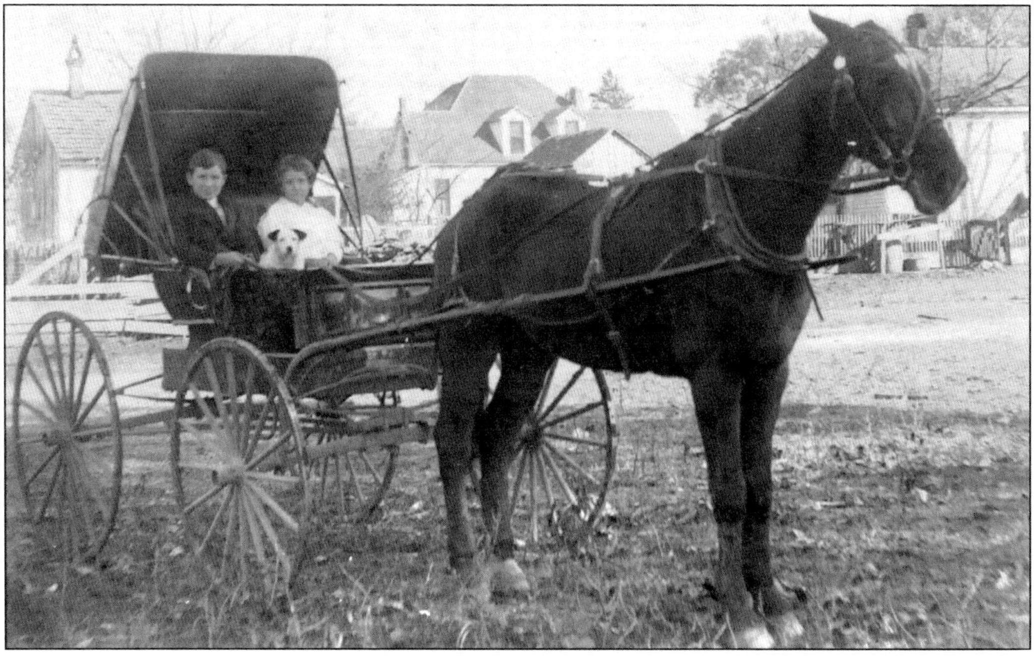

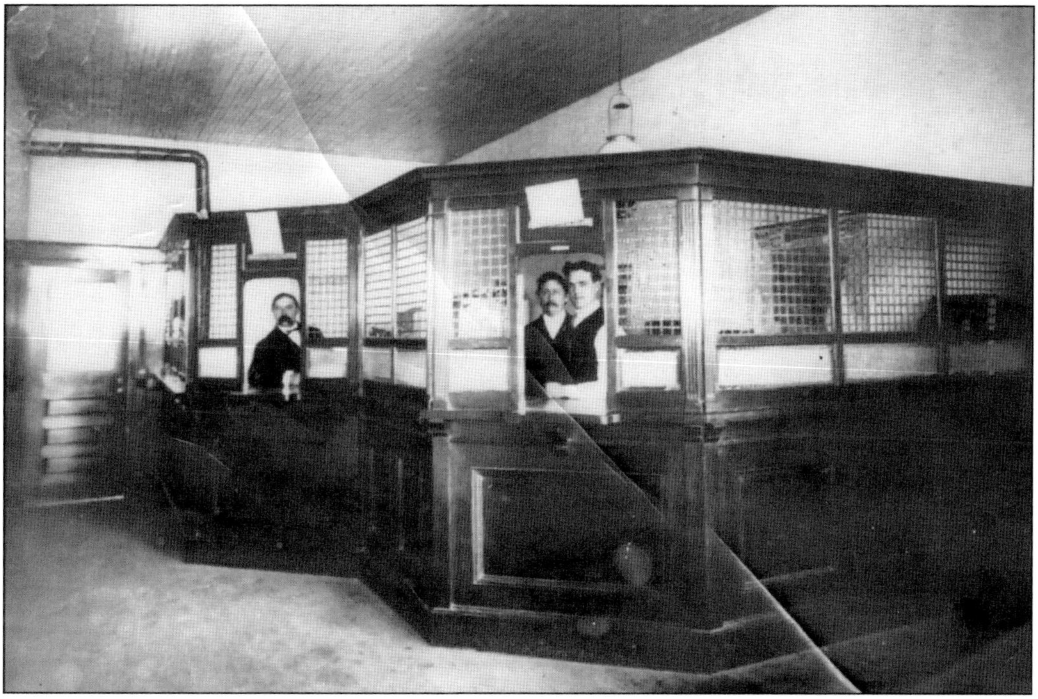

These photographs were taken inside the Bank of Holly Grove, established in 1903 by W. F. Branch. J. A. Walls was the first bank president, and James I. Matthews Sr. was the first cashier. James I. Matthews Sr. stands alone inside the bank in the 1920s photograph below. The Bank of Holly Grove remained open until being sold to the First National Bank of Eastern Arkansas on December 2, 2005. (Both courtesy of Danyelle Fletcher.)

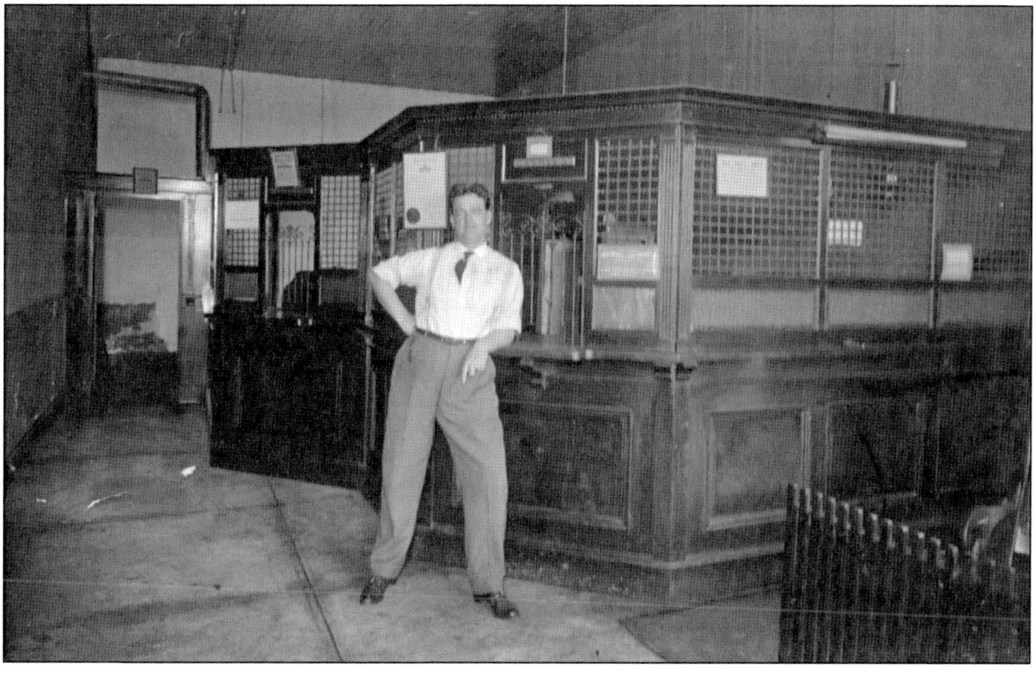

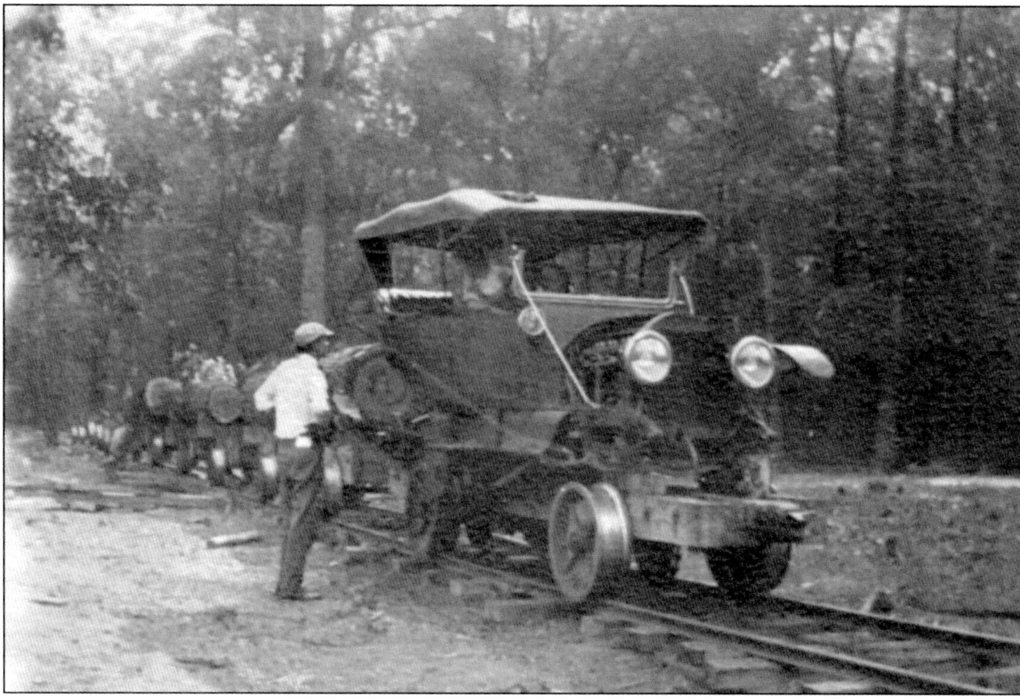

These photographs, dated July 14, 1918, show men at work on a logging railroad in the White River bottomlands, probably near Aberdeen. A car was converted into a makeshift locomotive to move the timber along the logging dummy line to the lumber mill. W. P. Brown and Sons owned vast tracks of land in the Monroe County bottomlands; however, their mill was located across the Cache River in Prairie County. (Both courtesy of Jo Claire English.)

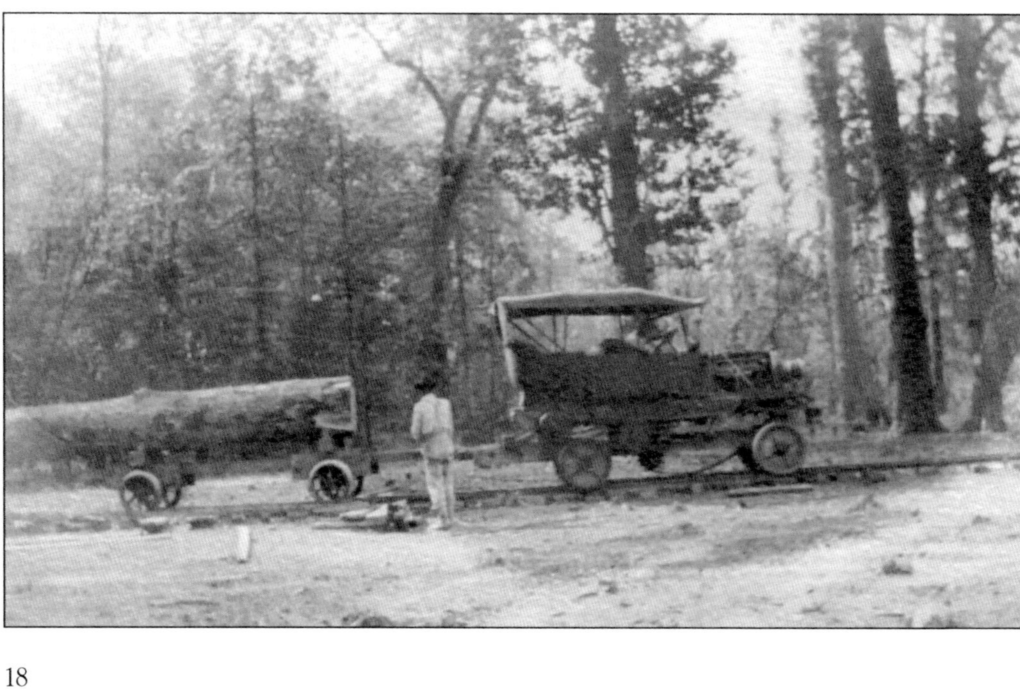

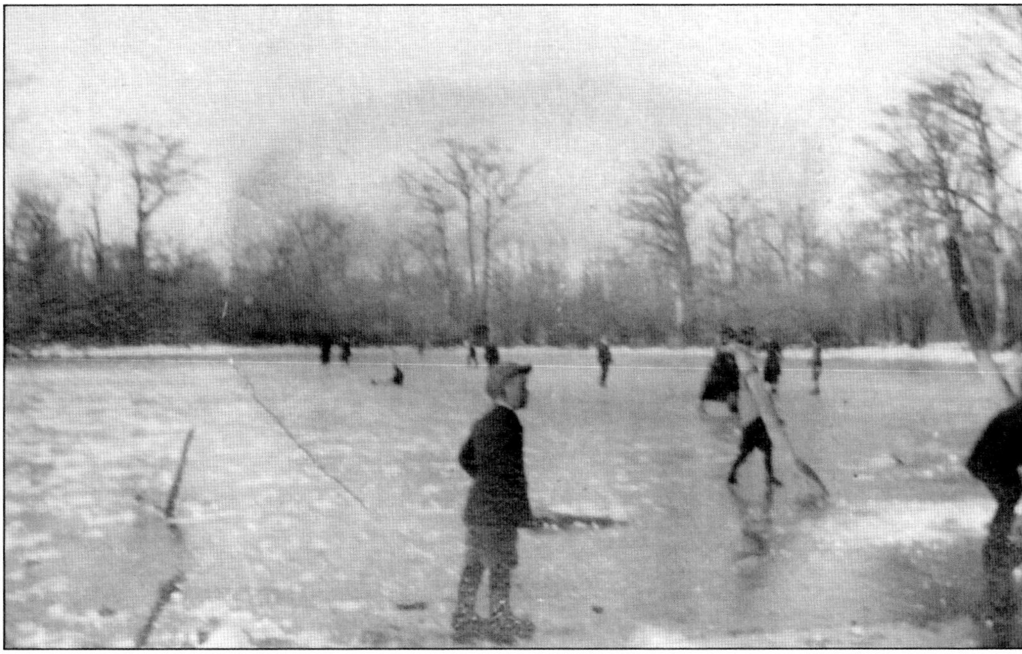

From January 10–12, 1918, the biggest snowstorm to hit Arkansas in the 19th century left no region of the state untouched. It buried Little Rock in 19.4 inches of snow and other northern parts of the state in up to 30 inches. Following this massive snowstorm was a severe Arctic cold front that produced the lowest temperatures of the 1900s with a record reading of 13 below zero. The White River froze over solid enough to let wagons and cars pass across at Clarendon. Children were captured above playing on the frozen river on January 12, 1918. Below, houseboats are docked on the icy bank of the White River by Clarendon. (Both courtesy of Jo Claire English.)

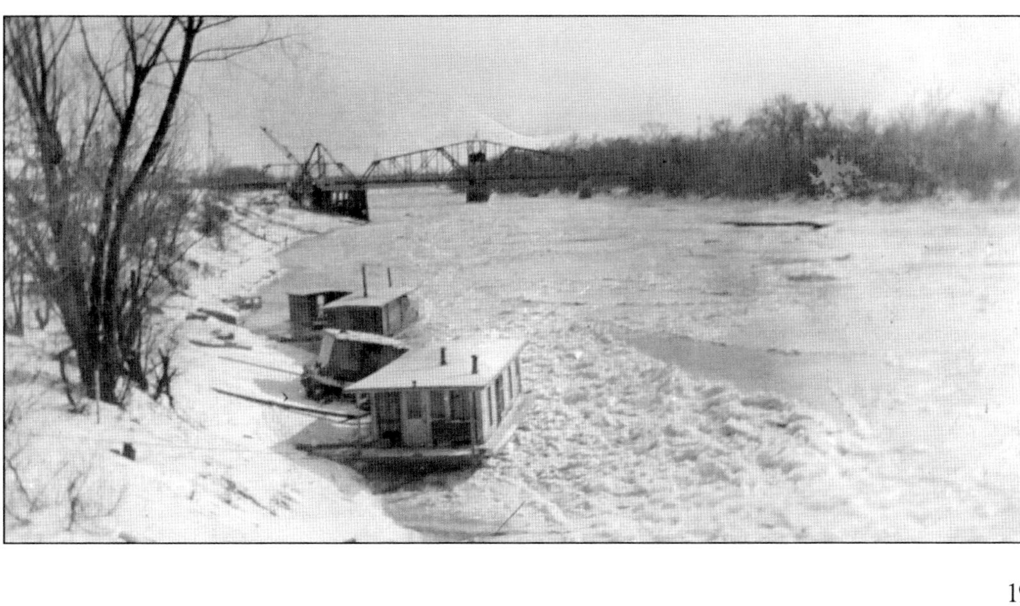

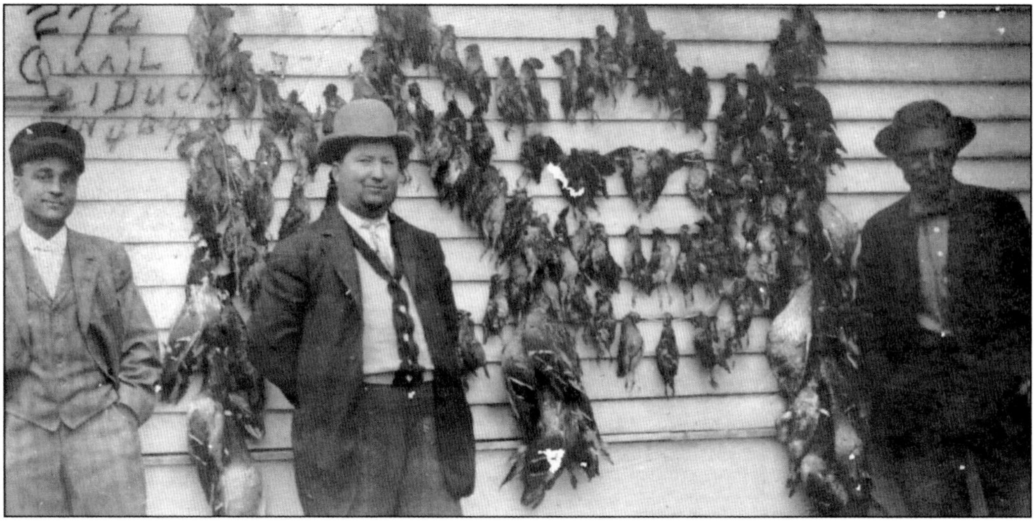

From left to right, Willie Mayo, Roy "L. S." Renfro, and June Davidson proudly pose with their impressive collection of 272 quail and 21 ducks that were harvested in one day in the woodland surrounding Holly Grove. (Courtesy of Danyelle McNeill Fletcher.)

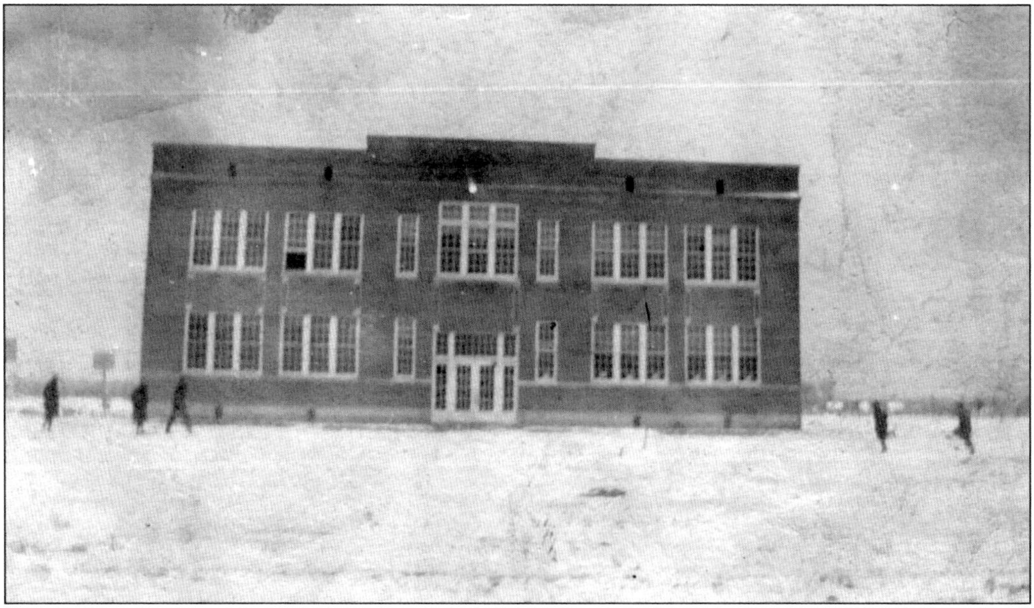

Pictured above in 1922 is the new Holly Grove High School for whites. In 1940, it was expanded by adding two wings, a gymnasium, and an auditorium. The Holly Grove schools were segregated until 1969–1970, well past the 1954 *Brown v. Board of Education* decisions and well past the integration of Central High in Little Rock. The school above was closed in 2005, and the children of Holly Grove now attend school in Clarendon. (Courtesy of Danyelle McNeill Fletcher.)

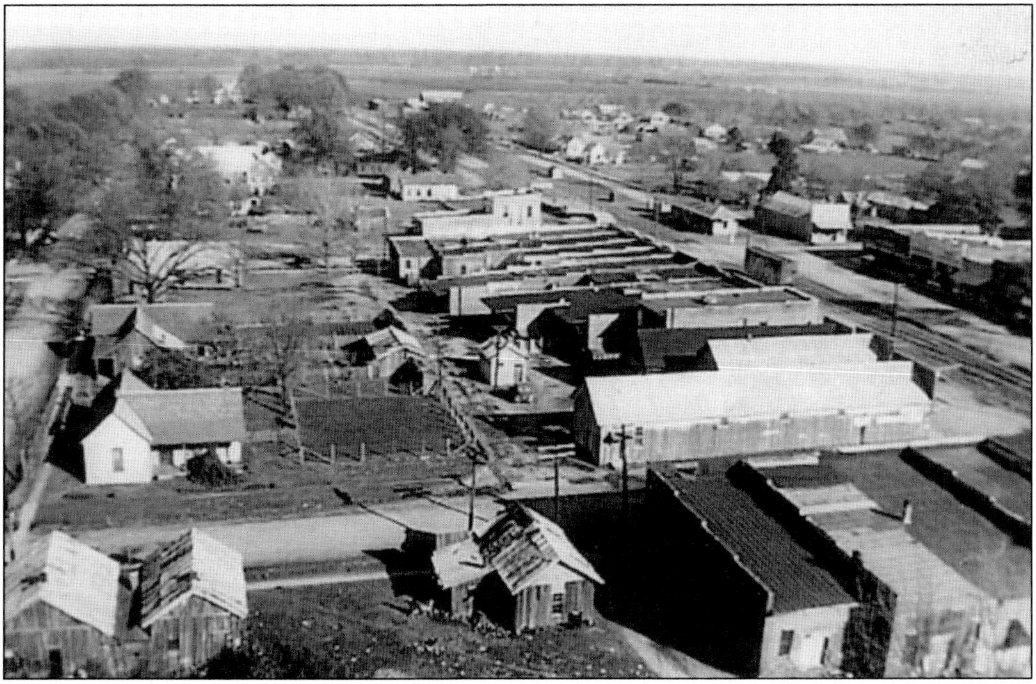

In 1836, Holly Grove, named for the large thicket of holly trees in the center of the town, was a small community of plantation families. The Arkansas Central laid track through the town in 1873, bringing a shift in the population from outlying areas to concentrate along the railroad tracks running through the center of the town. J. M. Smith and James Kerr, plantation owners, gave the land for the train depot. The holly thicket was cut down, and the new station was erected. The railroad offered a dependable means for getting farm products to market, bringing a boom to the community. (Both courtesy of Danyelle McNeill Fletcher.)

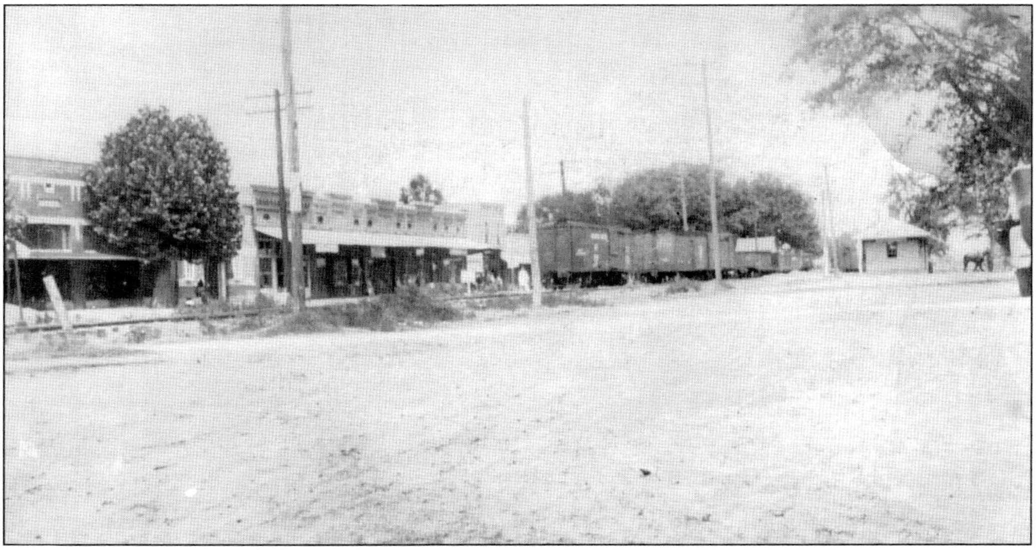

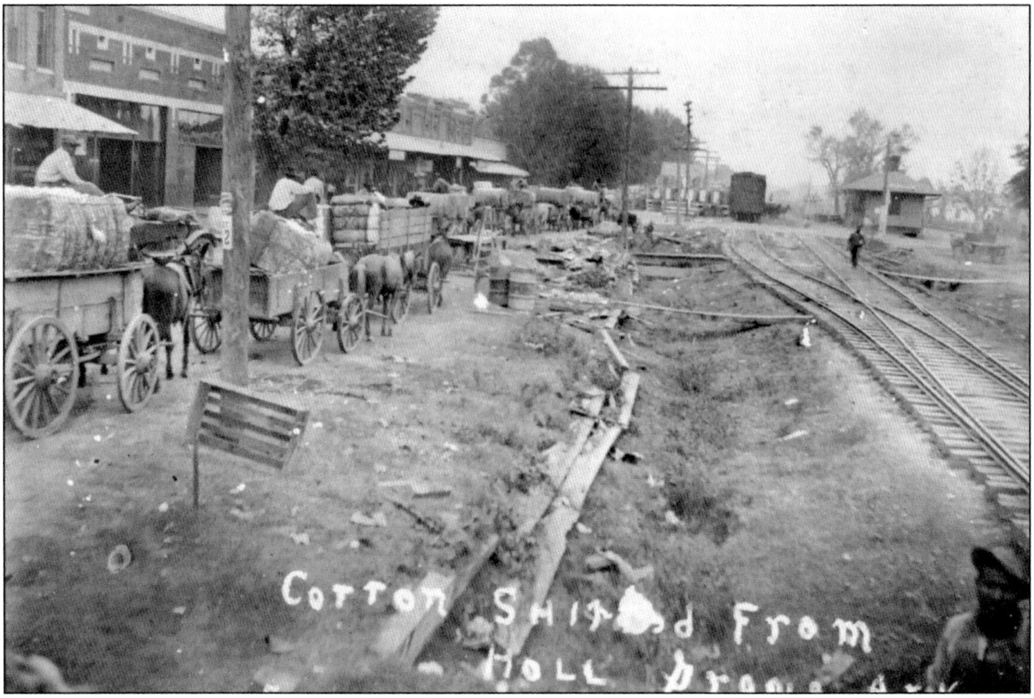

This 1937 caravan of wagons were loaded with bales of cotton headed to the cotton platform in Holly Grove for shipping. Cotton was at one time the biggest cash crop of the delta. A sharecropper's whole family, including children of a very young age, was put in the fields to chop and pick cotton. The children would not attend school until after the cotton harvest, which was usually sometime in December. (Courtesy of the Arkansas History Commission.)

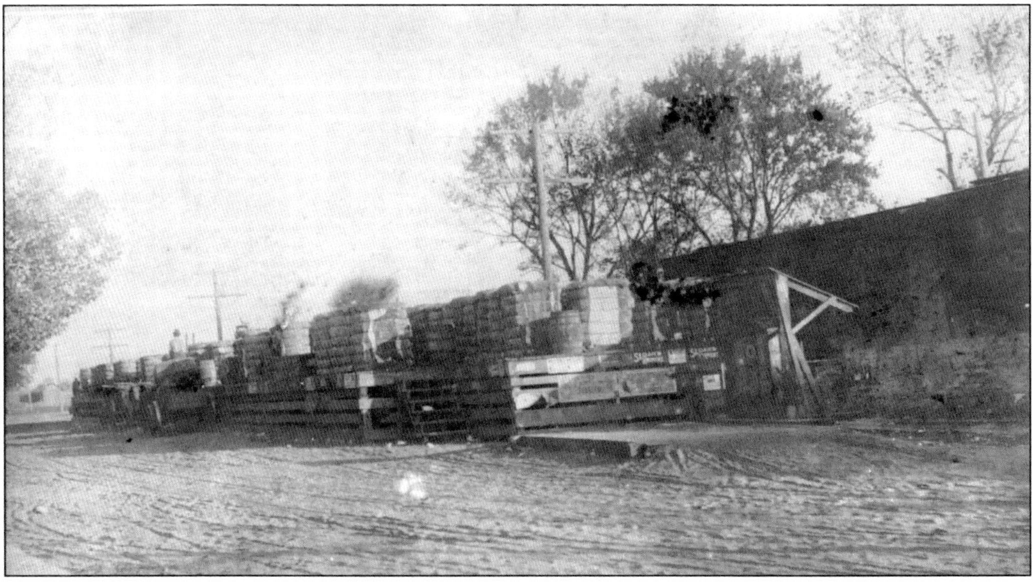

Here is a view of the cotton platform that stood alongside the railroad track for shipment to the market. This is the platform that the long line of wagons in the photograph above is waiting to reach to unload their bales of cotton. (Courtesy of Danyelle Fletcher.)

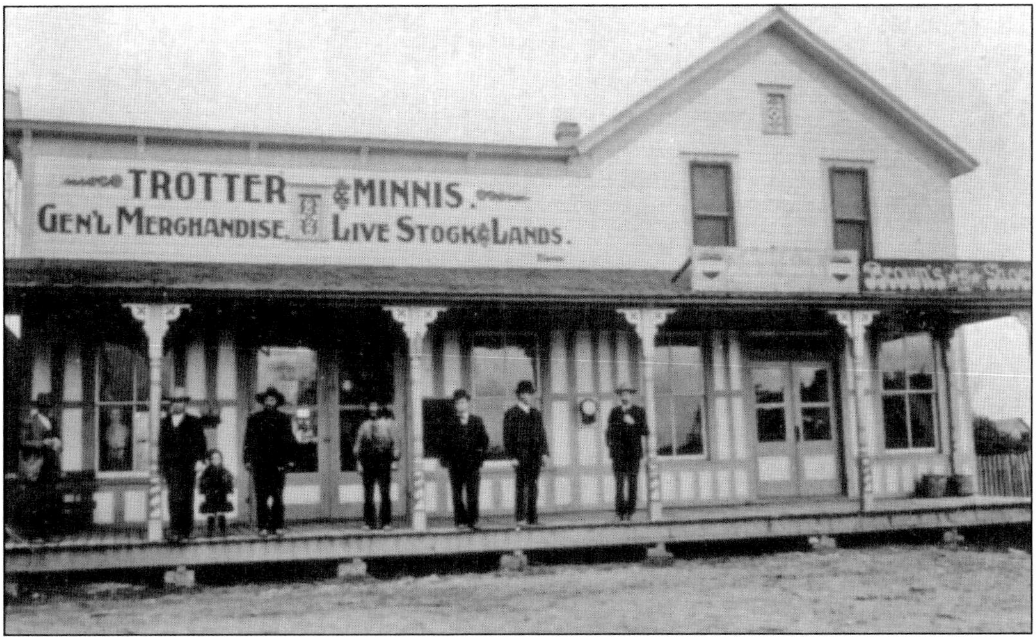

This photograph was taken in the early 1900s in front of the Trotter and Minnis General Store in Roe. The town is located near the county's southwestern border and has a current population of 125. It was thought to be settled as early as 1860 but not incorporated until the late 1960s.

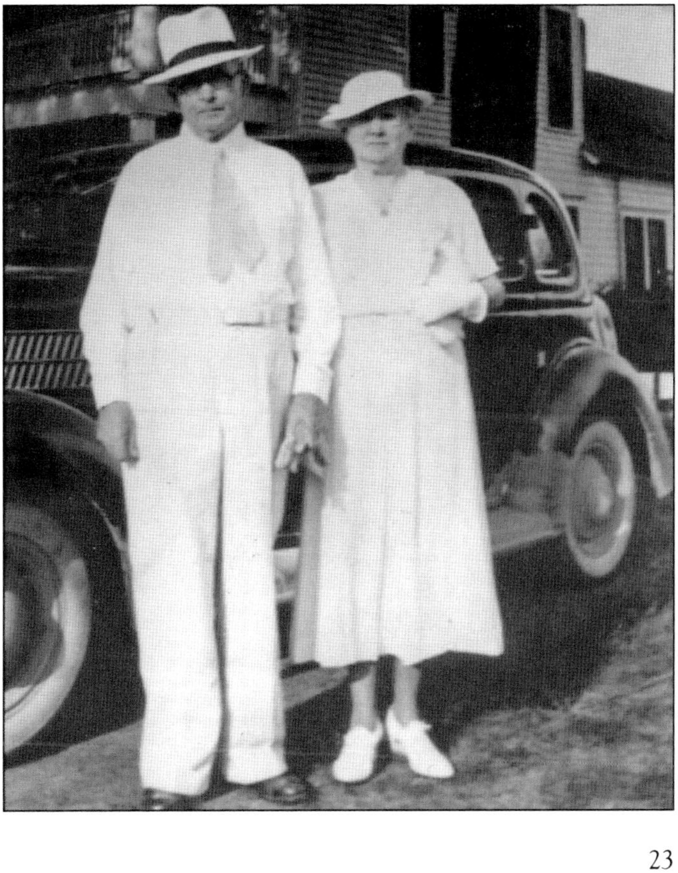

At right is a 1930s photograph of Jefferson Davis Minnis and his wife, Jodie. Minnis was a partner in the Trotter and Minnis General Store at Roe that began business in the late 1890s. His daughter, Jewell Minnis, inherited her parents' wealth and was herself a wealthy farmer and Brinkley schoolteacher. Upon her death, her Last Will and Testament directed 800 acres of farmland be placed in trust for freshman students at the University of Arkansas. So far to date, the trust has paid approximately $2 million to the university.

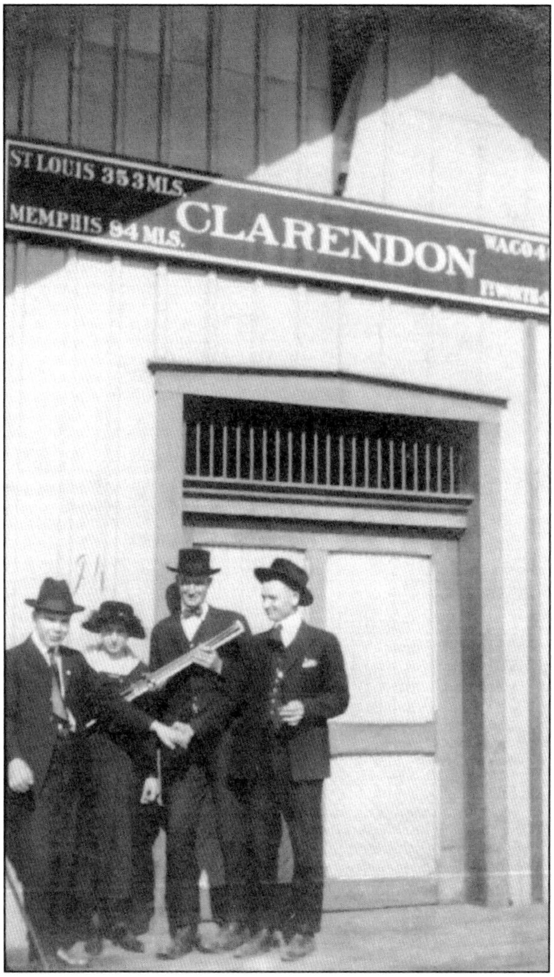

These early-1920 photographs were taken in Clarendon, a city served by the Cotton Belt and the Missouri Pacific Railroads. The city grew in importance as a lumber shipping point as soon as the Arkansas Central completed the rail line from Helena in the 1870s. The Arkansas Central was sold in 1877 to the Arkansas Midland Railway, which was later sold to the Missouri Pacific in 1917. The Missouri Pacific continued operation over the Arkansas Midland lines that connected Marvell, Pine City, Brinkley, Holly Grove, and Clarendon. The old Midland route serving Monroe County was abandoned in the 1950s, and all of the rails were removed by 1977. (Both courtesy of Jo Claire English.)

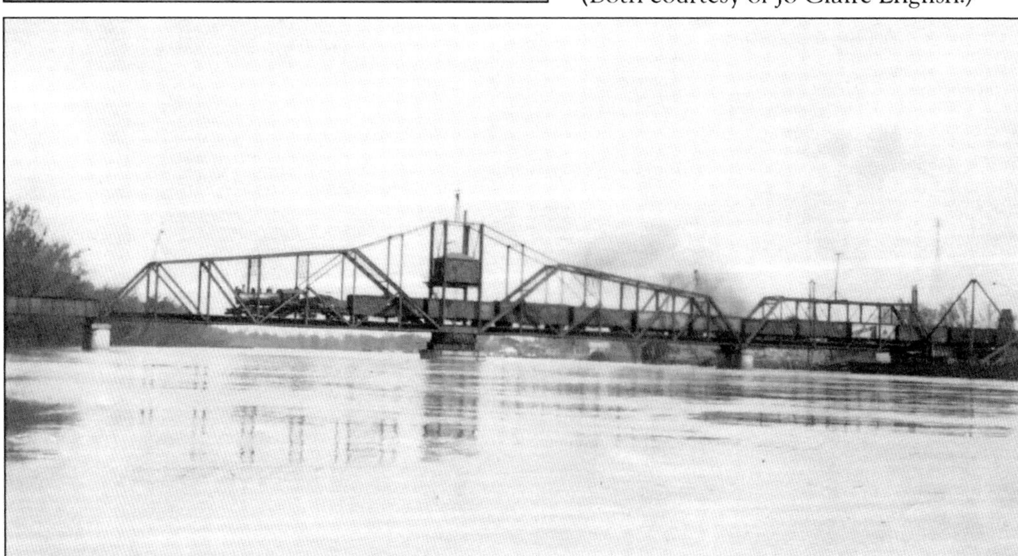

Two

The Cyclone of 1909

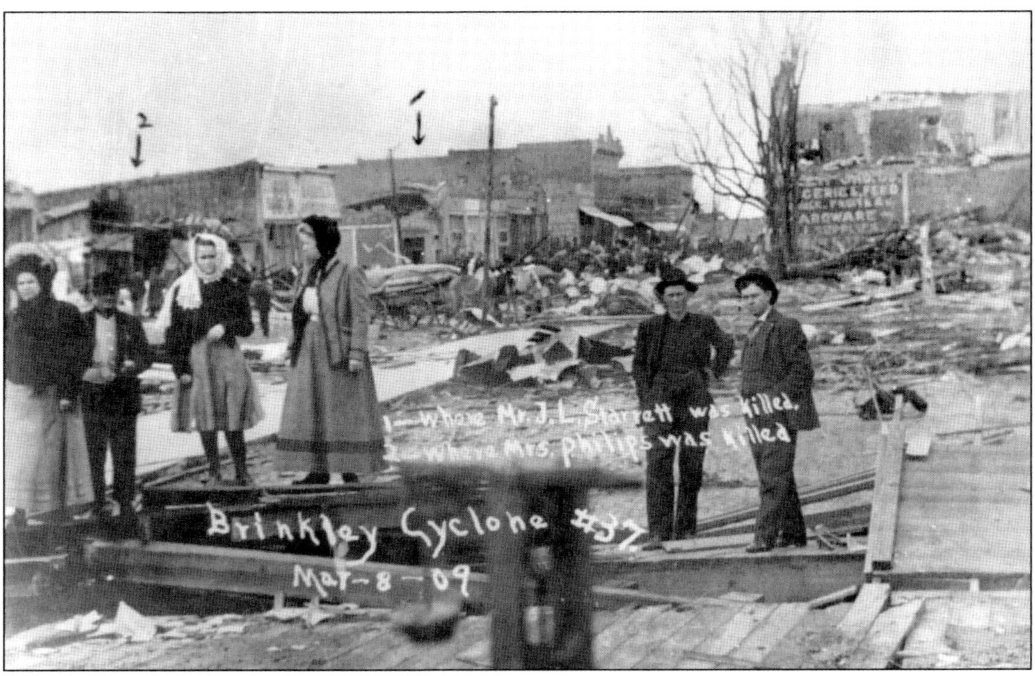

On March 8, 1909, a series of tornadoes swept through five Arkansas counties, killing 58 people and injuring over 600, while doing damages totaling millions of dollars. Brinkley was hardest hit and nearly wiped out of existence by a tornado that cut a swath almost a mile wide, with a path that extended 6 miles south of Brinkley and about 10 miles northeast of the city. Little was spared between these two points. Of approximately 1,000 homes, only 15 were left standing and one house of worship, St. John's Catholic Church, which in the aftermath was used as a morgue.

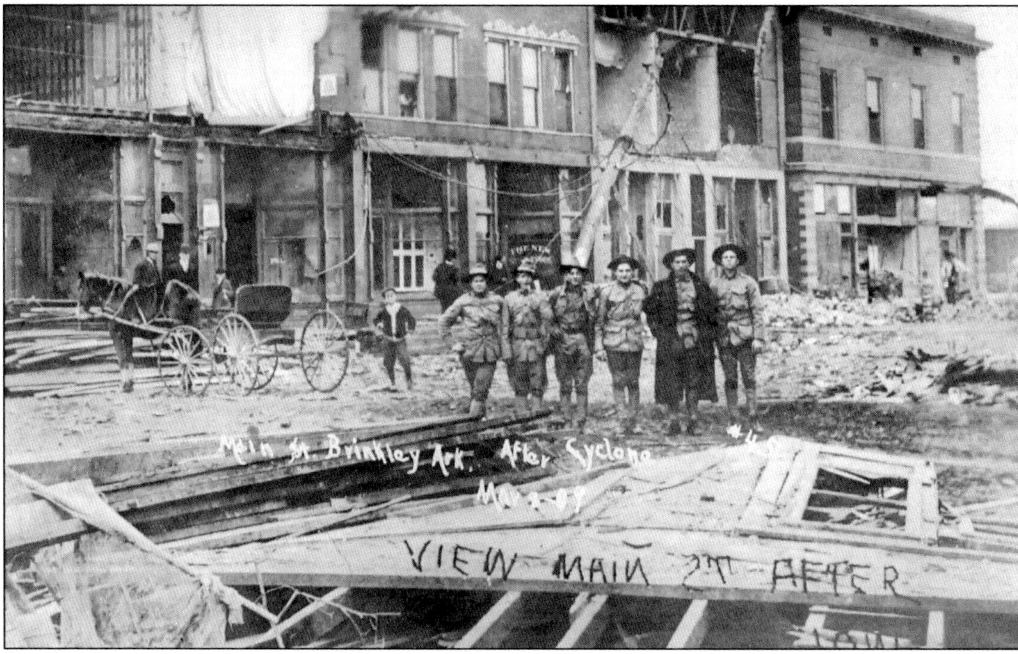

In the aftermath of the tornado, Gov. George W. Donaghey ordered the town to be placed under martial law with Sheriff Frank Milwee in charge. The State Guard, or militia, played a vital role in curtailing looting, enforcing a 10:00 p.m. curfew, setting up tents for the homeless, and assisting in clearing debris.

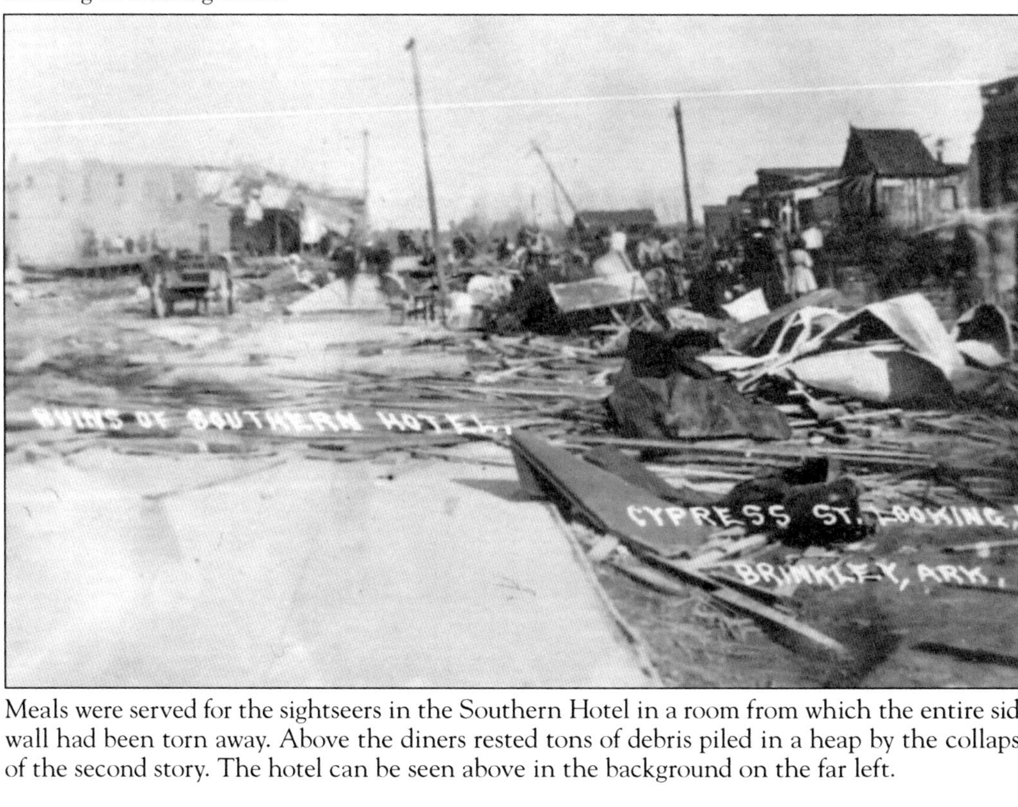

Meals were served for the sightseers in the Southern Hotel in a room from which the entire side wall had been torn away. Above the diners rested tons of debris piled in a heap by the collapse of the second story. The hotel can be seen above in the background on the far left.

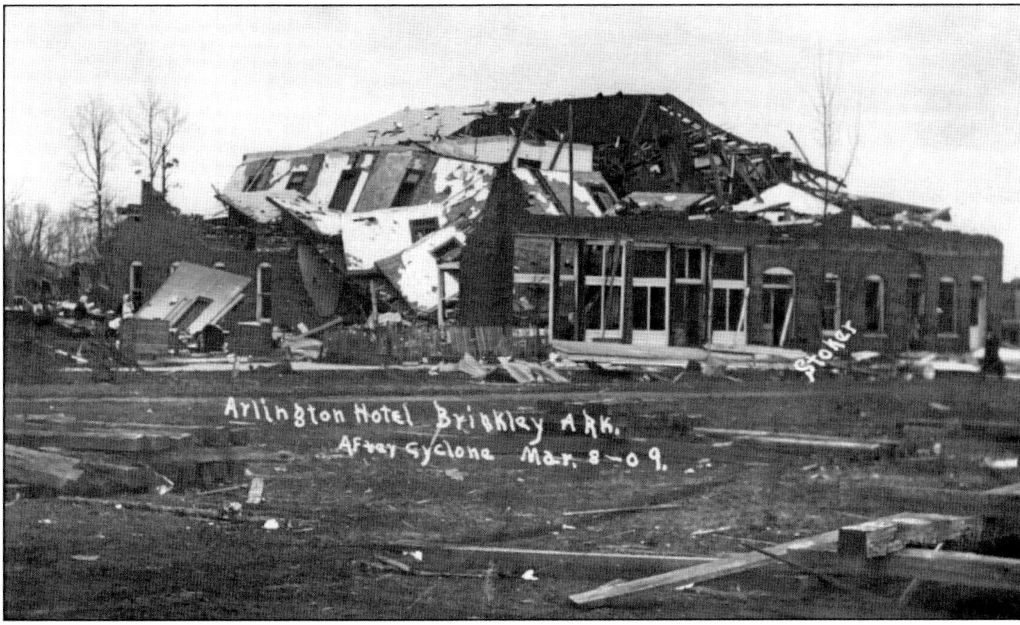

The city lost all of its hotels: the Arlington, the Hotel Brinkley, and the Southern Hotel. The Arlington Hotel's some 75 guests were amazingly spared when the entire top of the two-story hotel was destroyed. Through the years, the proprietor, Gus Rusher, had been putting his savings into improving and furnishing the hotel, only to watch his uninsured investment be swept away in seconds.

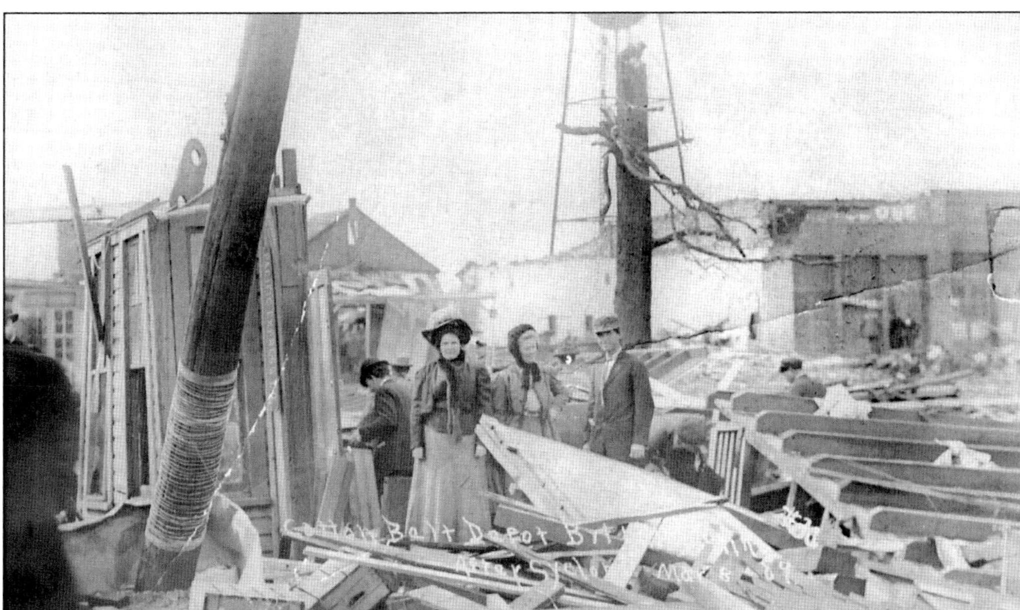

Traveling salesman W. M. Wilson stated to reporters, "There is one thing I do want to say, and that is, after the first shock, no one could have gone more heroically to the work of rescue than did the people of Brinkley; white and black, rich and poor were working side by side, doing all in their power to relieve the suffering of the injured and rescue those that were pinioned under the demolished buildings."

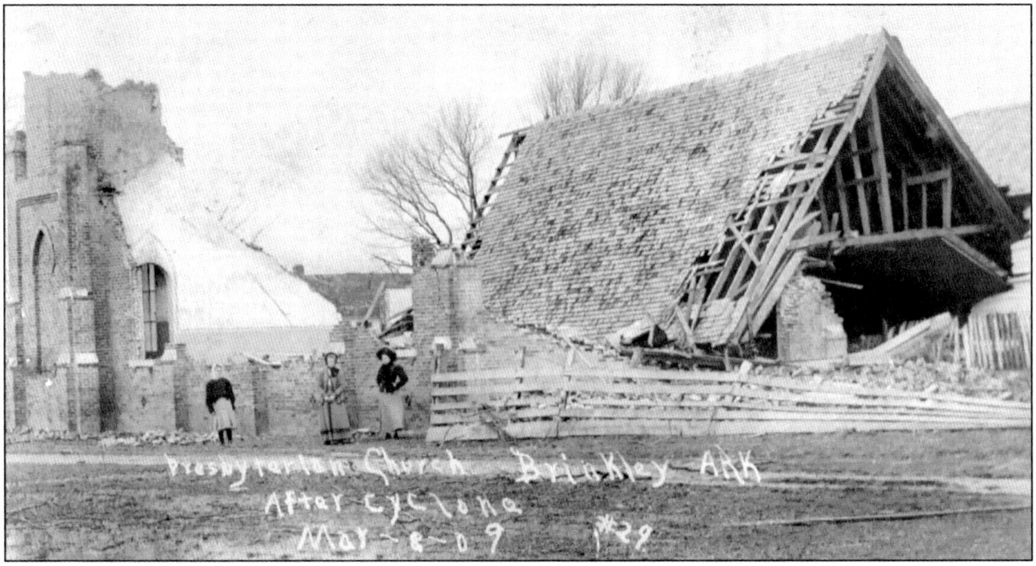

There were many accounts of miraculous escapes, many of which owed their salvation to the sturdy furniture of the day, such as iron bed frames. One account tells of five clerks and stenographers working in the Andrew Flora general store who escaped certain death as the two-story building's roof and walls collapsed into a heap of rubble 15 feet high, just by crawling under an iron bed in the back of the building. Another account is of two-year-old Robert Lee McKnight, son of Dr. E. D. McKnight, sleeping through the storm while the house was blown apart. The child was in an iron crib in a corner, and when the ceiling fell, the head and footboards held the weight of the wreckage above his head. The three children of J. C. Moshier owed their lives to other types of furniture. When the blast of the storm threw a chair in front of 12-year-old Hattie's face, sick in bed stricken with pneumonia, it protected her from the falling ceiling and walls. His other two children were spared when the upright piano was thrown over them by the storm, protecting them from the mortar and falling timbers.

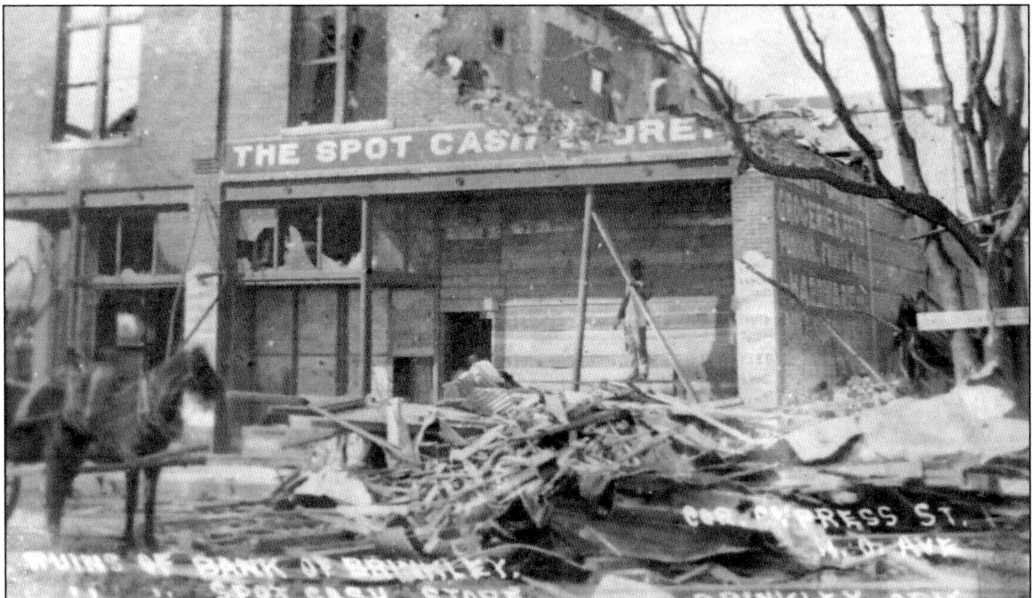

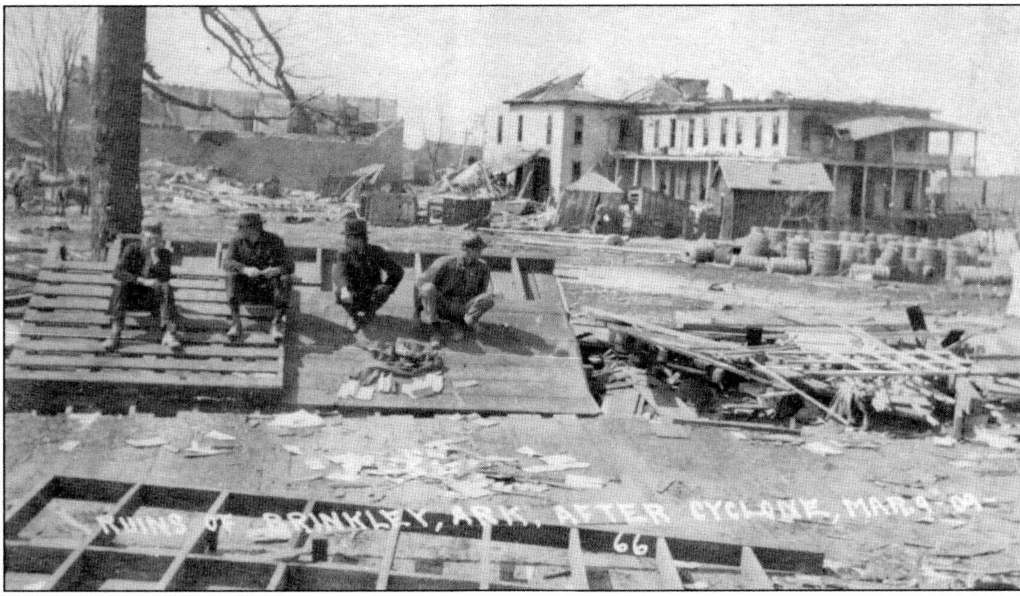

The *Woodruff County News* in McCrory, Arkansas, reported in its March 18, 1909, edition the following: "The cyclone that practically destroyed this city last week has passed into history, leaving all Arkansas engaged in the noble work of relieving the distress of the sufferers. The injured have been cared for and the immense amount of building material supplied by other cities is being used. The ruins and debris have been cleared away and the city will soon assume a more cheerful aspect." The April 2, 1909, edition of the *Brinkley Argus* proclaimed, "From early morning 'till late at night, the songs of the hammer, saw and other tools in the hands of an army of workmen are heard throughout Brinkley. They are engaged in apparently a mad rush to build a NEW BRINKLEY and 'do it now'. Besides the thousands upon thousands of dollars being paid out regularly each day in Brinkley, now there is every indication that even greater business is ahead."

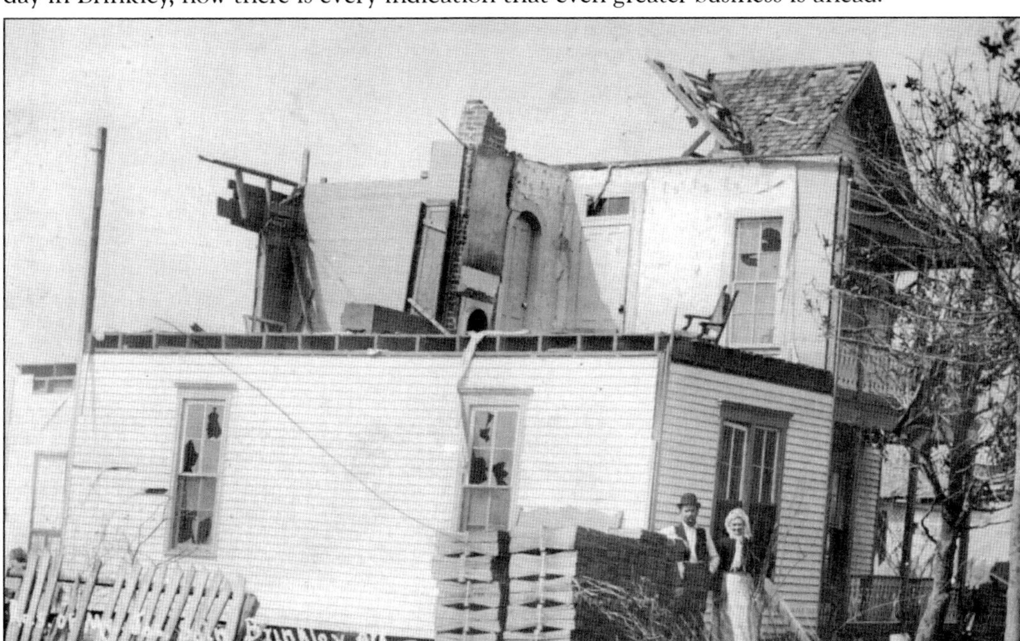

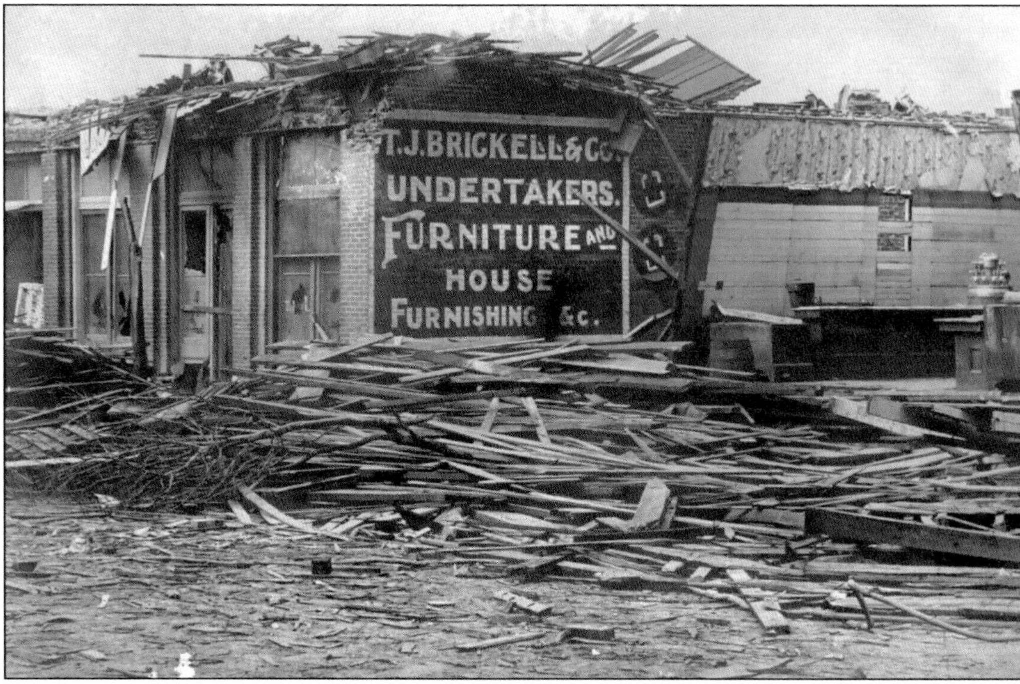

Tornadoes are the most destructive of all weather-related events, producing the most violent winds on earth, some over 300 miles per hour. They can be nearly invisible, marked only by swirling debris at the base of the funnel, and can reach heights of 60,000 feet into the atmosphere. The average tornado's path is about 4 miles on the ground, cutting a swath about 400 yards wide. The worst ones, like the one that hit Brinkley, can travel for 100 miles and can be as large as a mile wide. The March 8, 1909, cyclone was classified as a F4 on the Fujita Scale, which is defined as a devastating tornado (with wind speeds of 207 to 260 miles per hour) that levels houses and blows structures with weak foundations and cars for some distance.

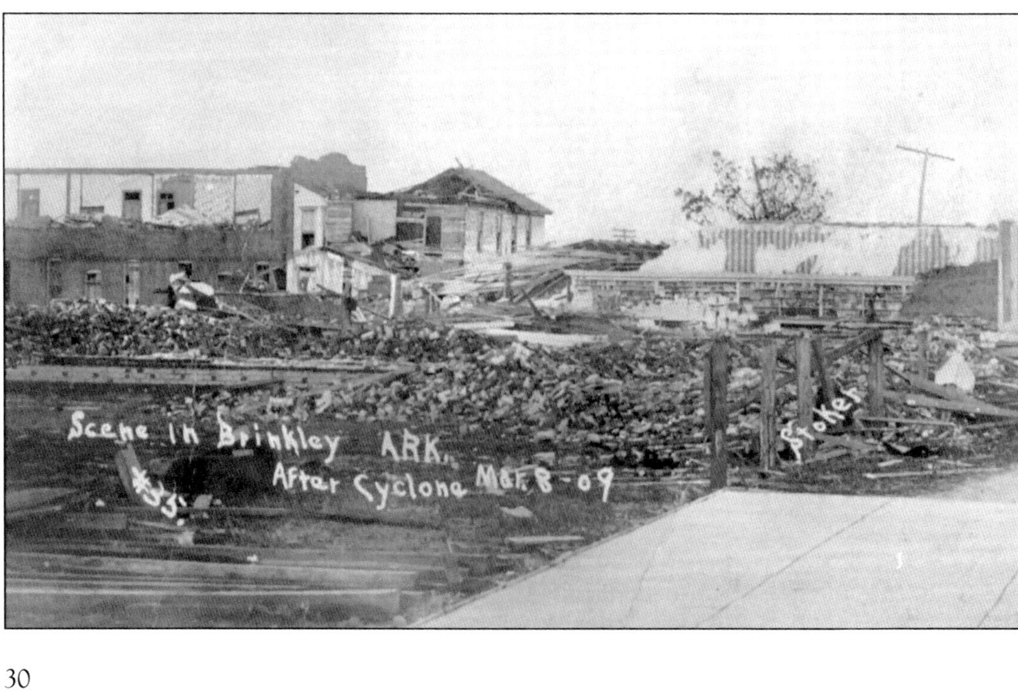

Three

The Great Flood of 1927

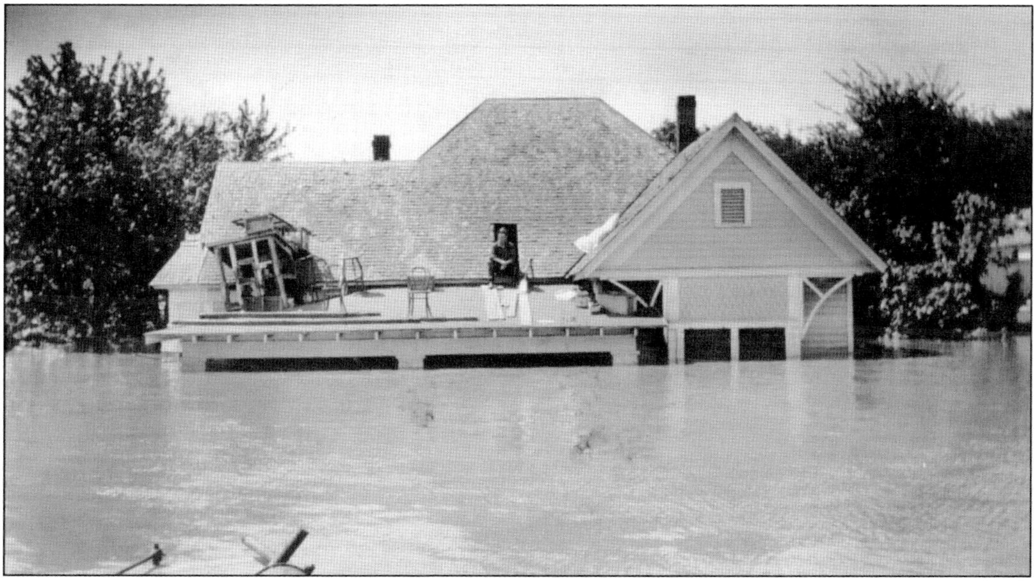

The flood of 1927 was the most destructive and costly flood in the history of Arkansas and the worst in the history of the nation. It afflicted Arkansas with a greater amount of devastation than any other state along the Mississippi River Valley. Pictured above is the McCabe home in Clarendon, with the owner sitting on the roof with what furniture he could salvage. (Courtesy of Jo Claire English.)

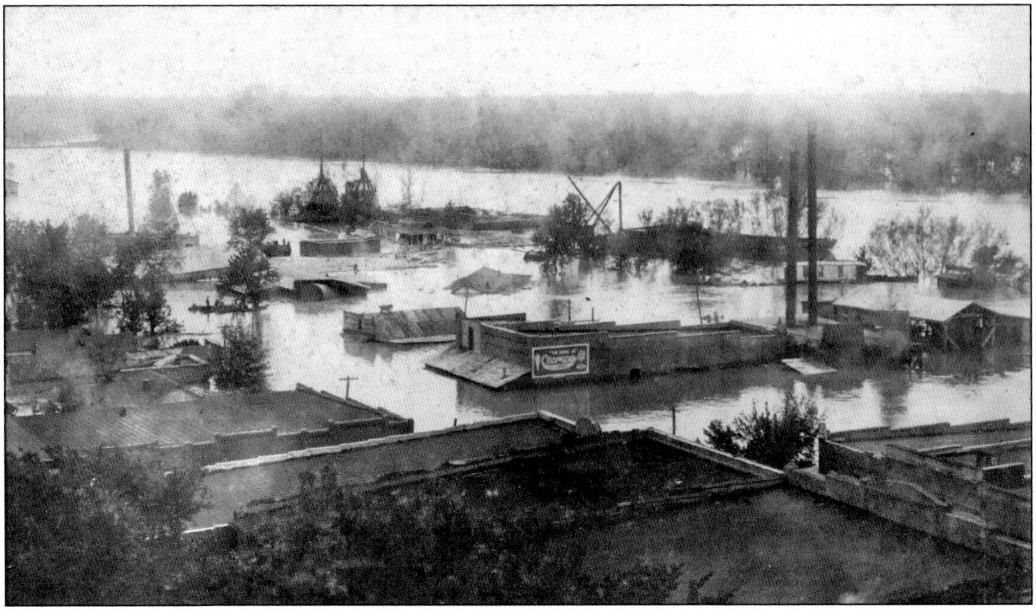

Above is a view of the flooded White River after it broke through the levees at 2:00 a.m. on April 20, allowing 38.5 feet of water to sweep over Clarendon. The water was recorded to have reached a depth of 16 feet on the city streets. April 1927 brought record rainfall, with more than 7 inches falling within just a few hours. The ground was already saturated from spring rains, and the Mississippi River was swollen from heavy rains in the upper Midwest. With no place for it to go, the Mississippi River backed up into the Arkansas, White, and St. Francis Rivers, causing massive flooding. The White River was recorded to have run backwards at one point as torrents of water rushed into it from the Mississippi. The mighty Mississippi River remained at flood stage for a record 153 days. Portions of flooded areas were underwater from April until September 1927. (Both courtesy of Jo Claire English.)

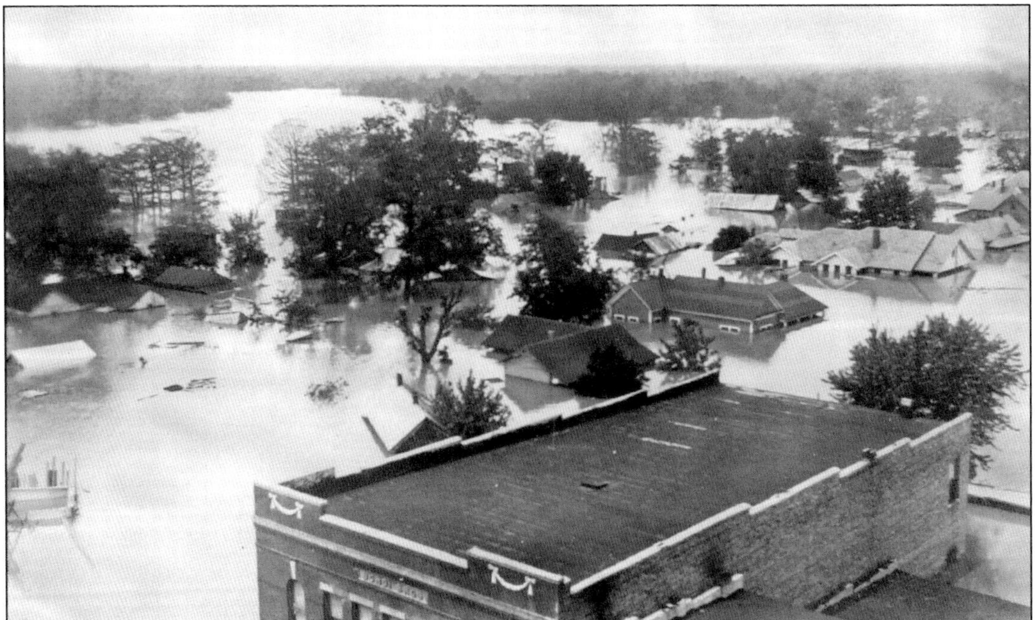

A young woman holds close what appear to be two small animals while being pushed to high ground by a man standing in waist-deep water on Madison Street in Clarendon. The wooden boat is loaded to capacity with a mattress, pillows, blanketing, and more than likely a few articles of clothing. (Courtesy of Jo Claire English.)

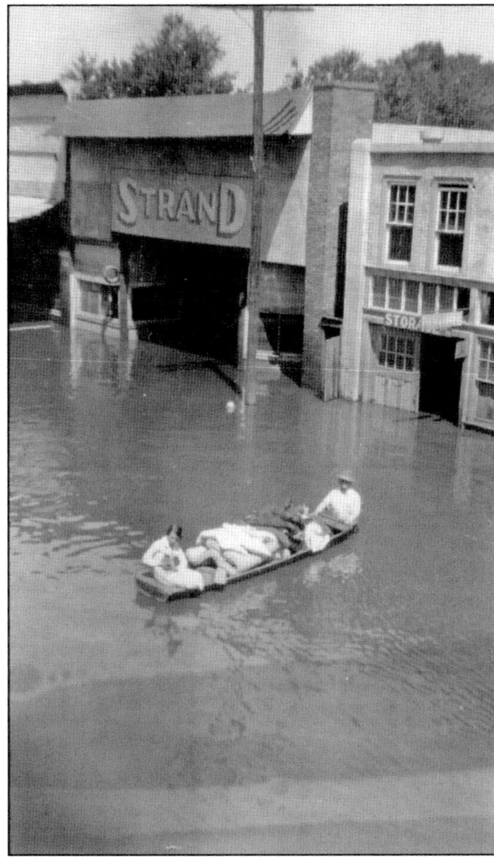

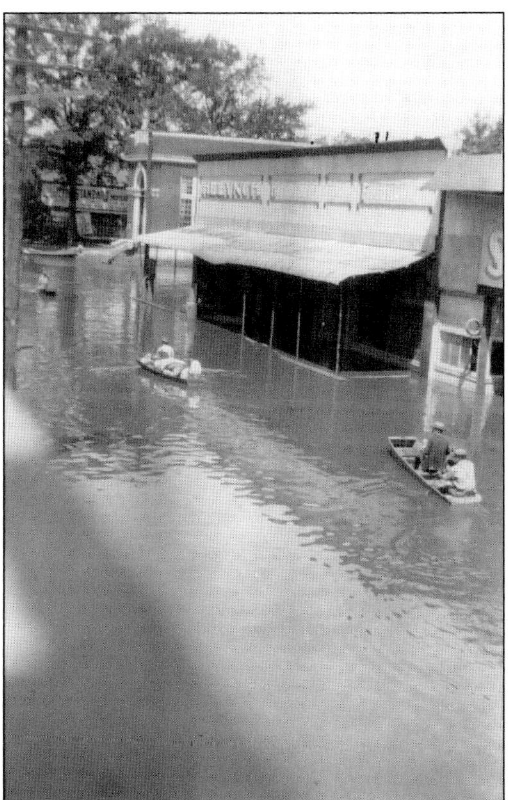

Rescue workers on Madison Street in Clarendon work to bring victims to high ground and shelter. A tent city was erected at Tom's Hill, where the Red Cross brought food and relief to the homeless families displaced by the flood. Many accounts of the tragedy state that had it not been for the efforts of the Red Cross, the disaster would have been much worse. (Courtesy of Jo Claire English.)

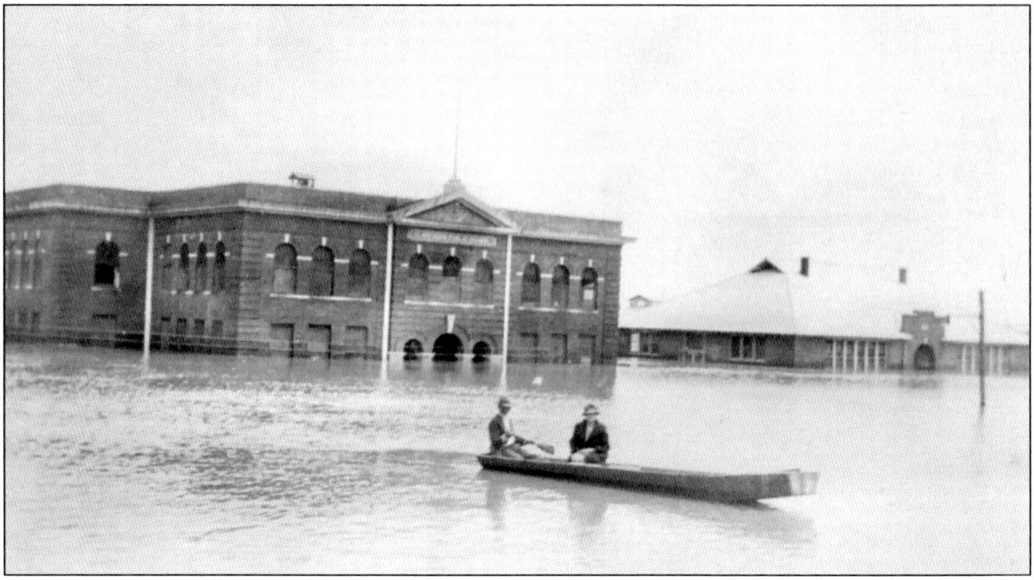

A Mr. Simmons and Sally Jackson, boating on the murky floodwater, survey the extent of the catastrophe. The Clarendon Public School in the background served as a safe haven for refugees fleeing the floodwater until they could be rescued by boat and taken to the Red Cross camp at Tom's Hill. (Courtesy of Jo Claire English.)

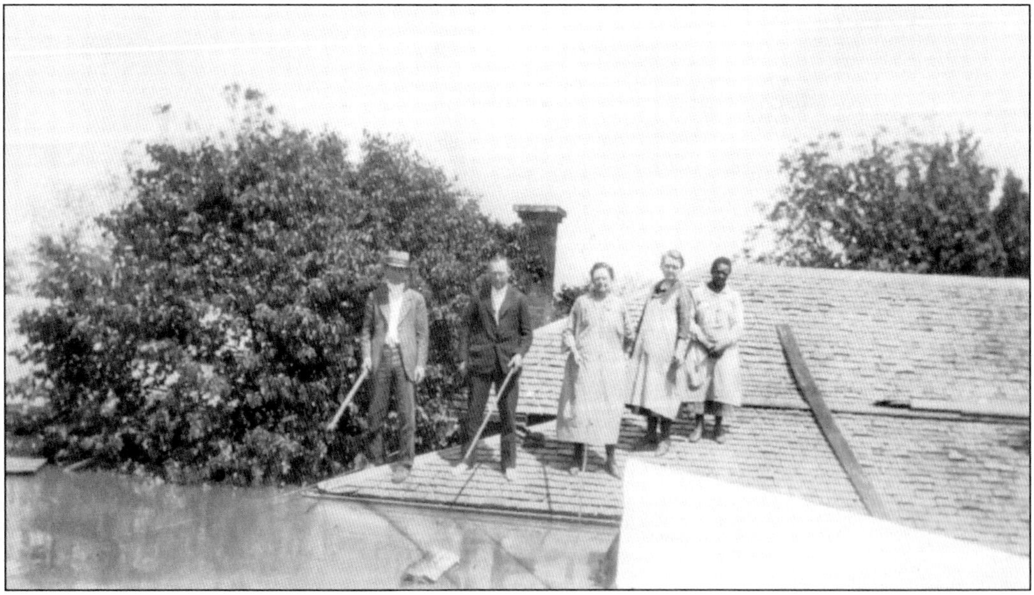

A Mr. Simmons, Rob English, and Sally Jackson are fishing with cane poles from the roof of Lucy's Boarding House in Clarendon, with boardinghouse owner Lucy Anderson and her maid, Rilla, viewing the fishermen's progress. The object to the right of Jackson is the roof of a shed washed against the house by the floodwater. (Courtesy of Jo Claire English.)

During the flood, Clarendon had to deal with the problem of looting. A state military company was called in, and on the same day, Guy Amsier, the secretary of the Arkansas Game and Fish Commission, arrived by motorboat from DeValls Bluff. He and his party transferred into a small skiff and paddled through the Monroe County Courthouse doorway, which is 6 feet above ground level. Pictured above is the courthouse underwater during the flood. (Courtesy of Jo Claire English.)

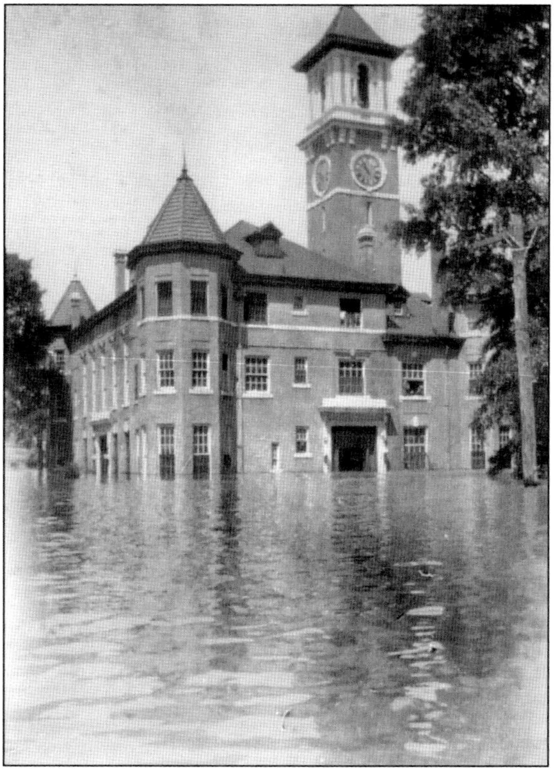

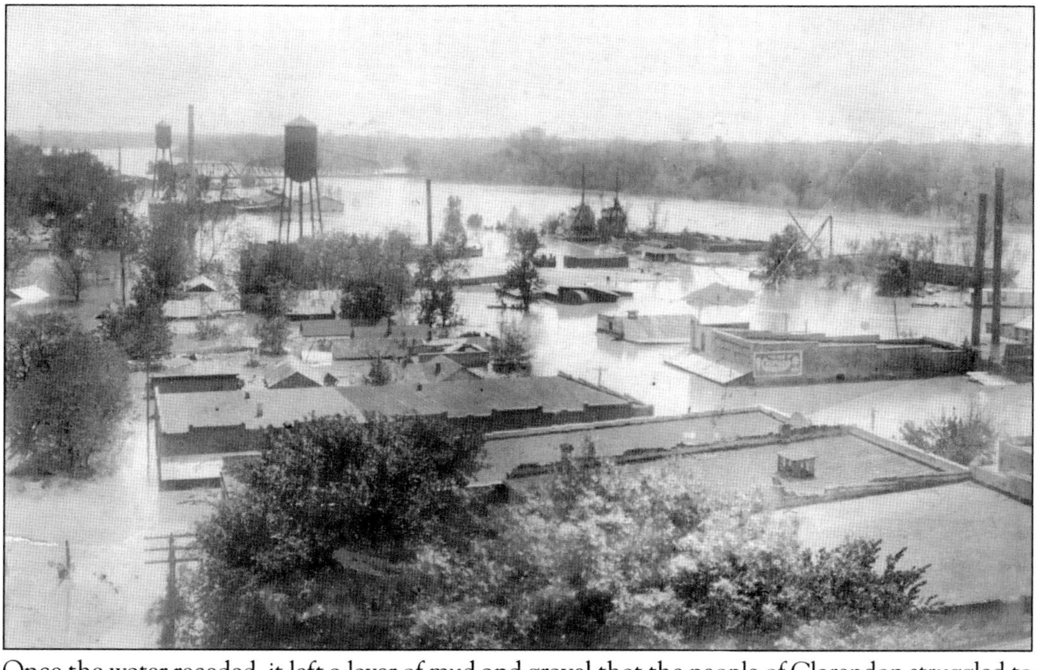

Once the water receded, it left a layer of mud and gravel that the people of Clarendon struggled to clean up. Sixty convicts were brought from the State Prison Farm at Tucker to help clean muddy debris from the streets. Water ruined most homes, and a terrible odor remained in the town for years. (Courtesy of Jo Claire English.)

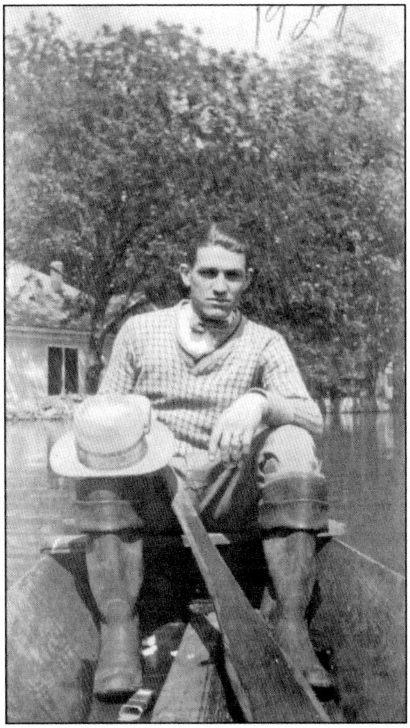
Holly Grove, like Clarendon, was submersed in floodwater from the White River. Dan A. McNeill had moved from Memphis to open a barbershop in Holly Grove. He is photographed here during the flood of 1927 while his shop lay under the muddy water of the White River. In later years he owned a bowling alley and a dry-cleaning business in the small community. (Courtesy of Danyelle McNeill Fletcher.)

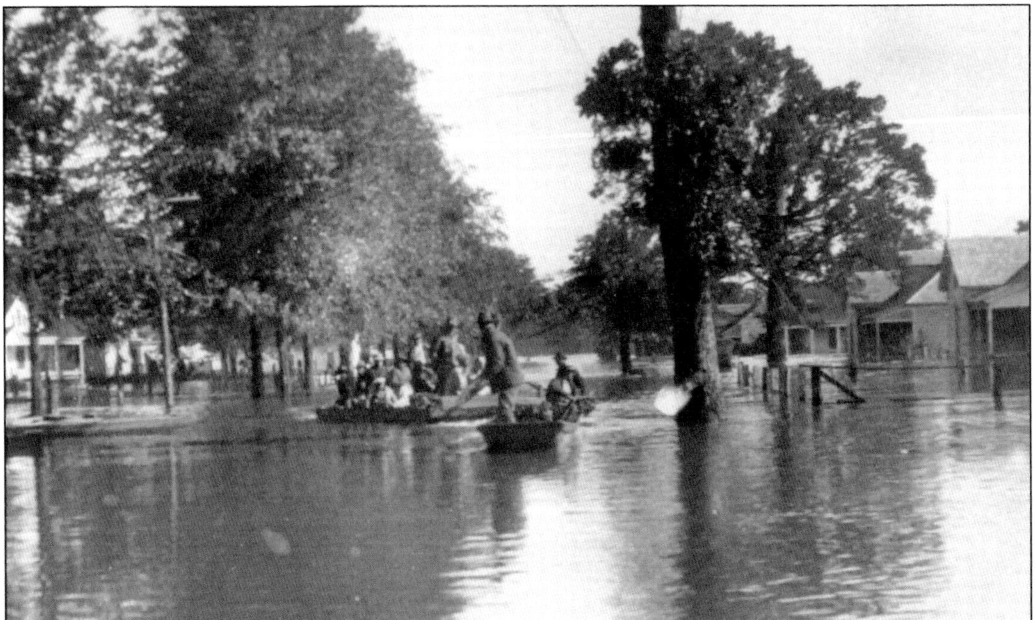
These unidentified men are floating down the flooded streets of Holly Grove. The Red Cross set up tent camps all across Arkansas to care for the flood victims. By the time the floodwaters receded, more than 325,000 refugees had been cared for in 154 Red Cross camps. They provided safe drinking water and food, gave hundreds of thousands of typhoid inoculations, controlled mosquitoes and malaria, disposed of dead animals, and gave medical attention to the sick and wounded. (Courtesy of Henry Wilks.)

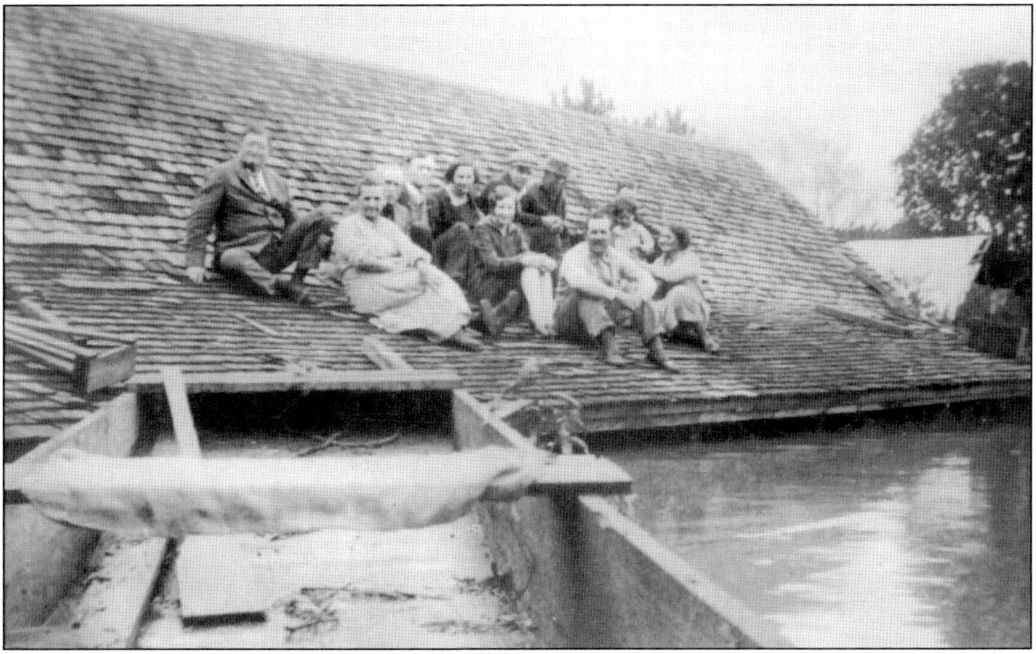

Although their situation seems desperate, the people congregated on this rooftop seem to be enjoying themselves while smiling for the camera. On May 5, the *Brinkley Argus* reported, "A merrier braver set I never saw, than these good people as they were setting about the task of coming again." (Courtesy of Jo Claire English.)

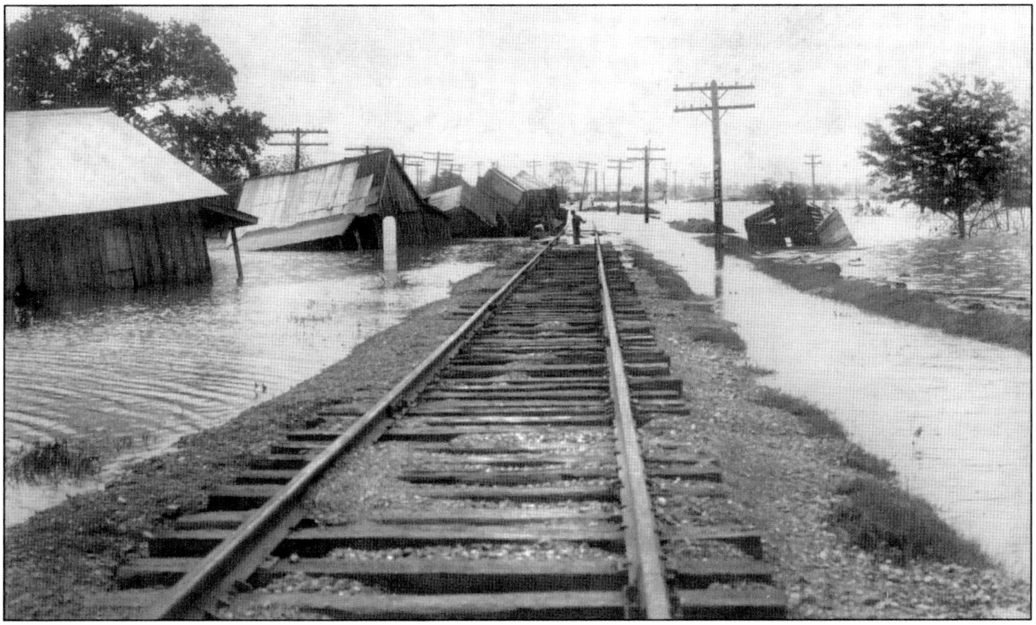

After the floodwaters receded, many Monroe County citizens returned to empty homesteads. Homes and barns were washed away by the floodwaters, and many lodged against railroad and road beds. Among the freaks of the flood was the washing away of a farm house on the Chaney Plantation that was replaced with a house floating in from the C. F. Greenlee Plantation. (Courtesy of Jo Claire English.)

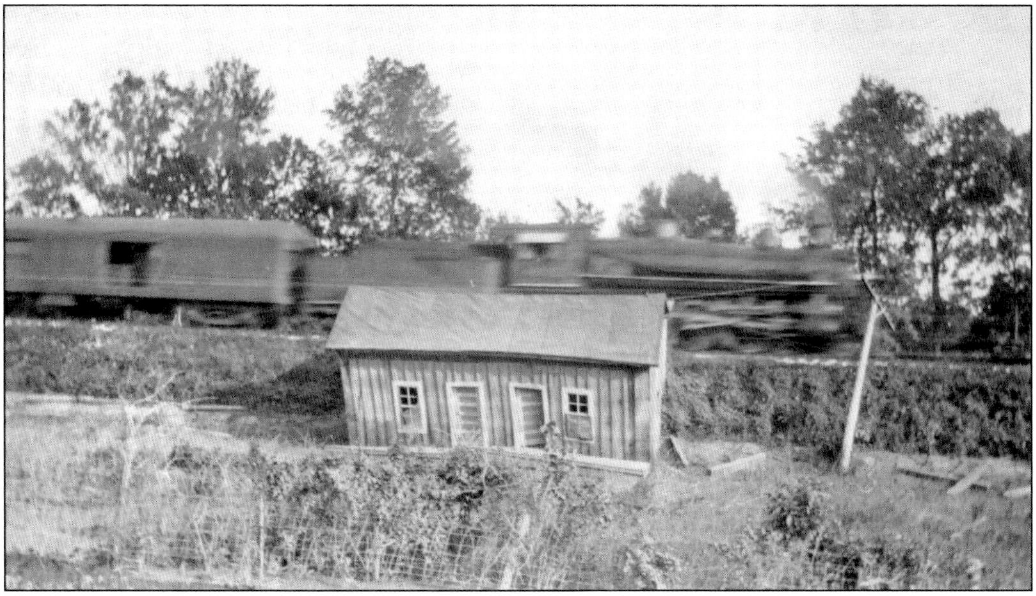

Everywhere in the county next to the White and Cache Rivers, scenes like these were commonplace. William Folsom of the *Brinkley Argus* made a trip to Clarendon when the water was receding to report on the damage, about which he printed in the May 5th edition, "The wreckage wrought is being revealed in all of its horrible hideousness as the water is going down. Houses washed into the street, plate glass fronts all crushed in, piles of wreckage washed into heaps in the stores and business places, and a deep covering of filthy mud over everything, terrible odors, arising from the putrid substances, all lend to cause you to wonder what on earth could be more terrible." (Both courtesy of Jo Claire English.)

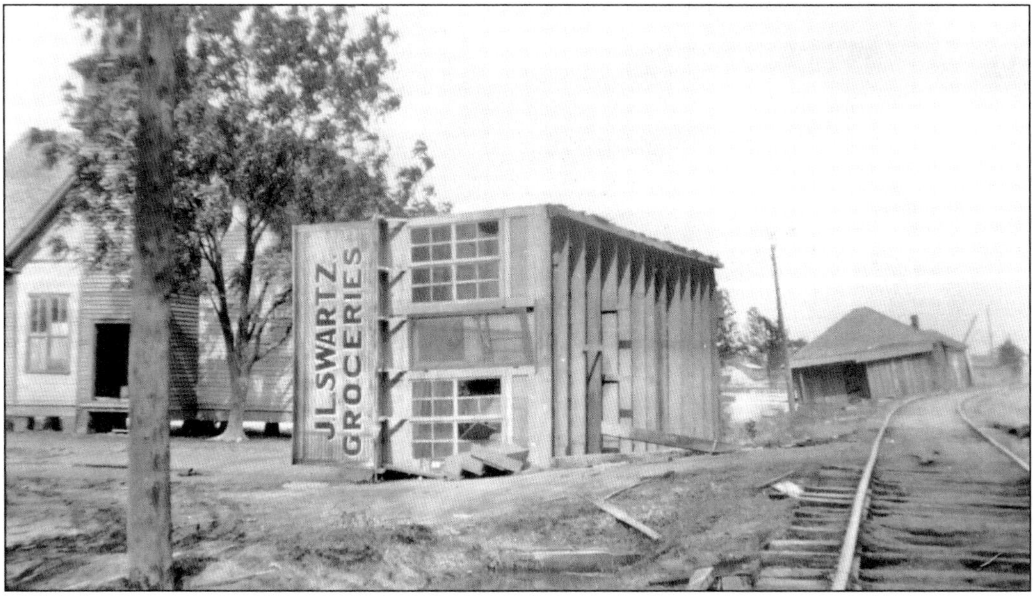

Four

AMERICA'S AMAZON

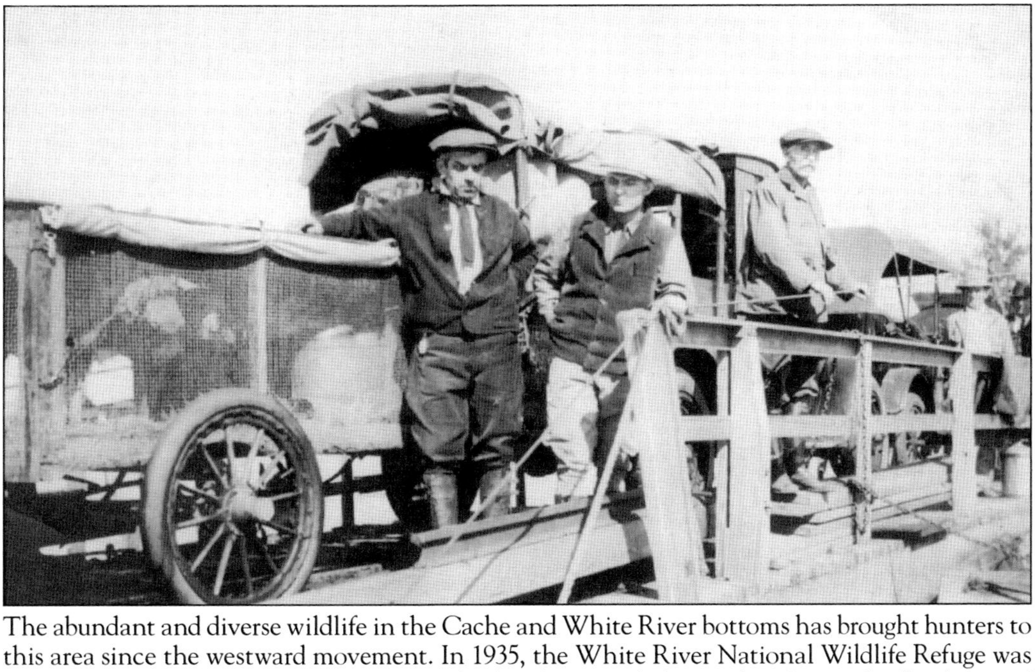

The abundant and diverse wildlife in the Cache and White River bottoms has brought hunters to this area since the westward movement. In 1935, the White River National Wildlife Refuge was established for the protection of migratory birds. The 90-mile-long refuge lies in the floodplain of the White River and is one of the largest remaining bottomland hardwood forests in the Mississippi River Valley. With over 300 lakes that are interlaced with streams, sloughs, and bayous, it is a haven for a myriad of wildlife and migratory birds. The 1916 caravan of hunters with their dogs in the photograph above are on the Cache River ferry on a hunting excursion in the bottomlands of Monroe County. (Courtesy of Billy Joe Holloway.)

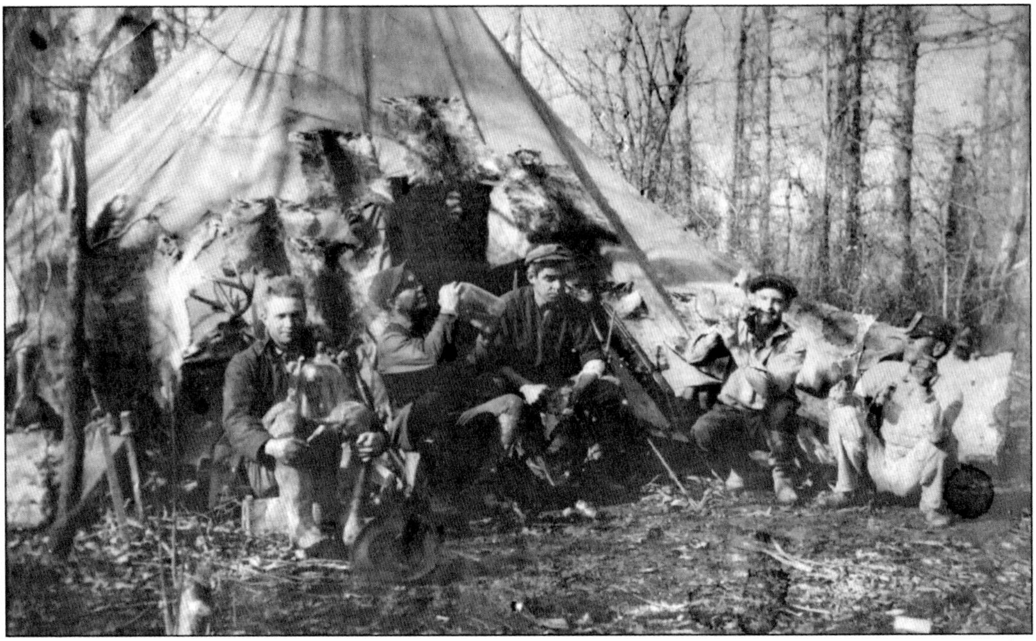

This primitive 1916 camp scene was photographed in the now Cache River Wildlife Refuge. The Cache River is a tributary of the White River and joins it at Clarendon. The name Cache is a Picardy word meaning "hunt" and is aptly named because of the abundant wildlife along the river. There are 53 mammal species, more than 200 species of birds, and nearly 50 species of reptiles and amphibians in the Cache River bottomlands. The only remaining population of black bears in Arkansas is found in this refuge. (Courtesy of Billy Joe Holloway.)

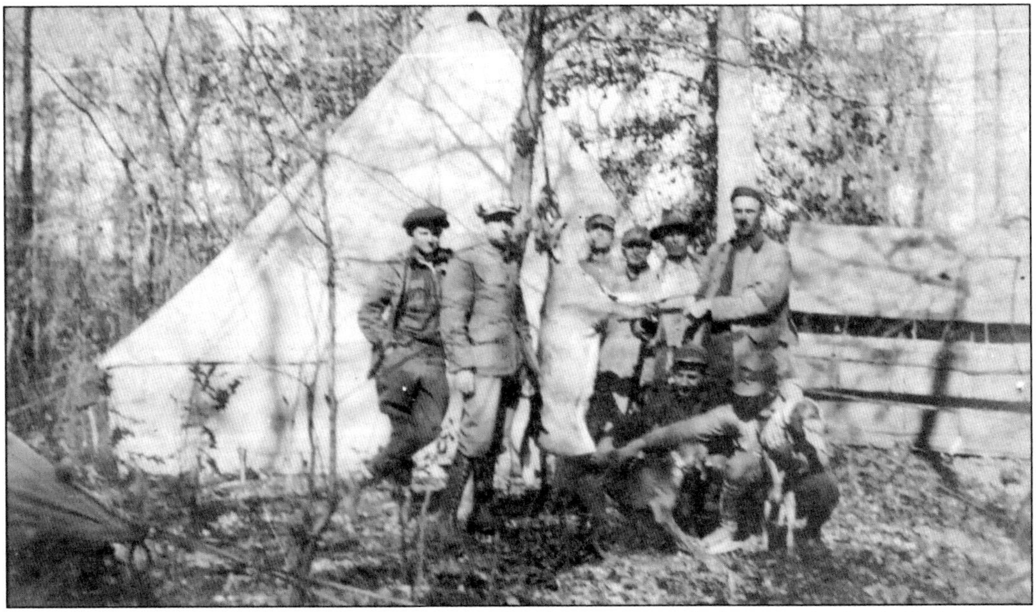

The 1916 hunting party near Robe Bayou poses for the camera with their trophy buck. Robe Bayou is situated in the Dagmar Wildlife Management area that received its name from a logging camp and small farming community located in this vicinity before the Great Flood of 1927. (Courtesy of Billy Joe Holloway.)

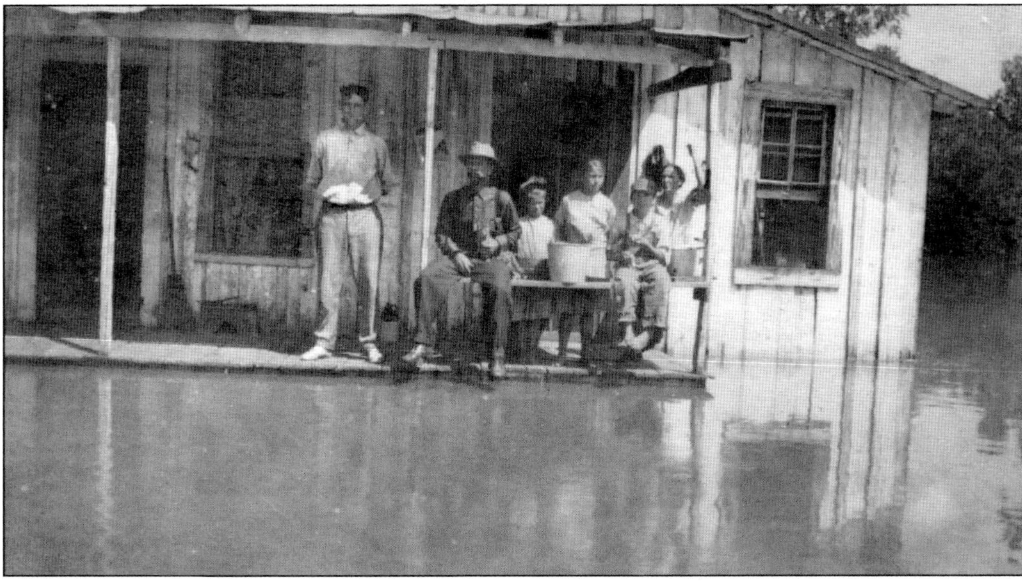

The Kim D. Lane family operated a boardinghouse for hunters and timber workers in the Cache River bottom. These *c.* 1916 photographs were taken during high water in the hardwood overflow area of Dagmar. The Cache River Wildlife Refuge contains the largest remaining tract of contiguous bottomland hardwood forest found in North America. After a tour of the refuges in 2000, former Secretary of the Interior Bruce Babbitt was quoted in the *National Wildlife Magazine* as saying, "I've got to tell you, I've never seen anything like this anywhere in the United States of America. The only place that's even remotely comparable is the Amazon, because of the same amazing phenomenon of rivers flowing through the forest." (Both courtesy of Billy Joe Holloway.)

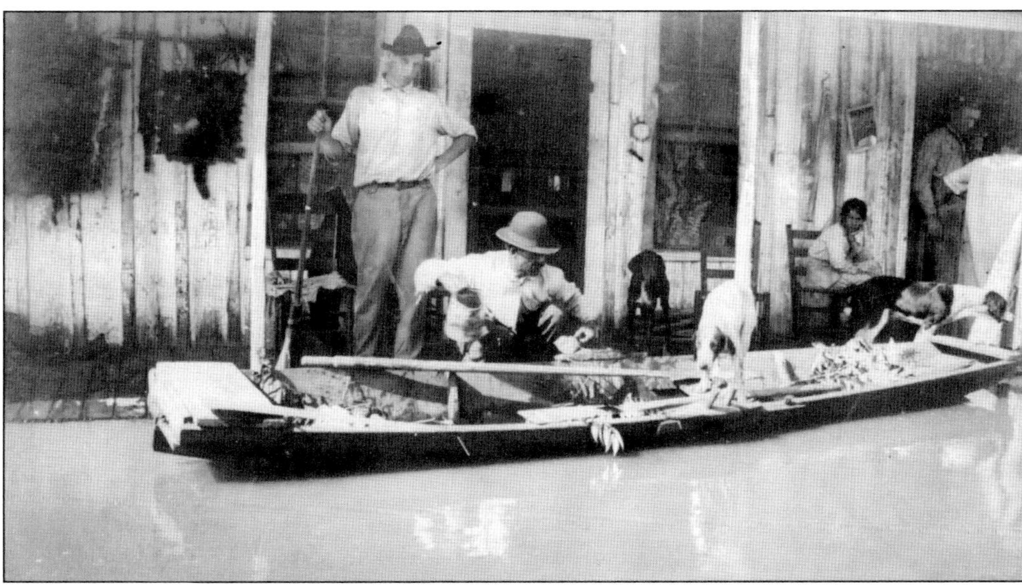

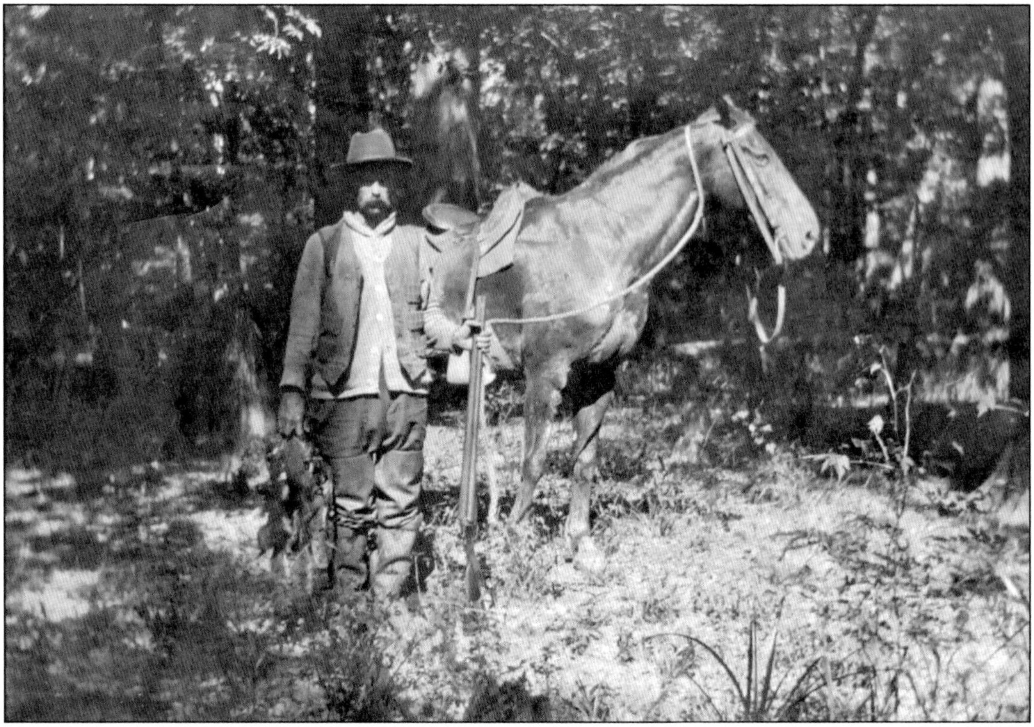

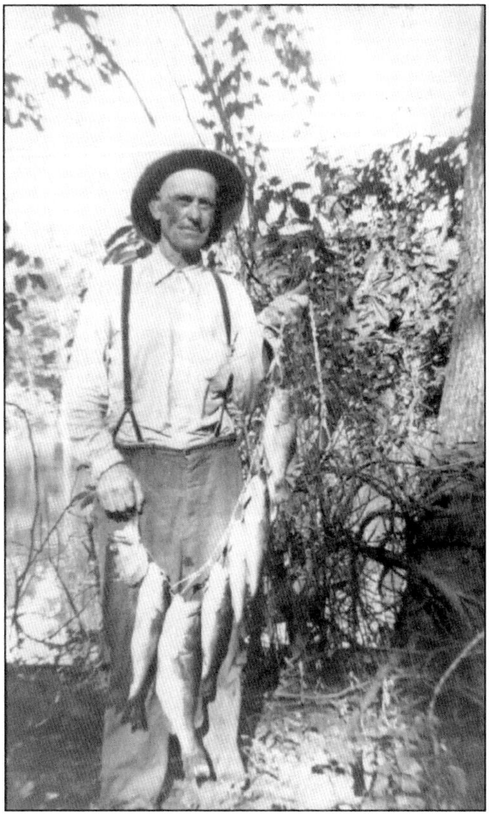

Kim Lane is shown above in 1916 with his horse, which, as the stories tell, would lead him home when he was lost in the vast river bottomlands. He is photographed at left in later years with his catch of fish from the Cache River. His hunting and fishing grounds are now the Dagmar Wildlife Management area, near the 160,000-acre White River Wildlife Refuge and the adjacent 45,000-acre Cache River Wildlife Refuge. Two centuries ago, the bottomland forests of the lower Mississippi River Valley covered 24 million acres through seven states. These were the "Big Woods" that author William Faulkner rhapsodized about in his novels three-quarters of a century ago. Only 20 percent of those great forests remain today. (Both courtesy of Billy Joe Holloway.)

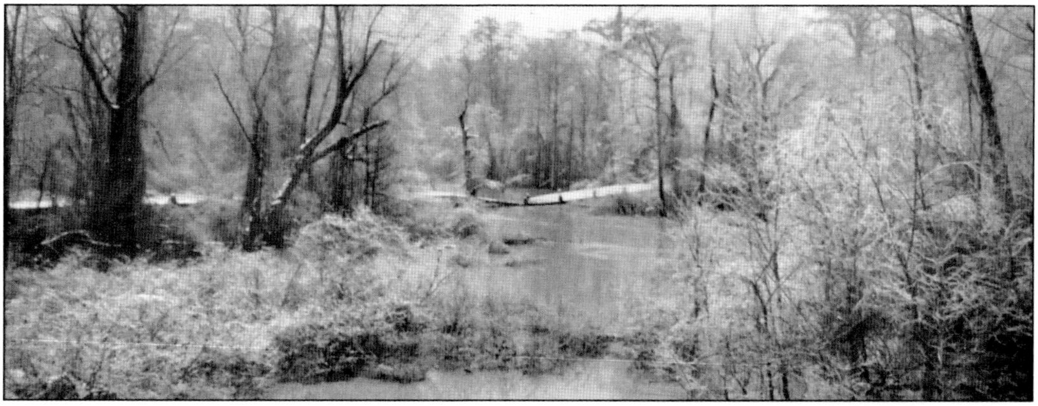

Pictured above is a view of Dagmar and the old Highway 70 bridge, and at right, a mighty bald cypress towers above the swamp where the ivory-billed woodpecker was sighted after it was believed to be extinct for over 60 years. The water beneath the cypresses' knobby knees holds a system of leaf litter, alluvial soil, and ever-changing water depths that nourish a complex web of life. University of Arkansas researcher Dave Stahle has documented 1,000-year-old cypress trees growing in the Dagmar Wildlife Refuge, noting there may be much older trees in the area. A study in 1995 found 21 mussel beds in the 90 miles of White River within the refuge, including the endangered pink mucket, and more than 100 species of fish. (Both photographs by and courtesy of Steve Hinton.)

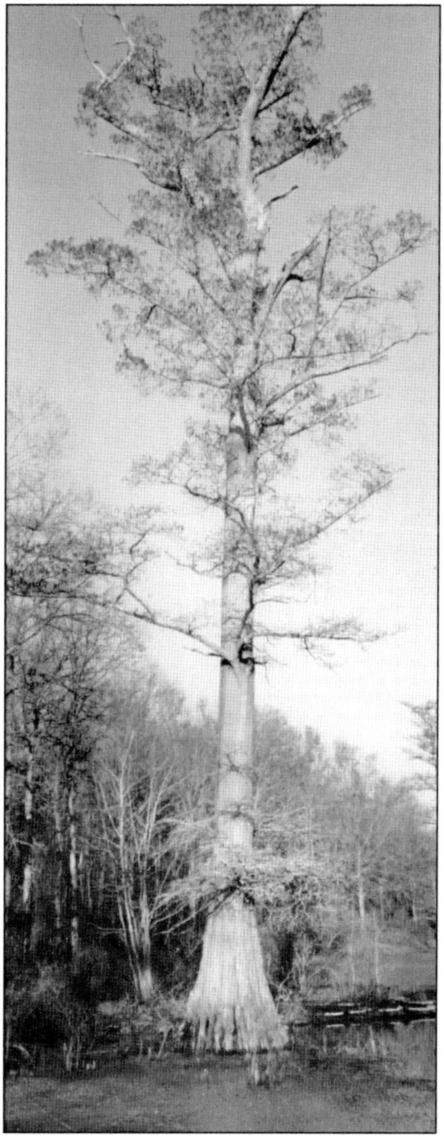

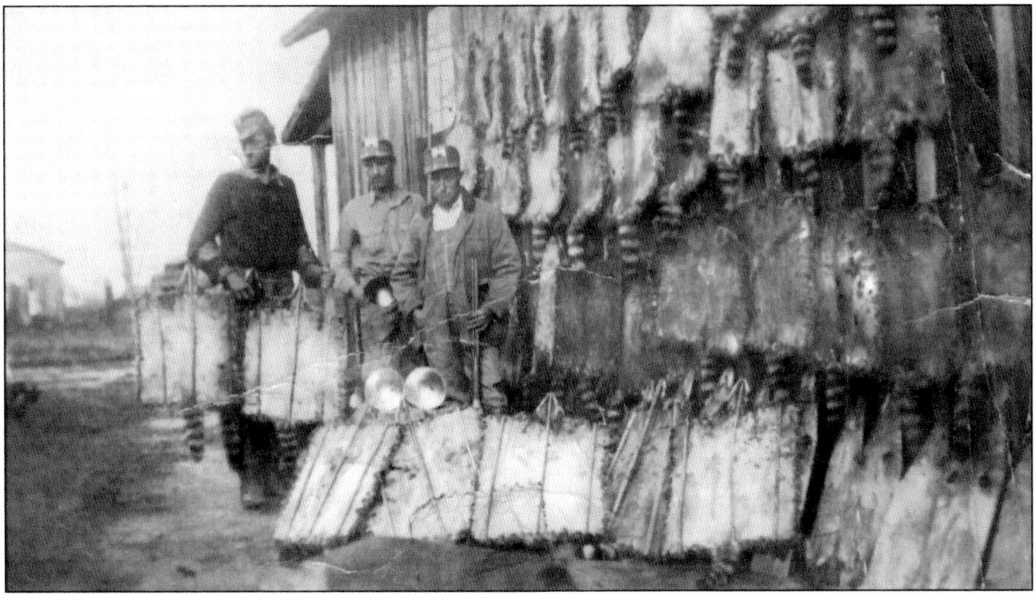

The White River travels nearly 720 miles and, in its early days, was prone to massive flooding during the spring of each year. Many people lived in houseboats, and there were even floating grocery stores along the river. These boats would buy fur pelts, such as the raccoon hides pictured above in this 1941 photograph of Arleigh Cook, Bill Kirtley, and Lenord Holloway (far right). Mussel shells were gathered from the bottom of the rivers by boats like the one pictured below. The boats were equipped with a lengthwise rack on each side that held 8- to 12-foot-long bars with strings tied to the bar every 6 to 12 inches, which held several "crowsfeet," four-pronged blunt hooks that would be dragged across the mussel beds. The mussels were used for food, and the shells were sold to factories for income. The factories along the White River in the early 1900s were the major source of pearl buttons for the world. (Above courtesy of Billy Joe Holloway; below courtesy of Jo Claire English.)

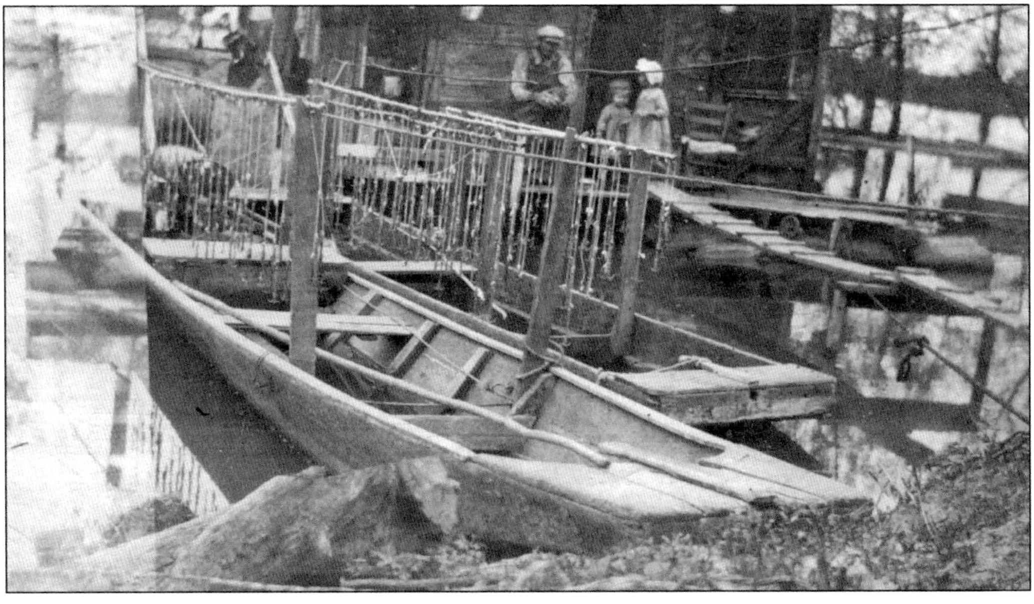

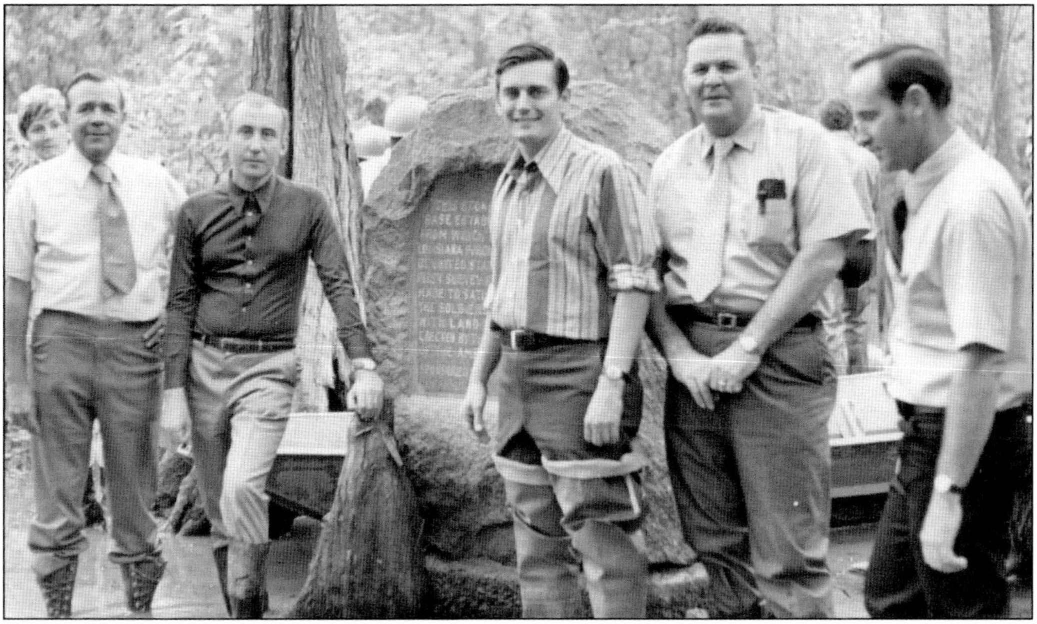

In the 1960s, dignitaries, including William Alexander (third from the right), stand beside the Louisiana Purchase Monument in the black-water swamp near Blackton, Arkansas. This point marks the origin of every township boundary and property line in 15 American states. The survey of the purchase was made to satisfy the claims of the War of 1812 soldiers with land bounties from a poor government who did not want to deplete the treasury.

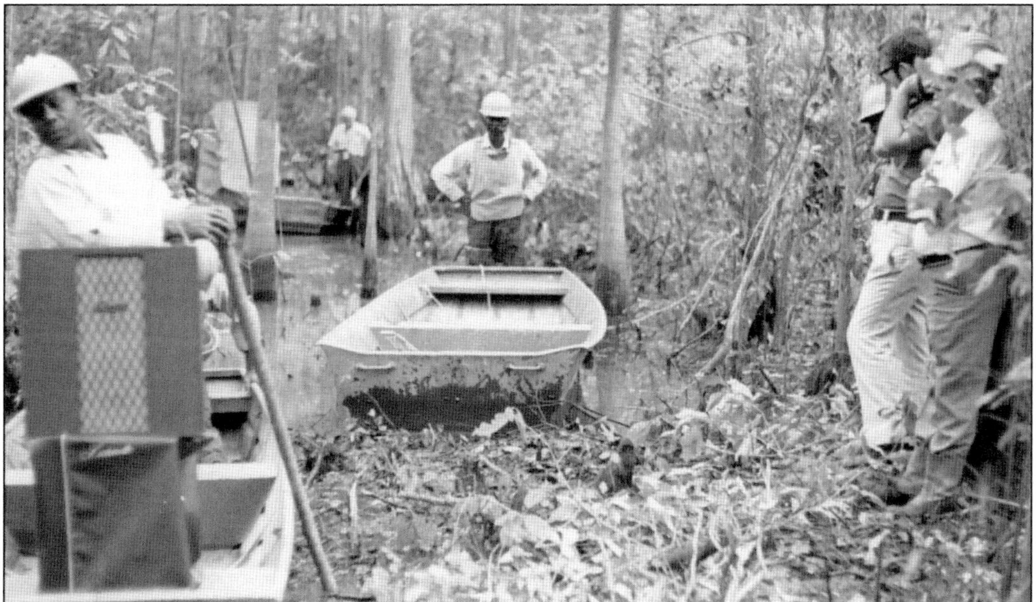

Arkansas Green Thumb workers built the 100-yard boardwalk to the Louisiana Purchase Monument from lumber donated by Potlatch Forests, Inc. For the first time in more than a century and a half, the people of the United States could see one of the vital stage settings in the events that transpired from the Louisiana Purchase. Green Thumb was a federal program designed to provide work for elderly persons whose income was below the poverty level.

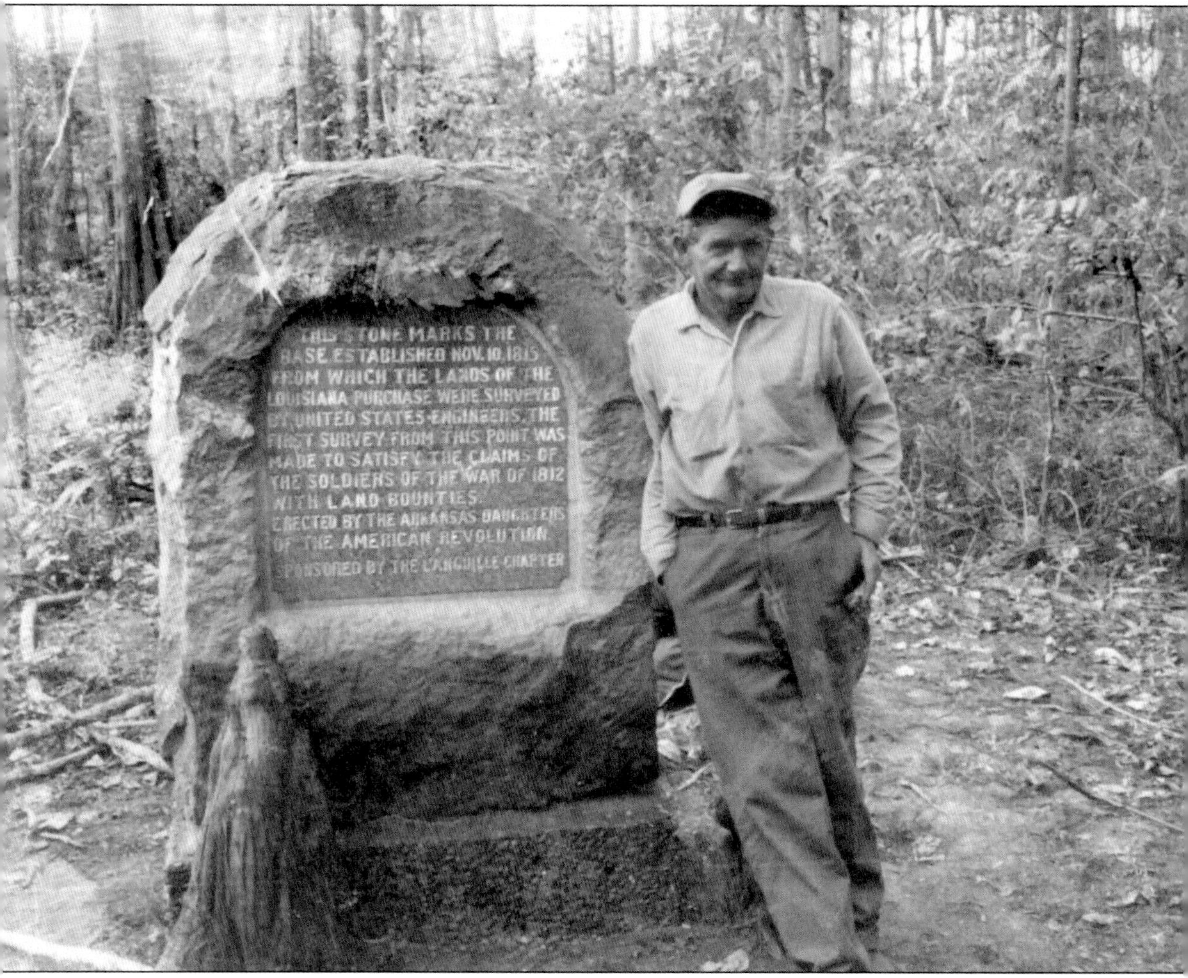

Udell Cupp is pictured above leaning against the Louisiana Purchase Monument placed in the black-water swamp by the Daughters of the American Revolution's L'Anguille chapter in 1926. After the dedication of the monument, the marker remained obscure until searchers rediscovered the landmark and lawmakers designated the initial point of survey of the Louisiana Purchase a state park in 1961. Cupp was a logging man who happened upon the marker one day during a dry season in the swamp. (Courtesy of Diana Cupp Howton.)

Five

EARLY ENTERPRISERS

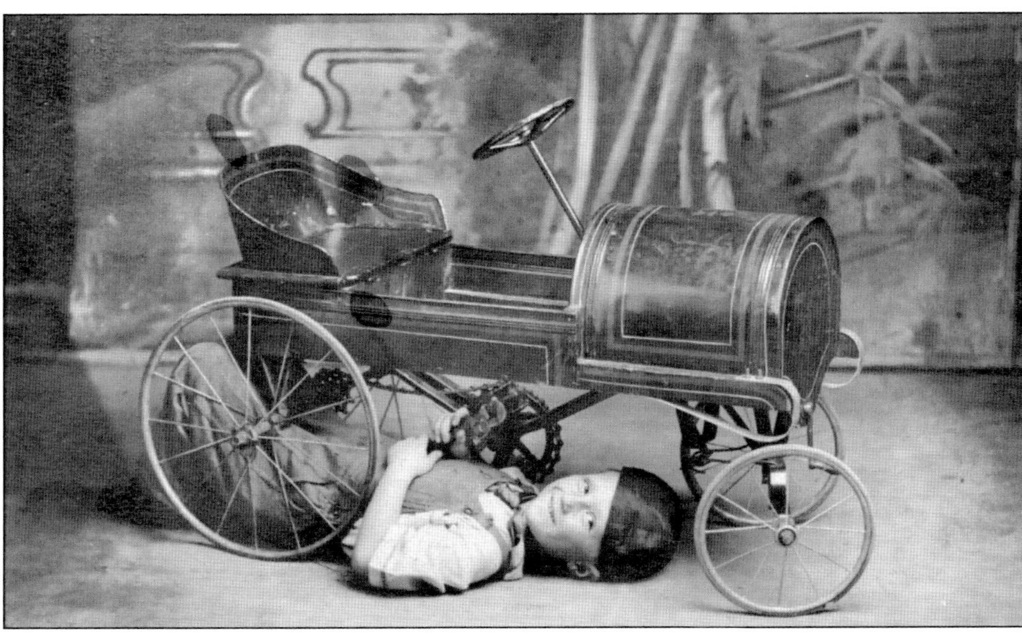

Fred T. Murphy Jr., in the photograph above, was the son of a prominent Brinkley doctor. While those who remember the younger cannot remember any occupation he held, they can recount what a fine doctor his father, Fred Murphy Sr., was and the city holdings he possessed. The office of Dr. Fred Murphy was in the two-story building on the corner of Main and Cypress Streets.

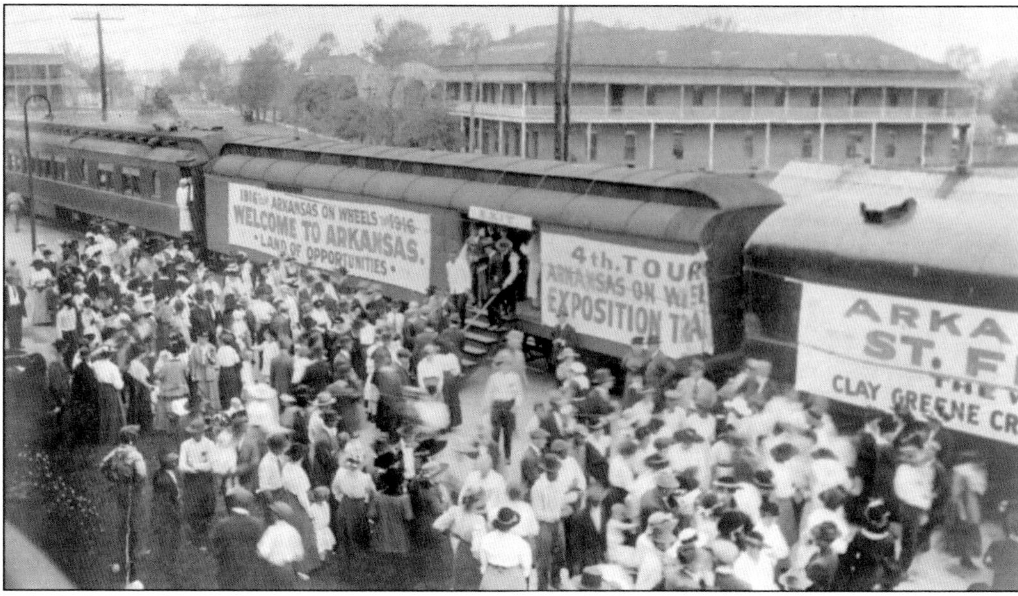

A little known but ambitious newspaperman, William B. Folsom, publisher of the *Brinkley Argus*, conceived an idea of promoting Arkansas with a show train in the year 1910. Arkansas on Wheels was, in effect, a traveling state fair with exhibits of every description, representing nearly every county in the state, all attractively displayed in three baggage cars. Hundreds of people were present on December 1, 1910, to bid bon voyage as Arkansas's most magnificent advertising scheme left for its trip through the Midwest, passing through Tennessee, Kentucky, Illinois, Iowa, Nebraska, Kansas, and Oklahoma. Brinkley, pictured above, was the only Arkansas stop for the traveling exposition. The traveling exposition was such a success that it continued until 1916. Below are the leaders of this and earlier trips, on the last Arkansas on Wheels exposition with W. B. Folsom pictured fourth from the right. (Both courtesy of the Arkansas History Commission.)

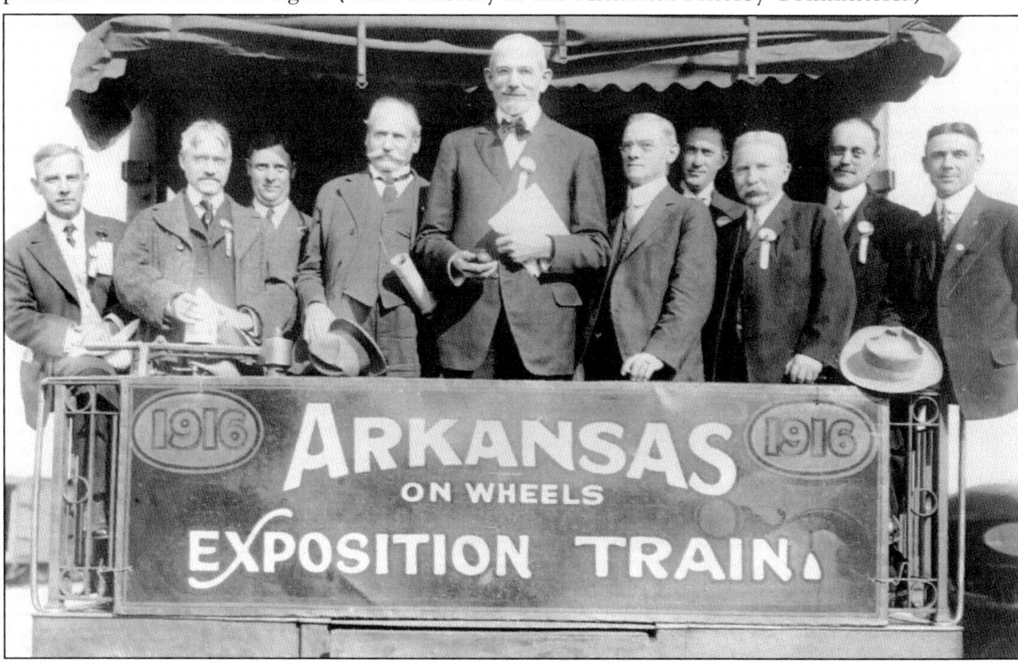

Pioneer hotel man Gus Rusher holds the hand of his grandson, Albert H. Rusher. The Roescher family came to Brinkley from Baden Baden, Germany, where they were innkeepers. In the 1890s, Gus Roescher purchased a hotel on Cypress Street and named it the Hotel de Arlington, which burned in 1901. Roescher rebounded and rebuilt the hotel on Cedar Street in 1903. It was destroyed by the cyclone of 1909. Still undaunted by misfortune, Roescher rebuilt the hotel. In 1913, the Brinkley House, owned by Capt. William S. McCullough, burned to the ground, and Roescher bought the property and built the grand Hotel Rusher. During World War I, anti-German feelings became so strong in the United States that Gus Roescher changed the spelling of his name to "Rusher." (Courtesy of Albert H. Rusher.)

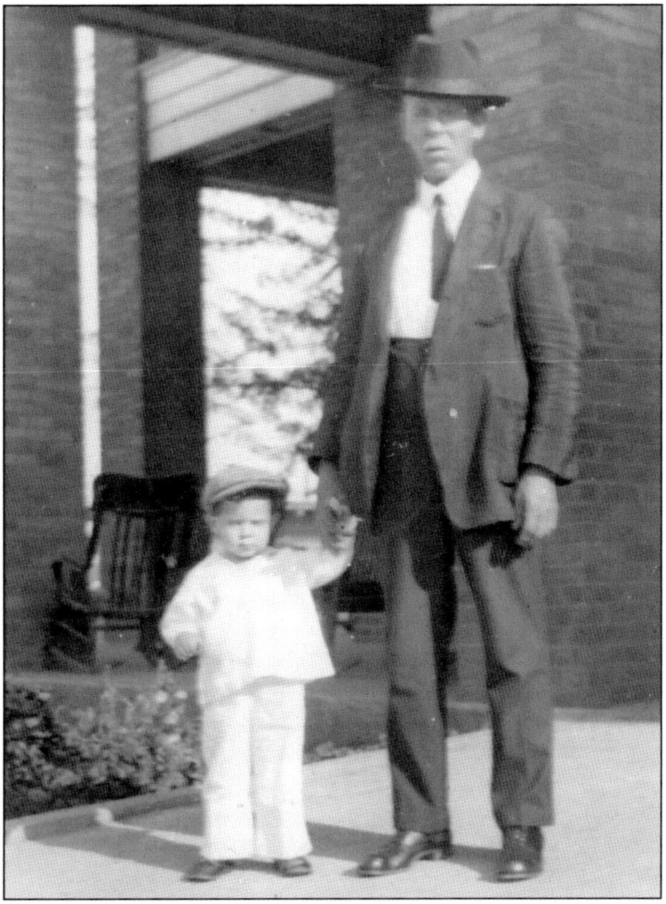

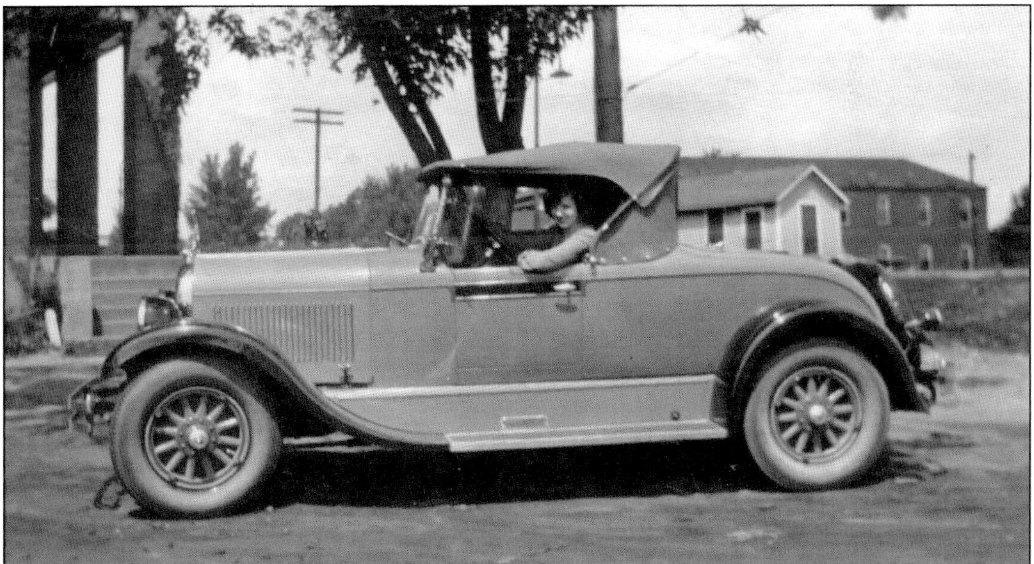

Dorcas Rusher, wife of Albert L. Rusher and mother of Albert H. Rusher, poses in her elegant new automobile in front of the Hotel Rusher in the 1920s. (Courtesy of Albert H. Rusher.)

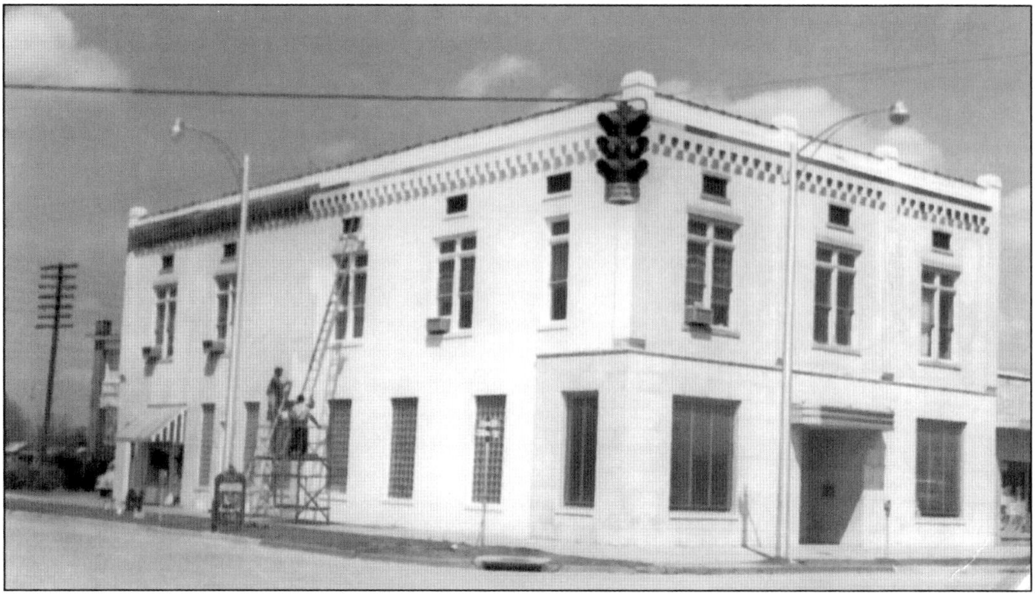

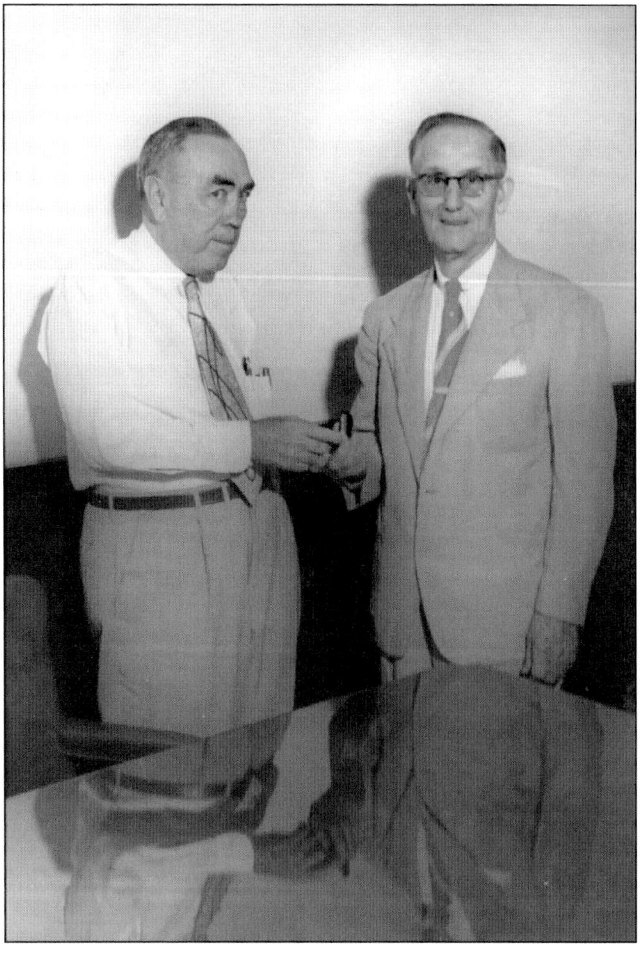

On January 16, 1903, the Articles of Agreement and Incorporation of the Bank of Brinkley were signed by W. E. Talley, H. C. Strong, H. A. Carter, V. V. Allen, T. L. Hefferman, James Gunn Sr., and Frank Andrews. The Bank of Brinkley was opened for business on March 11, 1903, and operated for 71 years on the corner of Cypress Street and New Orleans Avenue. During the early years, the bank occupied the front left section, Dr. Ed McKnight had his office in the rear section of the building, and Midkiff and Sons Funeral Home was located in the right portion of the building. The Sharp Law Firm occupied the second story. The photograph above shows the bank being remodeled after taking over the entire ground floor of the building. Pictured at left are W. W. Sharp (left), bank president from 1950 to 1955, and Frank Andrews, one of the original organizers, who was also vice president and secretary of the board of directors. (Both courtesy of Albert H. Rusher.)

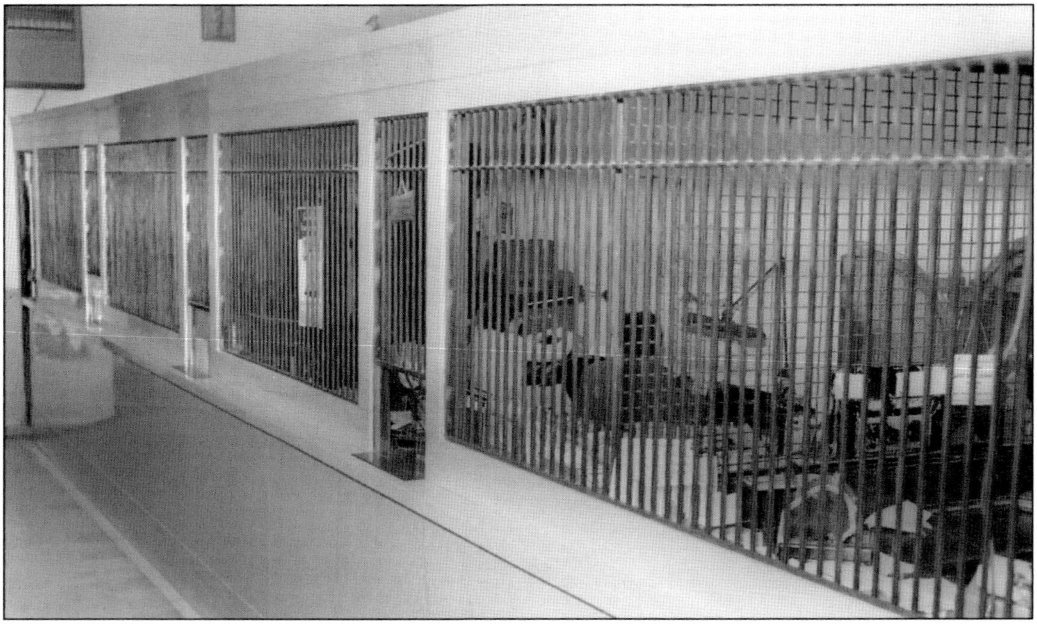

When the Bank of Brinkley opened in 1903, the original capital structure consisted of 800 shares of common stock at a par value of $25 per share, or a total capital stock amount of $20,000. In one week's time, it had increased to $25,000. By year's end, the total resources numbered $58,355, and by 1992, on the 90th anniversary of the bank, total assets were $65,362,132.60 and total deposits $56,568,430.08. The photograph above is a view of the teller windows during the 1920s and 1930s. The image below displays the remodeled teller windows during the 1940s and 1950s. The tellers from left to right are Dick Midkiff, Dorothy McKnight MacDonald, and Robert Moore. (Both courtesy of Albert H. Rusher.)

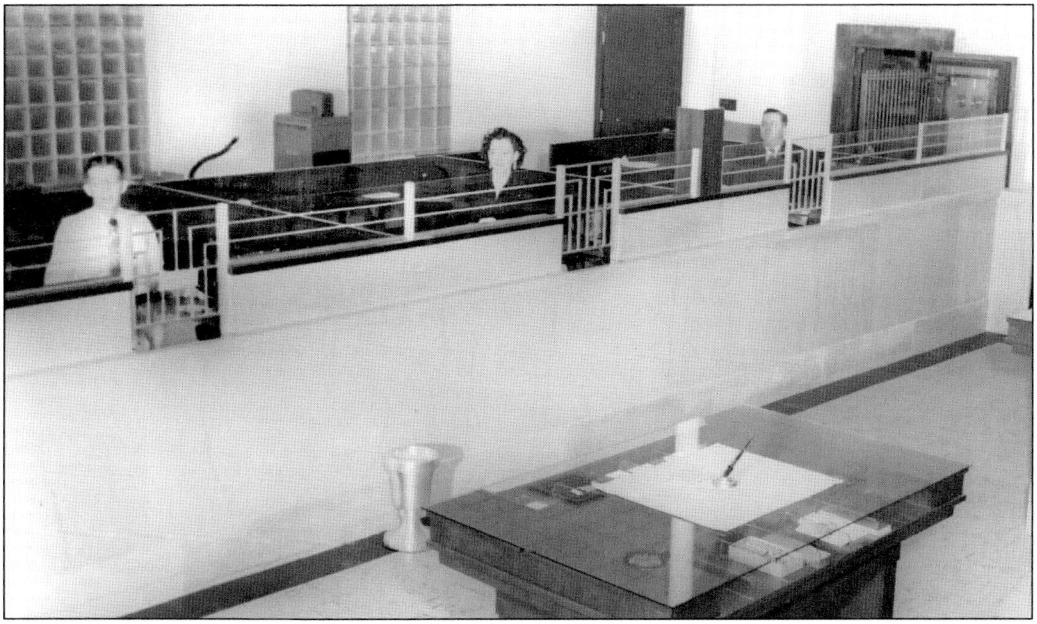

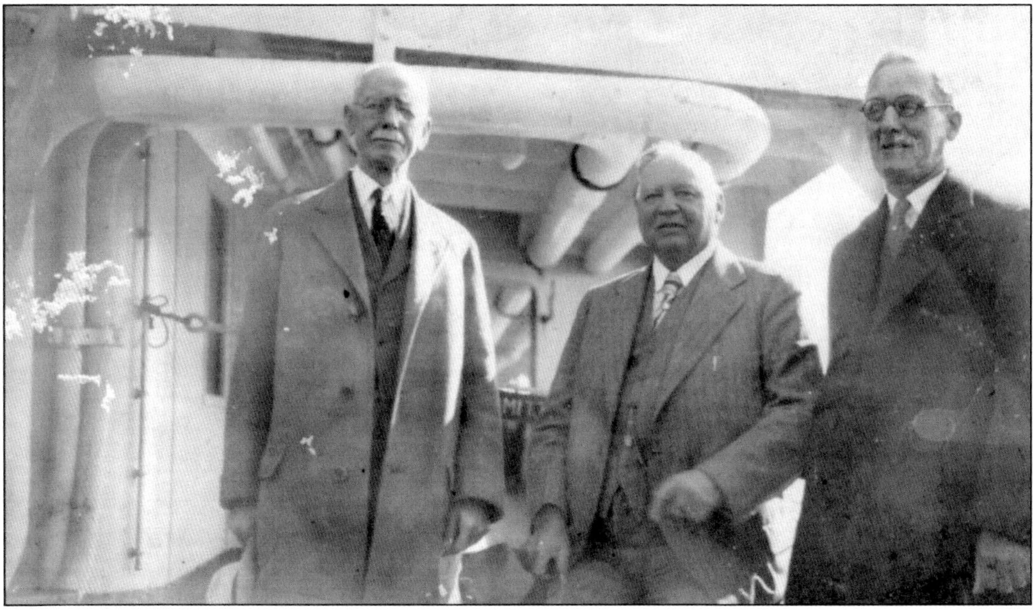

Brinkley's forefathers—Clarence Foster Greenlee ("the Judge," center), Frank Andrews, vice president of the Bank of Brinkley (right), and James Gunn (left)—are on a ship in San Jose, Costa Rica, in the 1930s. Gunn's uncle, John Gunn, never lived in Brinkley, yet he and William Black were considered Brinkley's founding fathers. Their vast landholdings and businesses were the foundation on which the town was built.

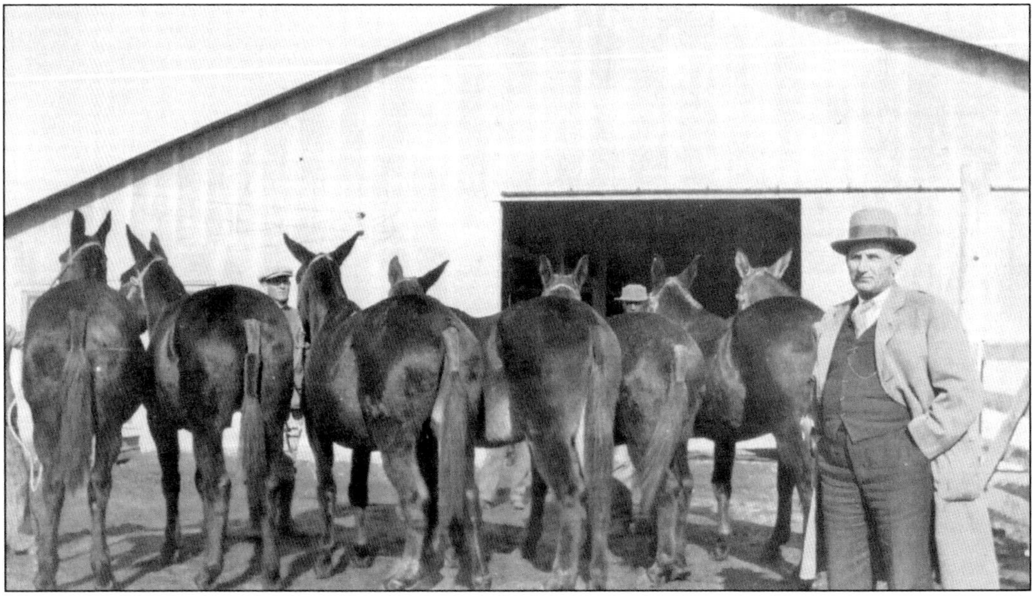

In the South, the mule dealer was the biggest man in town, and his barn was the center of trading activity. The delta was the boom place for mules in the 1930s, which were used as draft animals on the farms. Jim Goodson stands with his handsome mules in front of Goodson's Mule Barn, at the corner of Grand Avenue and Cypress Street. It opened for business in 1925 and closed sometime in 1935.

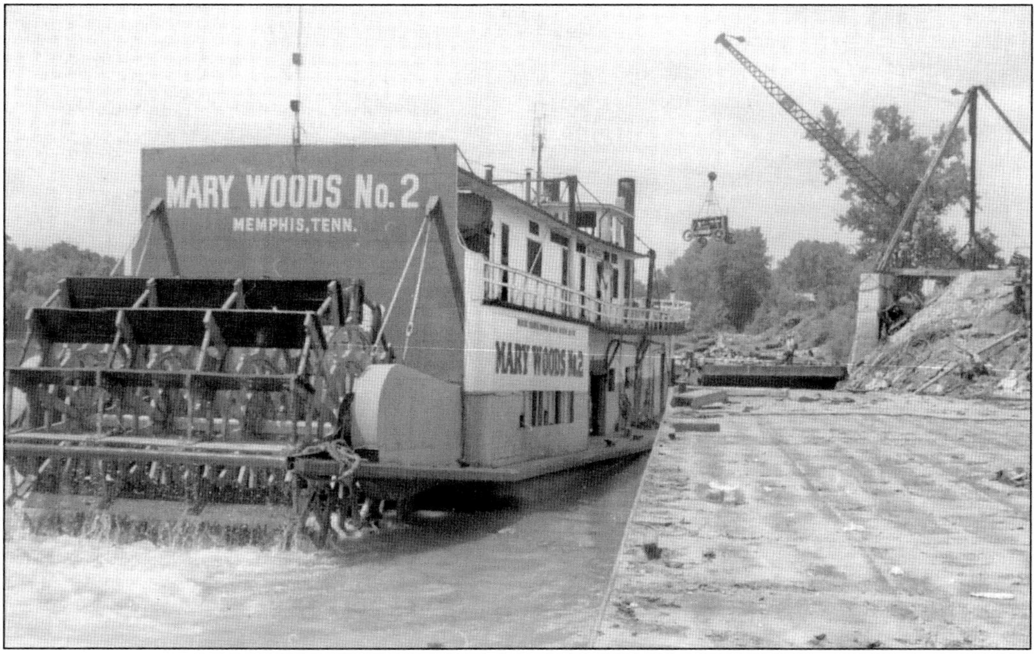

The steamboat above is the *Mary Woods No. 2*, owned by Eugene Woods Sr., founder of Woods Lumber Company in Clarendon. The steamboat's homeports were Memphis and Clarendon on the Mississippi and White Rivers. The crane in the background of the photographs is moving a vehicle to a barge to be transported downriver. In the late 1920s, when old Highway 70 was submerged by floodwaters between Brinkley and DeValls Bluff, motorists could drive over the "high and dry" road from Brinkley to Clarendon and then be placed by crane on a barge headed to DeValls Bluff. There they were unloaded and could continue to Little Rock on Highway 70. (Both courtesy of Jo Claire English.)

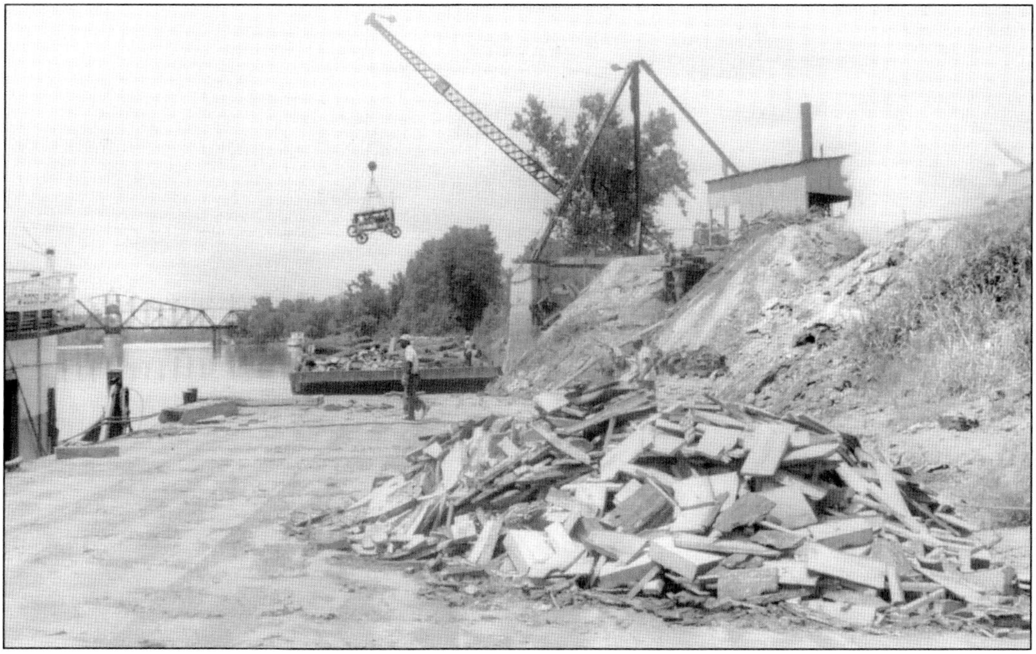

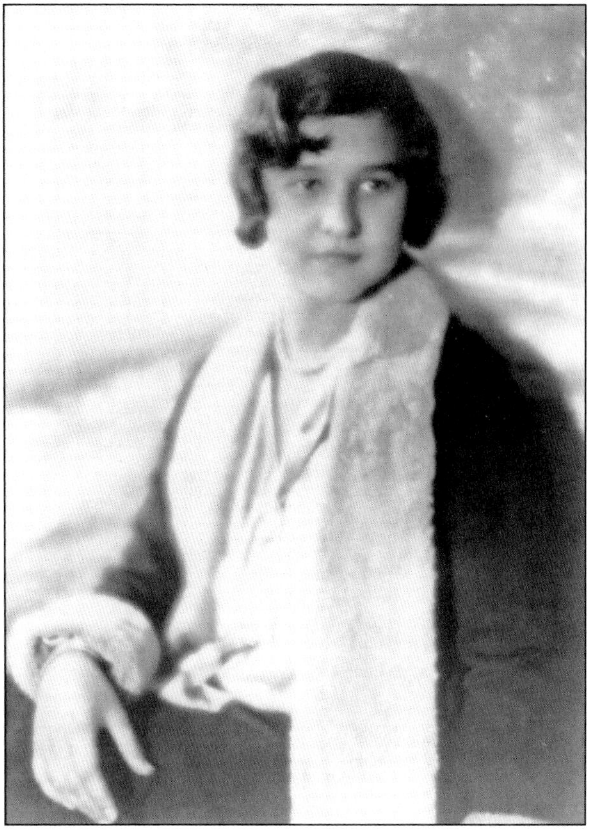

At left is a portrait of the lovely Mary Woods in the late 1930s. She was the namesake of her father Eugene Woods Sr.'s steamboat, *Mary Woods No. 2*, pictured below. Built in 1931 at a cost of $75,000, the *Mary Woods No. 2* was a steam-powered sternwheeler built for and operated on the White and Mississippi Rivers, towing steel barges loaded with logs for the Woods mills. She was the last steamboat to ply the waters of the White River at Clarendon and, after her conversion to diesel, the last paddle-wheel riverboat on the White. (Both courtesy of Jo Claire English.)

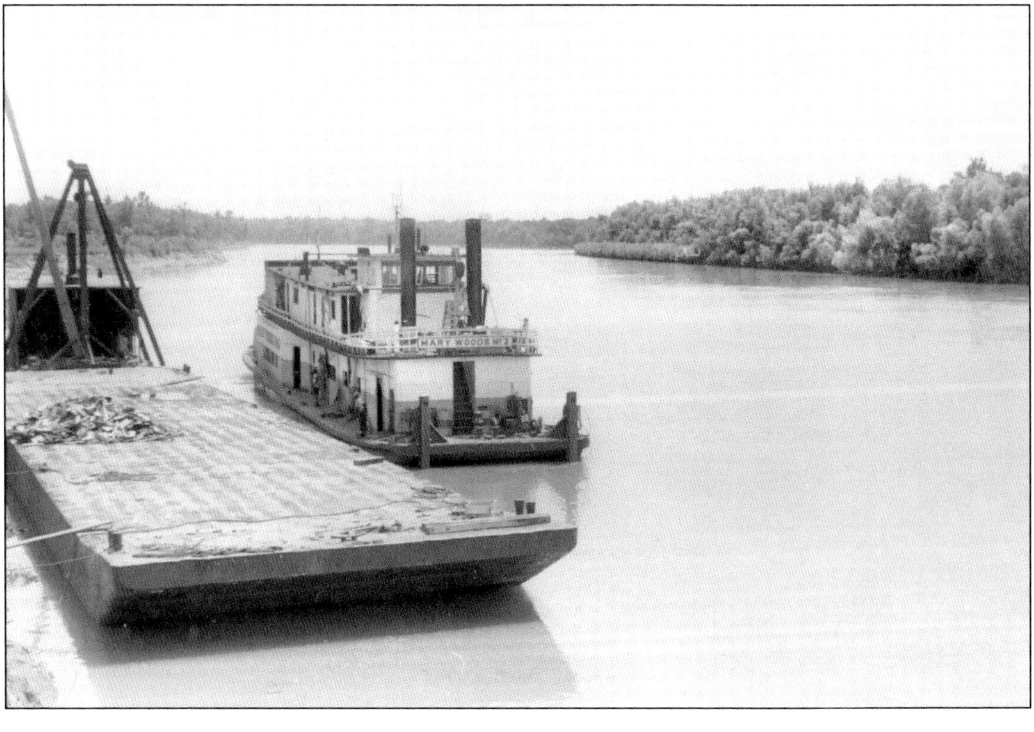

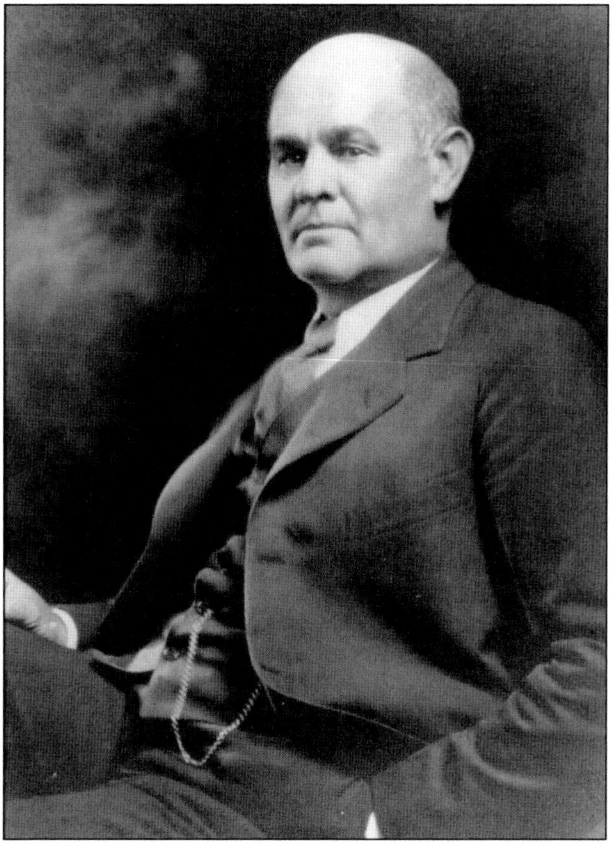

Eugene Woods Sr., owner of the Woods Lumber Company, had milling operations in Memphis and Clarendon. He was in the milling business for 69 years and maintained a home in Memphis as well as in Clarendon. Clarendon and Memphis were also the two original ports for the *Mary Woods No. 2*. He sold his Clarendon lumber and milling interests in 1959 to Potlatch Forests, Inc., along with his steamboat. Potlatch donated the boat to the State of Arkansas, and it was docked at the Jacksonport State Park in a slough of the White River. (Both courtesy of Jo Claire English.)

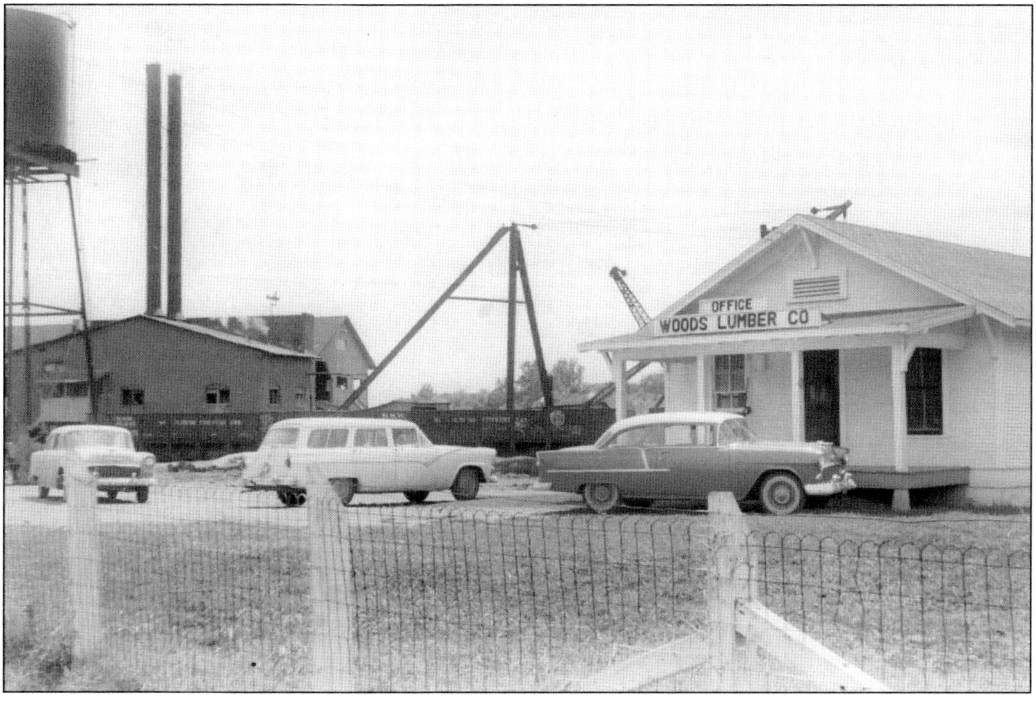

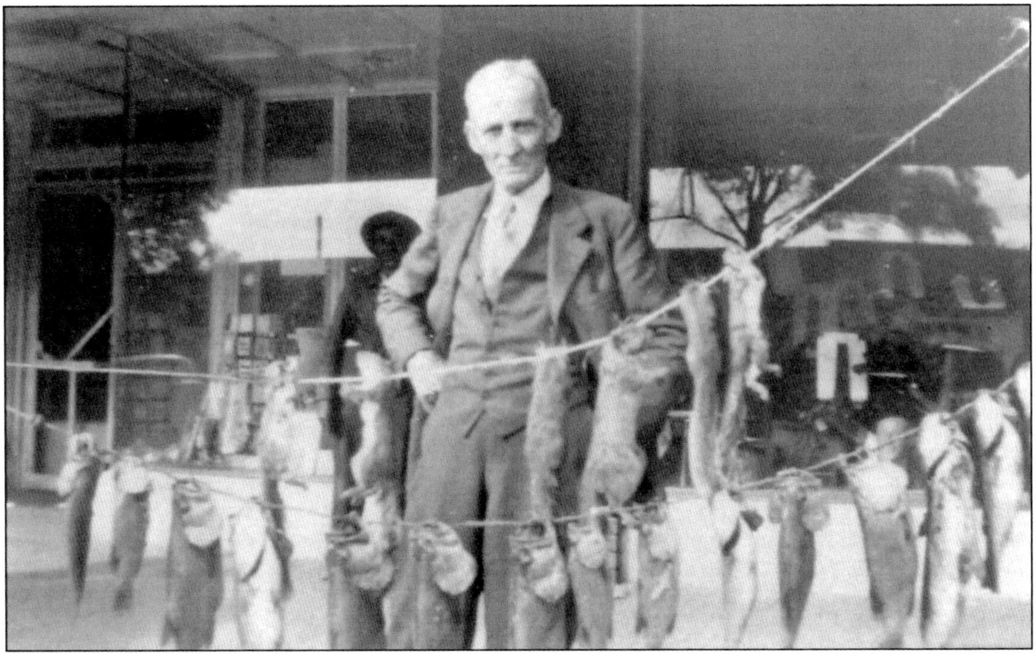

Proprietor William A. Johnson stands in front of his mercantile store in Holly Grove with a stringer of fish and squirrel. Holly Grove lies 75 miles southeast of Little Rock and 10 miles southeast of Clarendon. The Johnson Brothers general store dated back to the early 1900s and was listed in the *Polk's Arkansas State Gazetteer* in 1912–1913. (Courtesy of Henry Wilks.)

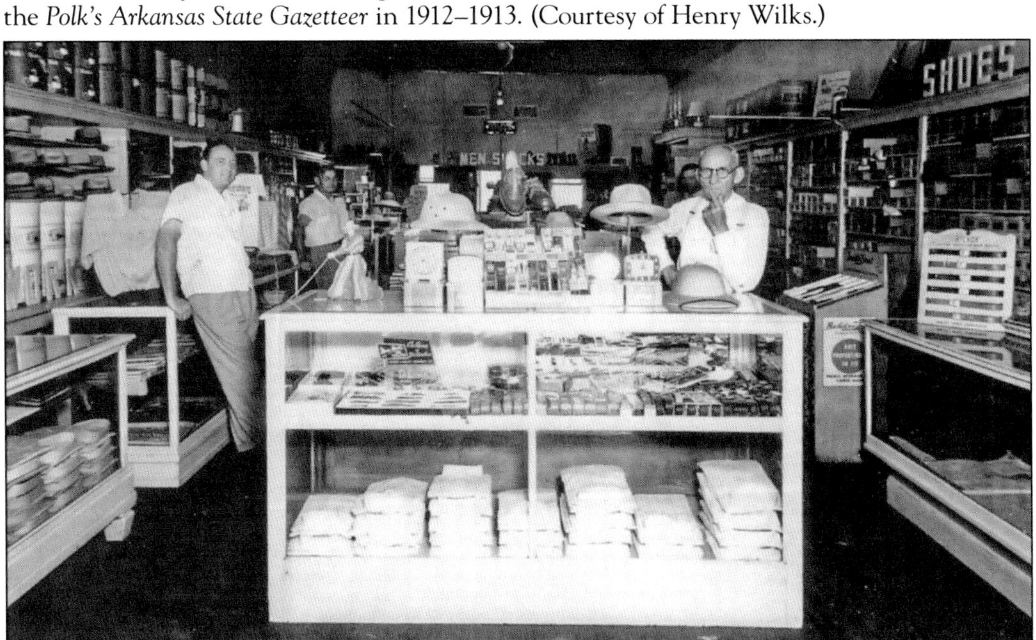

This inside shot of the W. A. Johnson Mercantile and Dry Goods Store was photographed in the 1950s. To the right is W. A. Johnson, and on the left is his son, Bill, who later operated the Esquire men's store in Brinkley for many years. Bill Johnson also operated a nightclub at Deep Elm, south of Holly Grove, which featured popular entertainers such as recording artist Blue Steel. (Courtesy of Henry Wilks.)

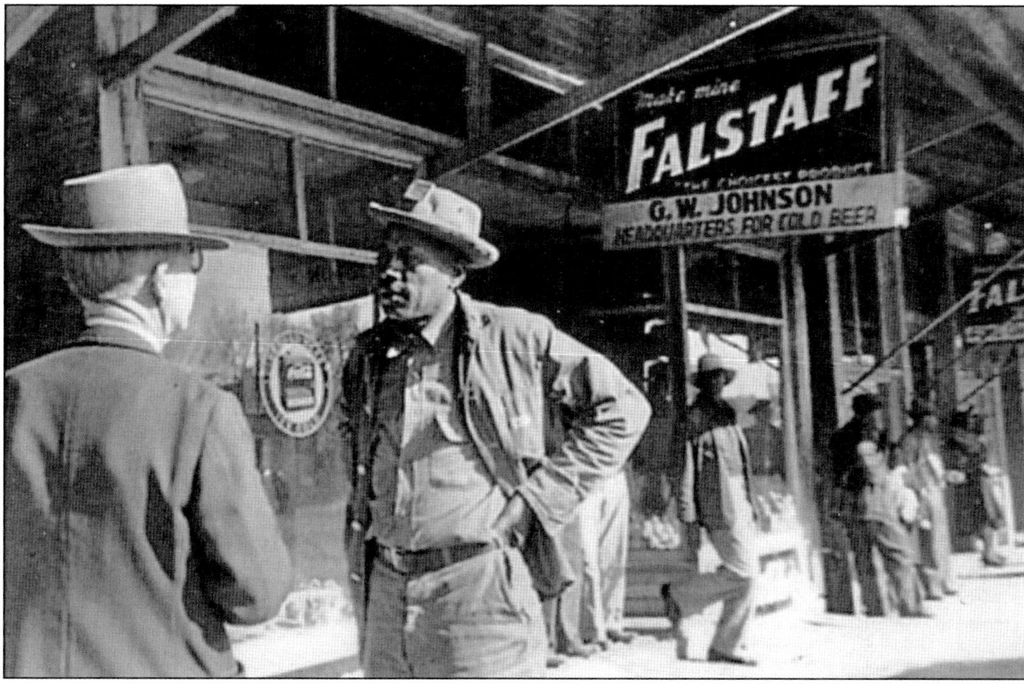

This 1950s Holly Grove downtown street scene is next to G. W. Johnson's juke joint. The sign in front touts it as "Headquarters for Cold Beer," and in its heyday, it was a thriving nightspot for the locals, featuring live bands, cold beer, and dancing. (Courtesy of Henry Wilks.)

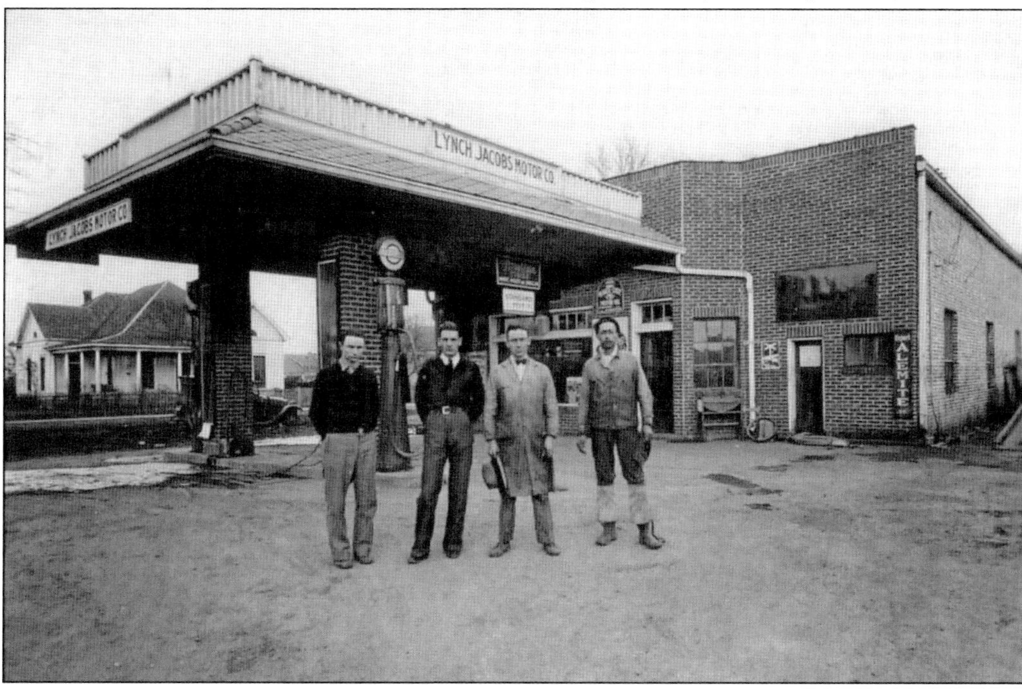

The Lynch-Jacobs Motor Company in Holly Grove is captured above in 1929. From left to right stand Herman Webster, Andrew Fitzgerald, Ellis King, and a man identified as "Red." (Courtesy of Henry Wilks.)

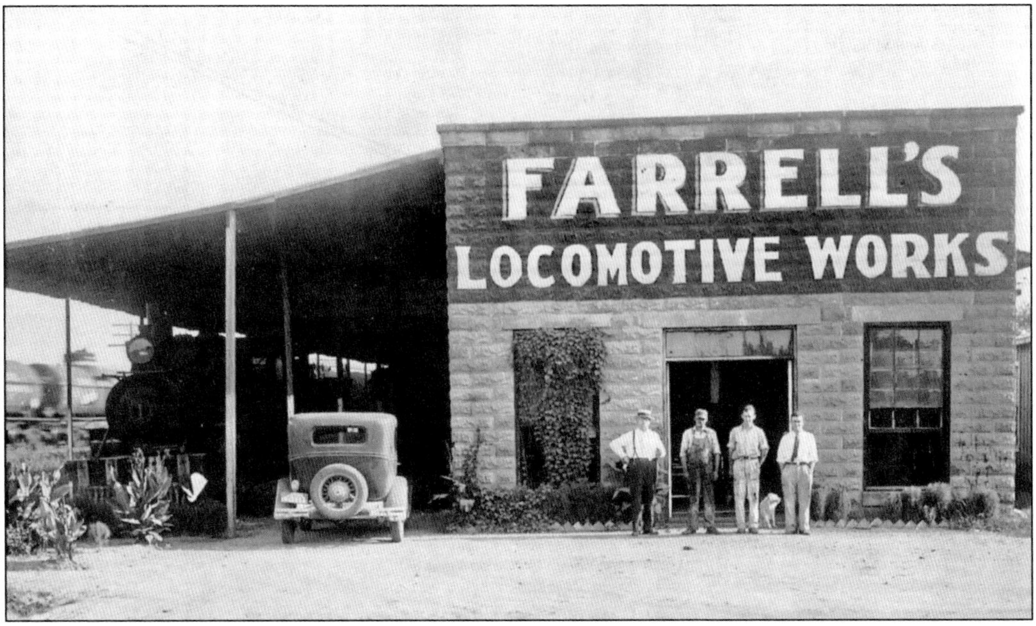

From left to right, J. J. Farrell Sr., Lon Lane, Hank Farrell, and Paul Farrell stand in front of Farrell Locomotive Works. Farrell Sr. originally built the Farrell Machine and Boiler Works in 1898; it was destroyed by the tornado of 1909. He quickly rebuilt and opened a new business, Farrell Locomotive Works, which primarily engaged in rebuilding locomotives but also repaired cotton gins, sawmill equipment, and well pumps. (Courtesy of Frances Farrell.)

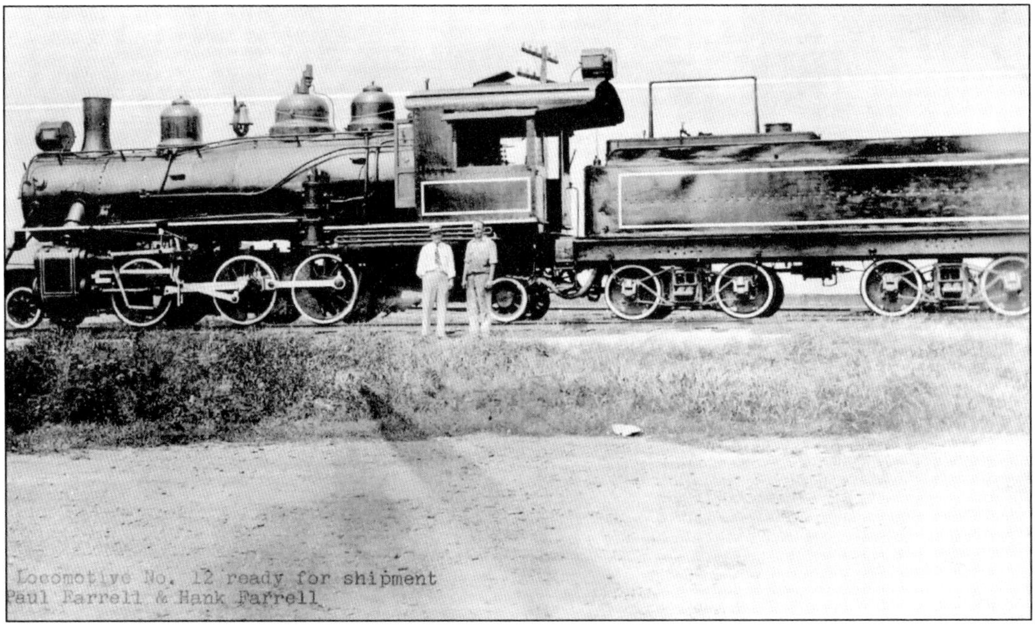

Paul Farrell (left) and Hank Farrell stand in front of a locomotive that was ready for shipment. During World War II, the Farrell brothers rebuilt locomotives for the U.S. government because of their success in rebuilding locomotives without using priority materials. The locomotives were used not only by the army and navy plants, but also in foreign lands that supplied the allies with critical materials. (Courtesy of Frances Farrell.)

Six

THE COUNTRY FOLK

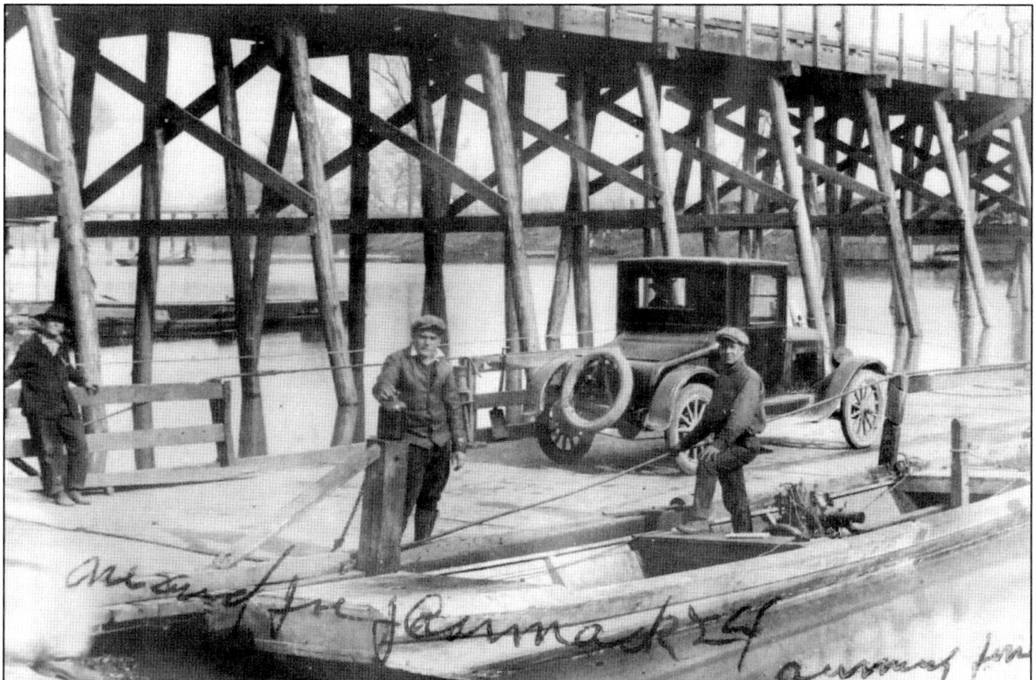

From left to right, Jack Harris, Joe Carmack, and Oliver Sayger were photographed working on the Cache River ferry in 1924. The Bankhead Highway (old Highway 70) opened on Christmas day that same year, making the need for a ferry to cross the river obsolete and, at the same time, putting these men out of work. (Courtesy of William Sayger.)

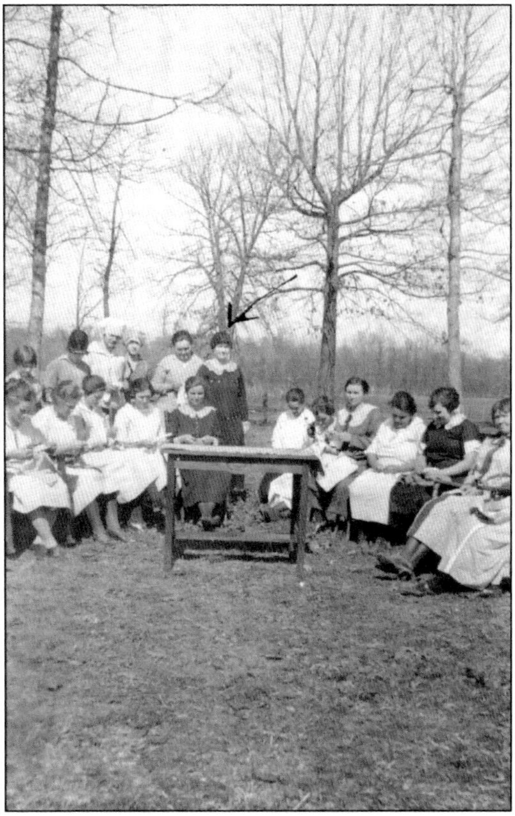

This 1925 photograph shows the Monroe County Home Demonstration Club with local leader, Addie Owens, marked by the arrow, demonstrating the latest techniques in clothing work. Home Demonstration Clubs brought rural women information and new ways to make household tasks lighter and homes more pleasant.

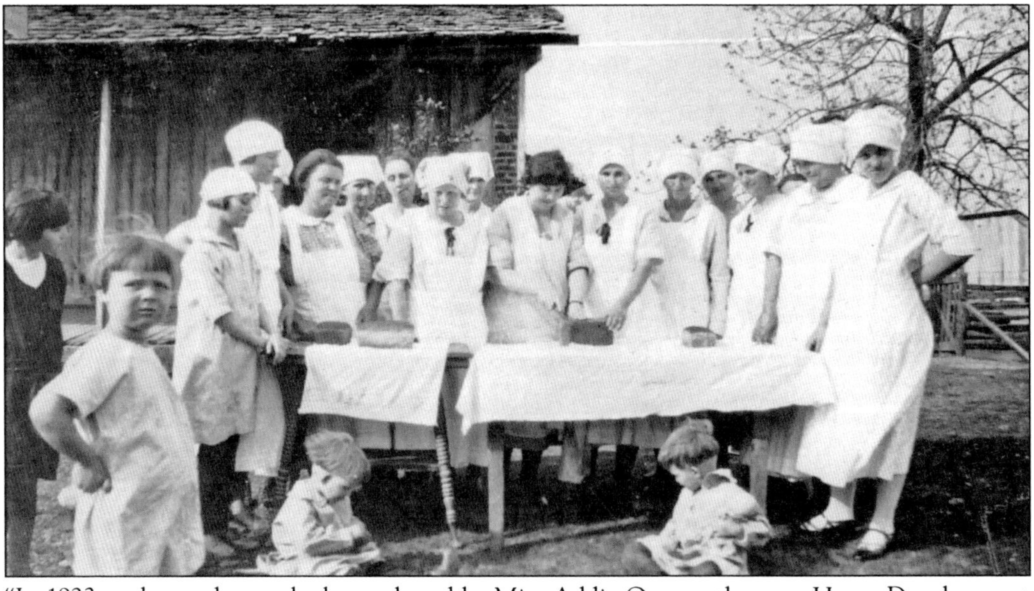

"In 1923 we learned to make better bread by Miss Addie Owens, the new Home Development Club agent," was the notation under this photograph in the Allendale Home Demonstration Club scrapbook. Local leaders demonstrated up-to-date information and recommended practices on different phases of homemaking, such as food preparation, clothing, and home furnishings, to improve family life in the rural farming areas in Arkansas.

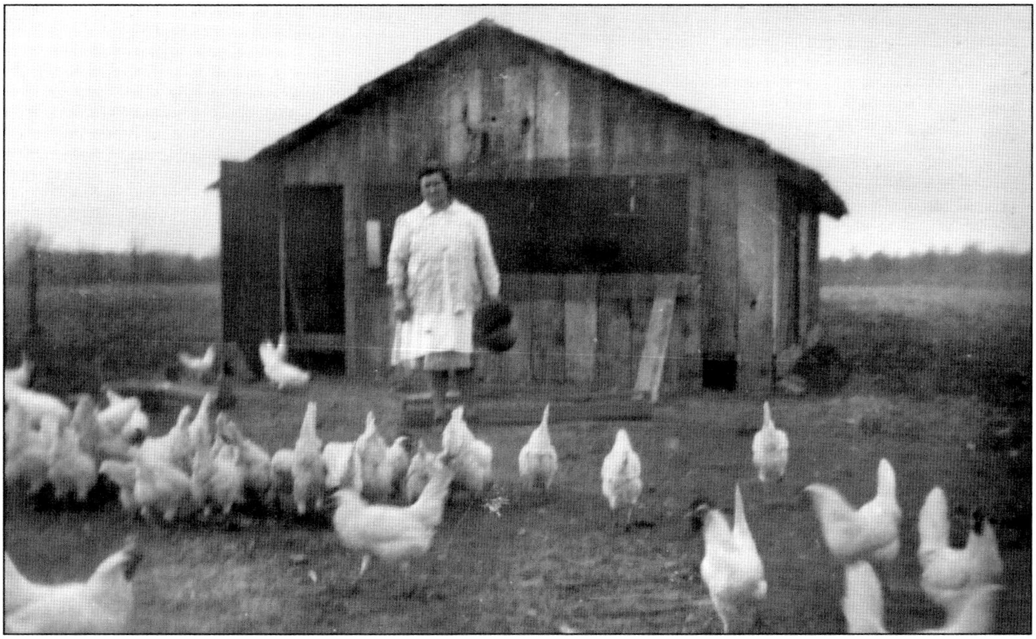

In 1934, Mrs. Geter (Corine Stigler) Miley made good with her poultry as poultry leader in the Allendale Home Demonstration Club. The $165 Mrs. Miley cleared from her poultry flock in 1933 paid for many improvements in the Miley home. She pampered her kitchen with a new built-in cabinet, sink, closet for food storage, and a mop and broom closet. A new pressure cooker was the most important of the several new pieces of kitchen equipment Mrs. Miley bought.

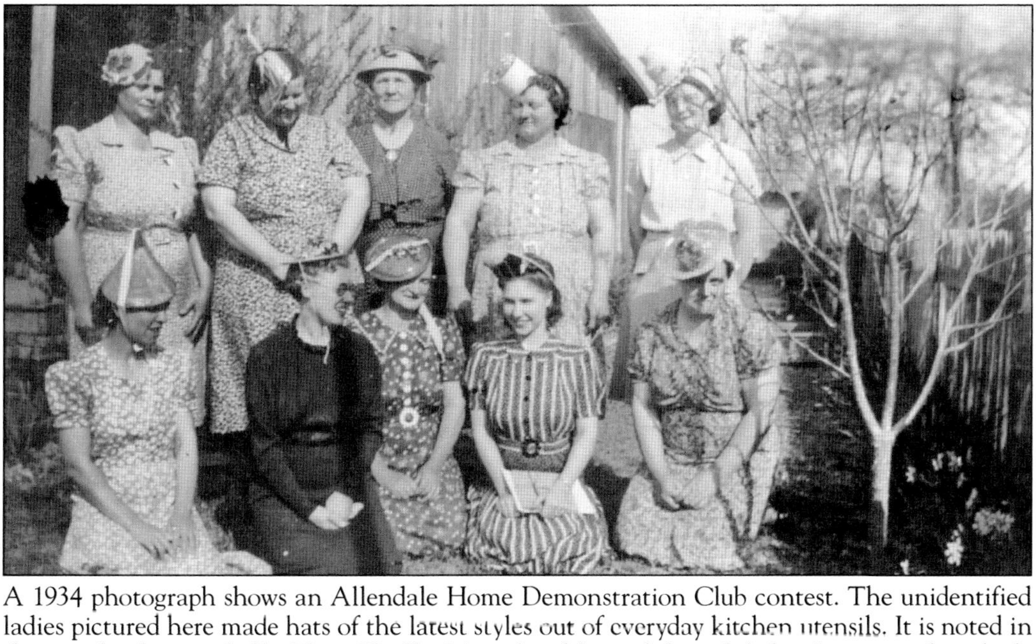

A 1934 photograph shows an Allendale Home Demonstration Club contest. The unidentified ladies pictured here made hats of the latest styles out of everyday kitchen utensils. It is noted in the scrapbook compiled by Flora Chaffin Moorehead (seated, far right) that "we enjoy these little contests from time to time." Other contests included cotton dress making.

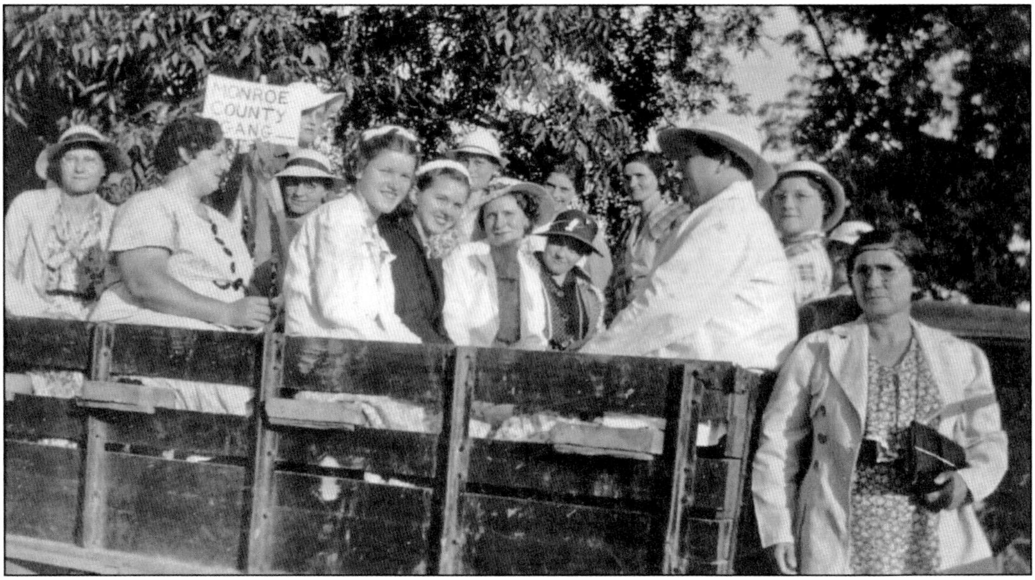

Fourteen members of the Allendale chapter of the Monroe County Home Demonstration council traveled some 68 miles to Camp Pike, Arkansas, in the back of this old truck in September 1934 for their state camp. Activities included Colonial dance, bookbinding, rug making, archery lessons, pressing cotton garments, and "quiet games for club meetings."

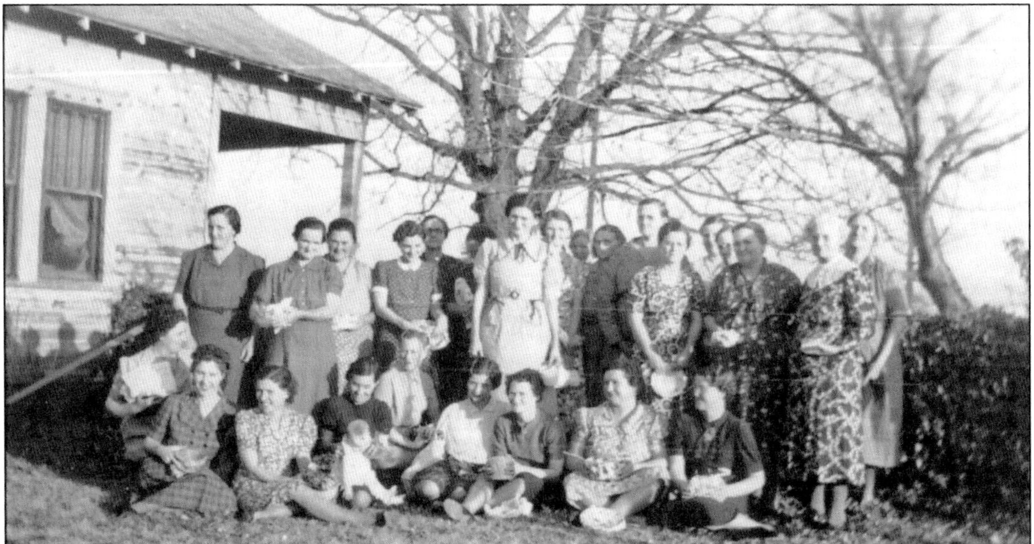

A Home Demonstration Club Christmas Party was held at the home of Flora Moorehead in 1941. During the home demonstration era, the county Home Demonstration agent traveled throughout the county and presented educational demonstrations in the various communities. Few women worked outside the home, and homemakers were seeking information that would help them primarily in the home. The major program focus was on food production, food preparation, and food preservation.

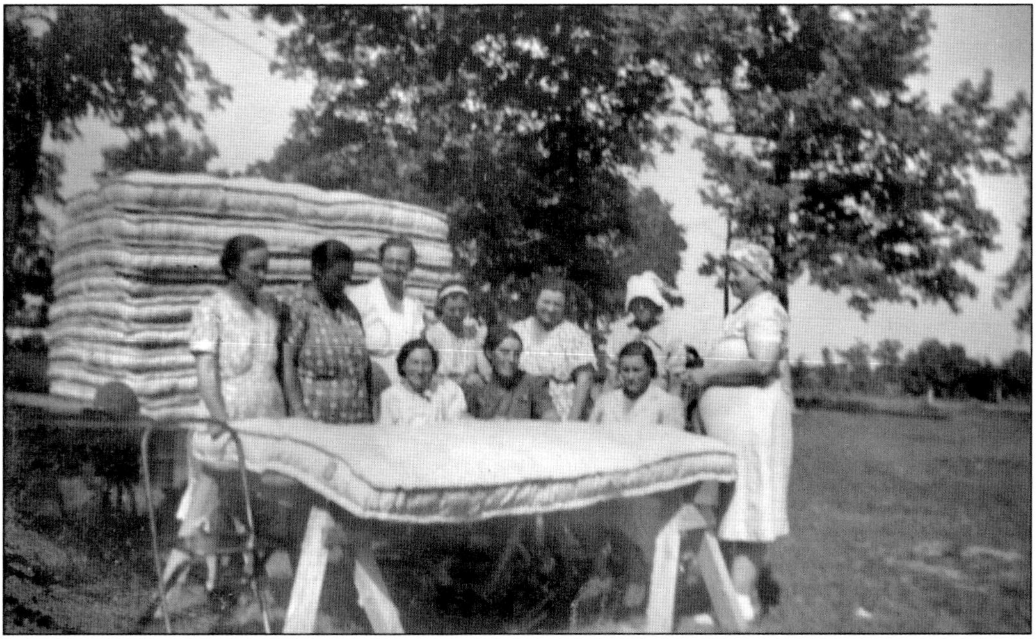

Above is a 1936 photograph of unidentified members of the Allendale chapter of the Monroe County Demonstration Club learning to make comforts and mattresses for their homes. A handwritten list by Flora Moorehead in the club's scrapbook noted a few of their Home Demonstration programs as community work in landscaping, community social activities, home arts and handicrafts, better homes, yard improvements, clothing, gardening, poultry, foods and nutrition, food preservation, home dairy, gardens for backyards, home industries, home management, health in the home, first aid in the home, and recreation. In addition, Flora Moorehead noted, "We have improved our homes in many ways. Our ways of living, our health and in handling our finances. We stand by and support our church and Sunday school, which dates back as long as there has been an Allendale community." The Allendale club was one of the oldest in Monroe County.

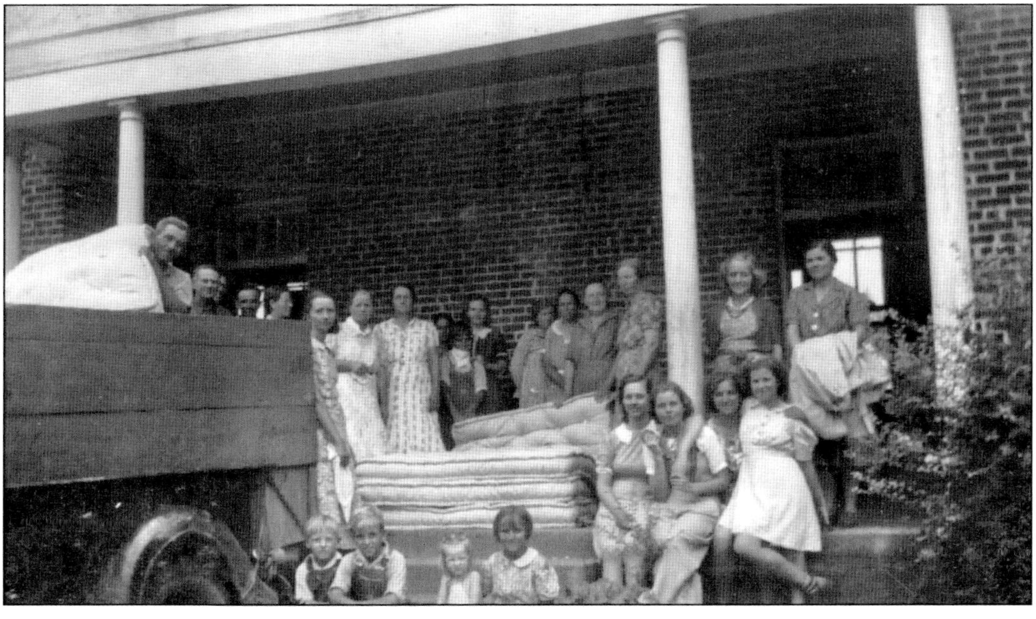

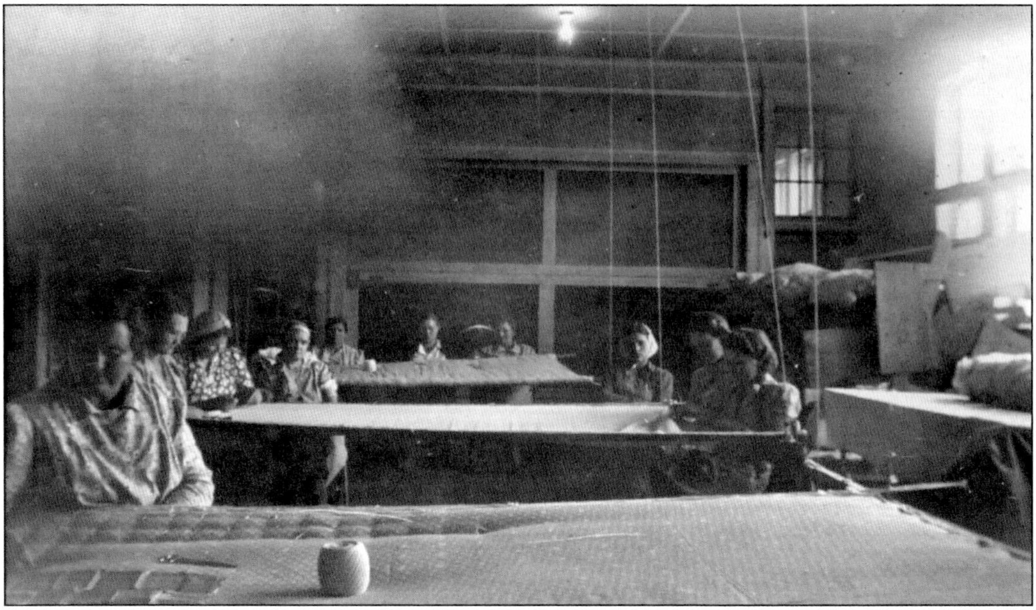

Mrs. Charles (Edna) Chaffin's most outstanding work in the Allendale Home Demonstration Club was the work she sponsored in the mattress and comfort making program. Mrs. Chaffin had been active in the extension work since 1918 and recalled that the program was accelerated in 1932 when Addie Owens became the agent. "Home Demonstration work has proved to be most beneficial to farm women of Monroe County. The program has answered the farm women's need through all times, including the years of depression and years of prosperity. The younger you get into the program, the more years you will have to learn improved methods of workmanship and serving your community," reads a quote from Mrs. Charles Chaffin in the April 28, 1949, issue of the *Monroe County Citizen*.

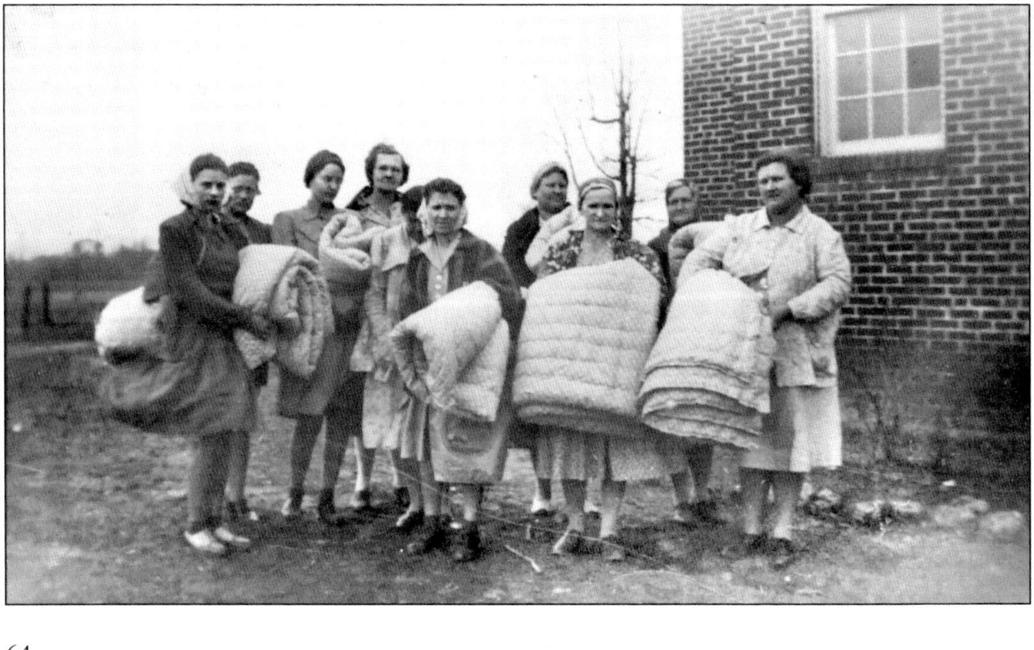

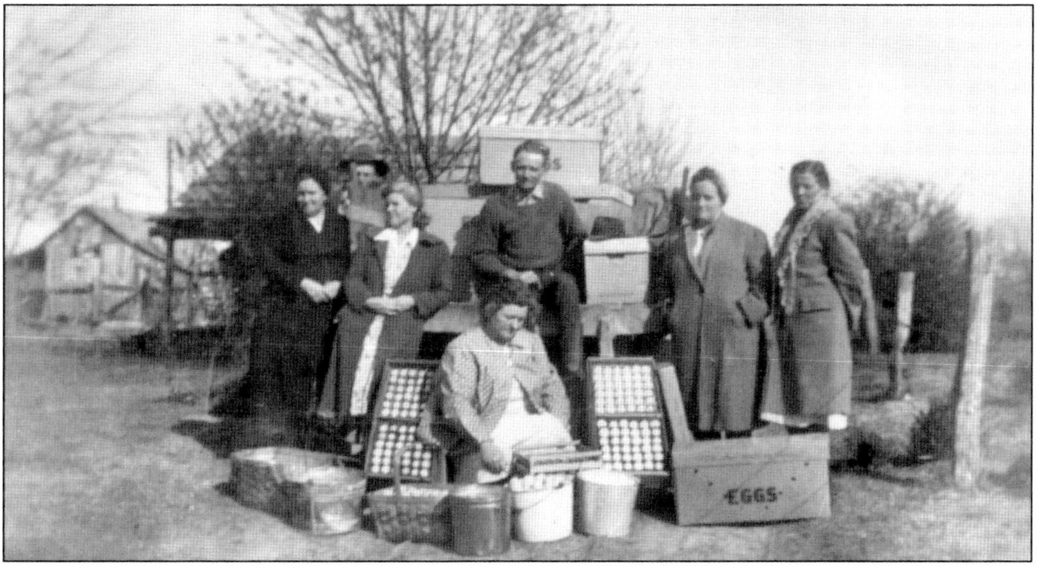

The Home Demonstration Club of Allendale sponsored a home egg market in February 1944. During that time, approximately 2,300 dozen eggs were sold by the club members without having to go to "town," which was a long, laborious trip over the rugged, muddy roads of the area before they were paved.

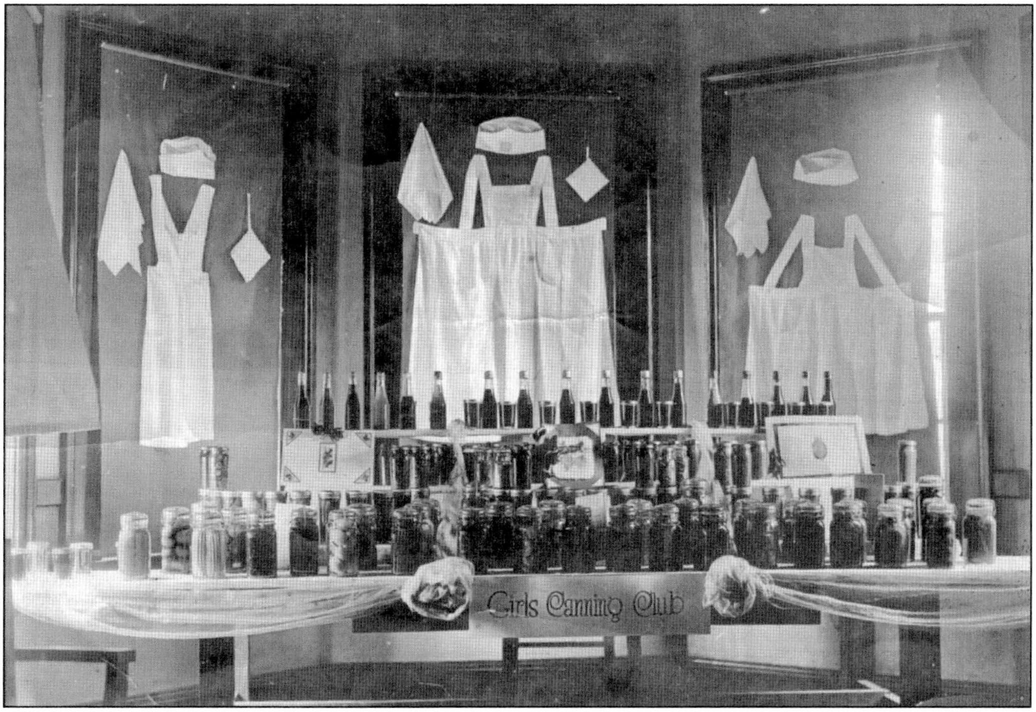

Food preservation by the homemakers of rural Arkansas was crucial to every household in order to provide food through the months when the gardens lay dormant. Pictured above is Leone Henard's exhibit for the Girl's Canning Club at the county fair in Clarendon.

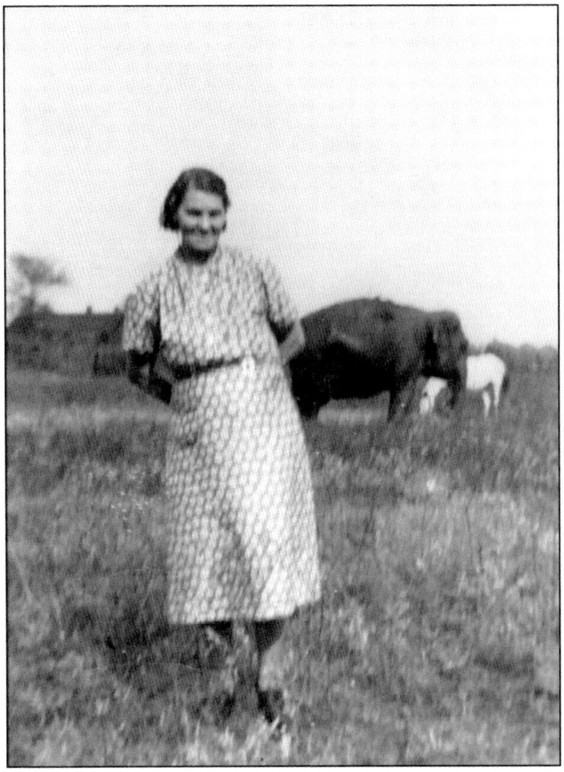

Elephants are not native to Monroe County, so this image would lead one to believe that the circus must have been in town. Anna Gaisbauer happily poses in front of the pachyderm in this 1940s Brinkley photograph. (Courtesy of Steve Hinton.)

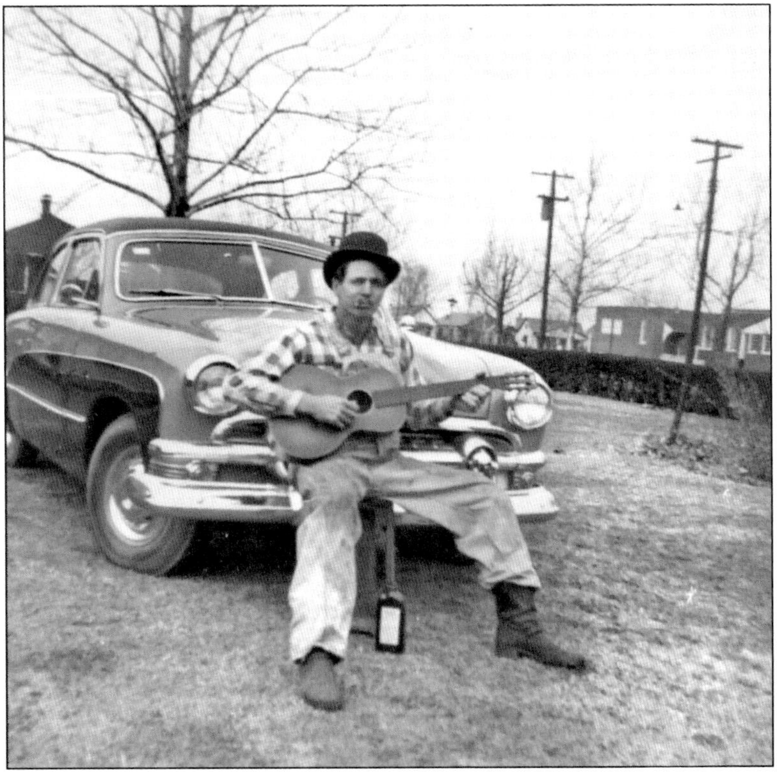

Jesse J. Miles enjoys a nip and some guitar picking in this quaint 1950s photograph. He was married to Kathryn Wiesle Johnston, the sister of Angela Wiesle Hinton of Brinkley. (Courtesy of Steve Hinton.)

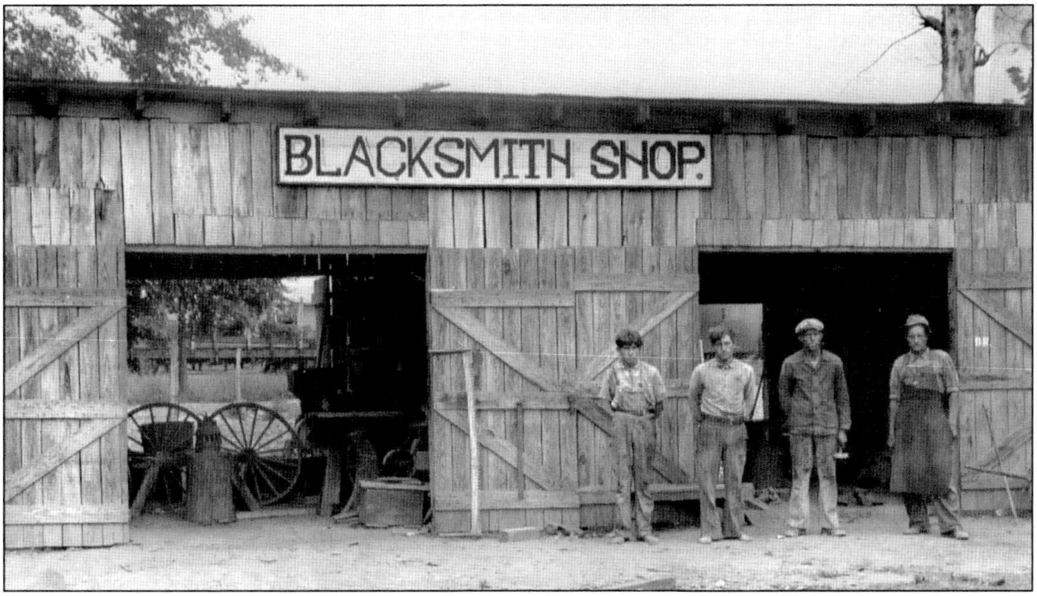

The blacksmith shop of John Leo Wiesle and his brother-in-law, John Deuerling, was located on the corner of Cedar Street and North Grand Avenue in Brinkley. Deuerling built the shop while Wiesle was fighting in the military during World War I. The blacksmith shop remained open until Wiesle's death in the early 1960s. He was best known to the community as Doc Wiesle because of his skills as a veterinarian. Above is John Deuerling (right), with his sons, from left to right, Carl, Andrew, and Herman. (Courtesy of Steve Hinton.)

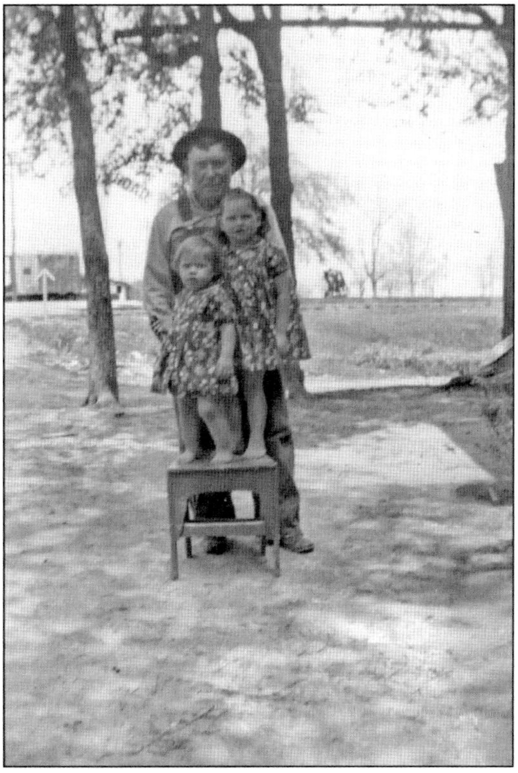

John Leo "Doc" Wiesle Sr. stands with two of his granddaughters, Jeanette Wiesle (left) and Joyce Wiesle, in this 1950s photograph. He was the father of nine children and grandfather to 25 children. (Courtesy of Steve Hinton.)

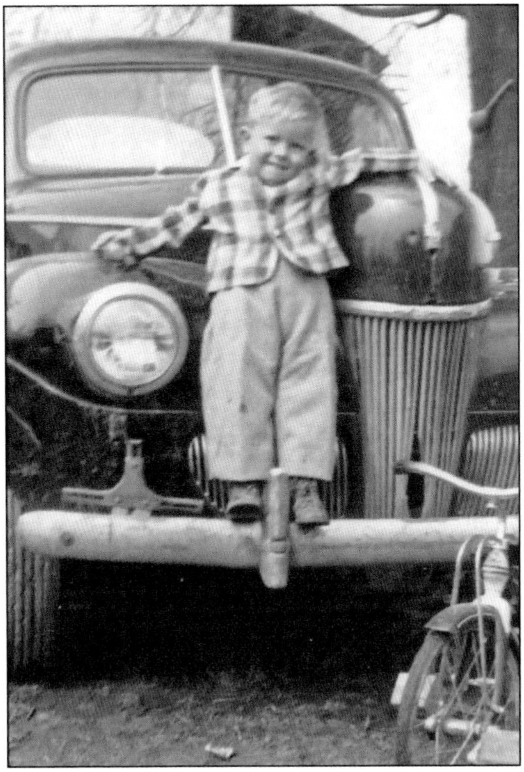

Clarence Wiesle was born August 27, 1947, to John "Doc" and Elizabeth Wiesle. The youngest of nine children, he was born when both of his parents were in their 50s. He is pictured at left on his father's car in the late 1940s and below serenading the camera. He began work in the construction business when he reached a working age and continues his carpentry business in Brinkley and the surrounding area. (Both courtesy of Steve Hinton.)

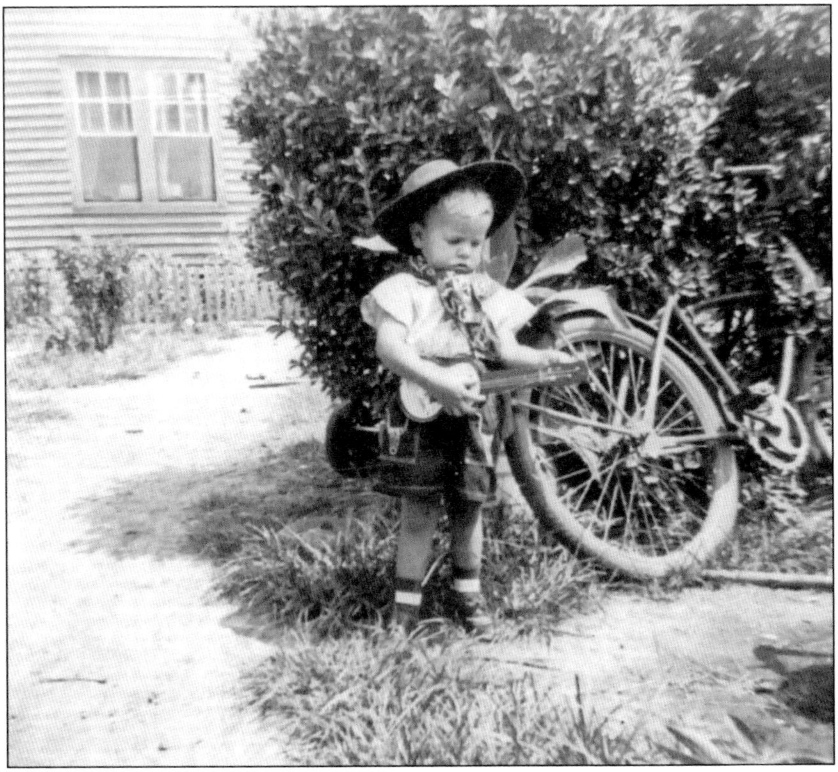

Seven

FARMING THE DELTA

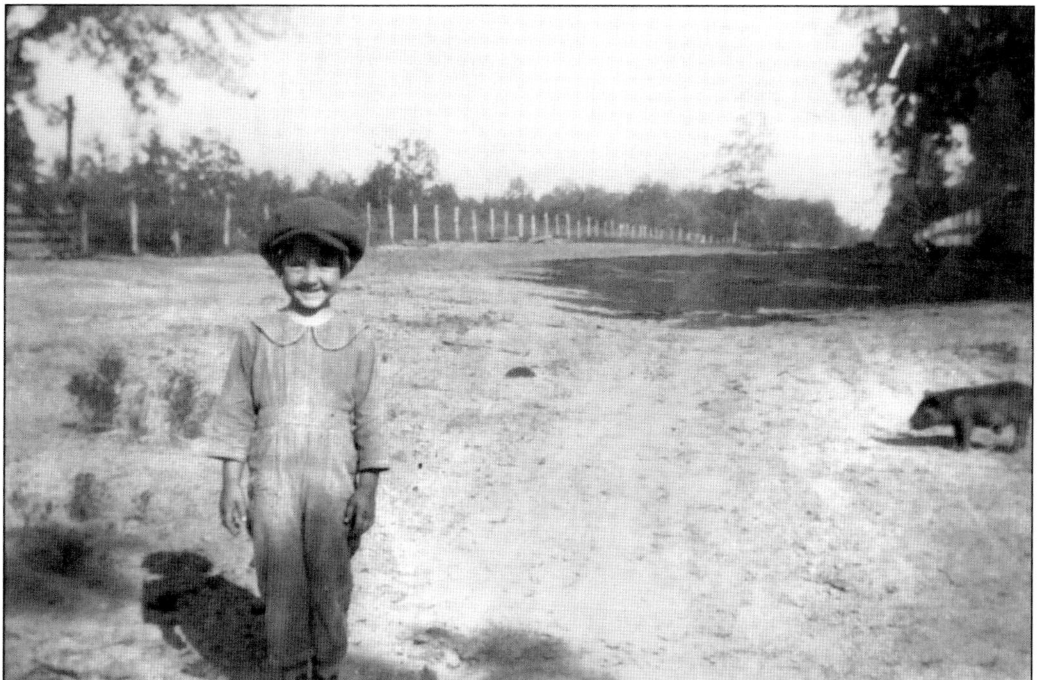

Floyd Henard of Zent proudly stands for the photographer in this 1932 photograph. The 1930s were hard for Americans, but for the Arkansas farmer, the Depression started with the Flood of 1927. A drop in housing construction and a downturn in the forestry industry followed the flood. Just as rural Arkansas was adjusting to those losses came the financial upheaval from the 1929 stock market crash, killer tornados, and the drought of 1930–1931. While not as severe as the Dust Bowl conditions, the drought's effects were devastating. It became as legendary as the flood.

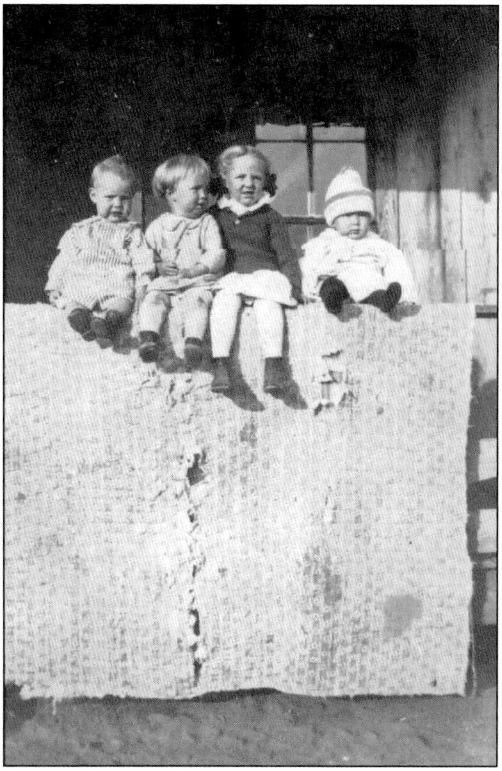

Sharecropping was a tenancy lease by poor farmers who leased farm property from a landowner for a share of the crops. The leases were small acreage operations, and the tenant family members provided all of the labor to plant, cultivate, and harvest the crops for 50 percent of the harvest. Title to the crop was held by the landowner, who could sell it without consulting the sharecropper and take whatever portion of the farmer's harvest he deemed owed him. In the early 1930s, the sharecroppers faced "nickel cotton" and the locked doors of banks, causing an exodus of the tenant farmers to the North. Today almost all Monroe County farmers rent some of the land they cultivate. Modern tenant farmers have become larger operations to achieve economies of scale and marketing clout that make the Arkansas farm operations the nation's most productive. The unidentified children at left, and Mamie Smallwood with her infant child below, are on a sharecropping farm in Zent in the 1930s.

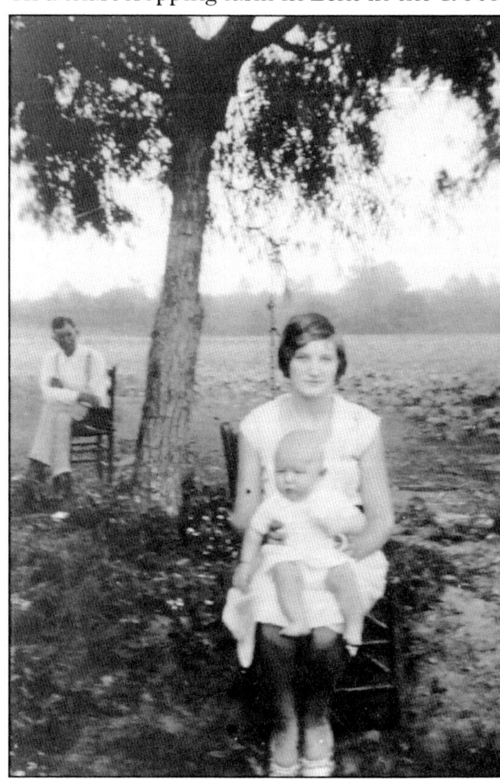

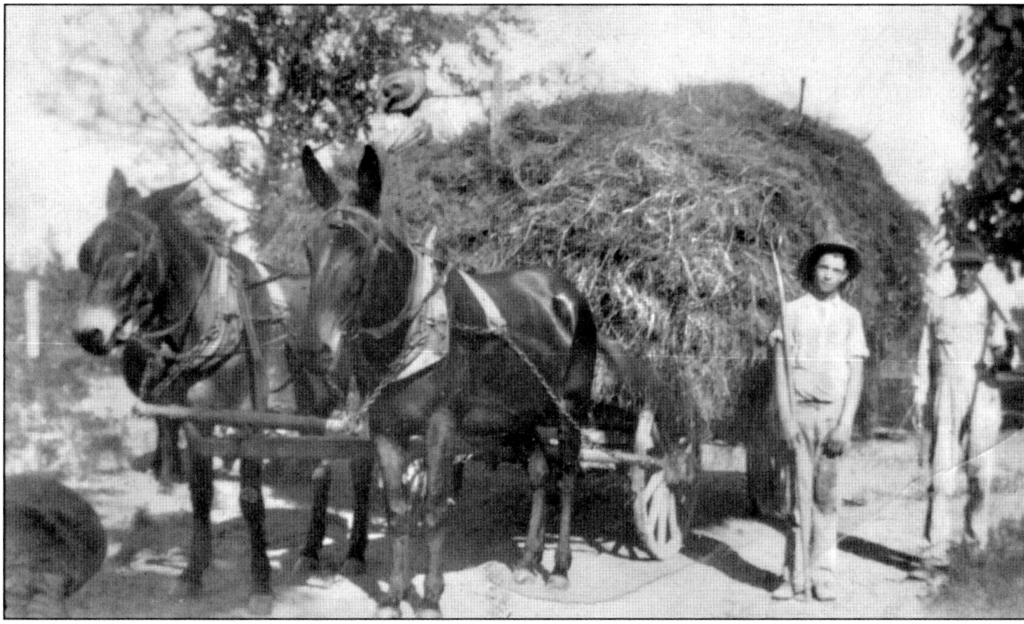

The revival of the plantation system after the Civil War brought the expansion of cotton planting in the South. Mules made up one-third of the draft animal population, with their numbers peaking in 1925 at 4,465,000. The effects of tractors began to be felt in the Southern economy with the increased demand for farm products during World War II. When small farmers did not return after the war, landowners were forced to rely on machinery, transforming agriculture in the delta. Cotton had been the bellwether crop, but by the end of the war, rice and soybeans had won a loyal following. Farmers realized the ease of growing these crops gave a greater economic return, and they were willing to make a long-term commitment by acquiring new equipment, such as tractors, planters, and harvesters. Herman Henard and his father, Jordon Henard, are pictured above with their mule team in Zent. Tommy Deuerling is pictured below on an early "rice tractor" in 1935. (Below courtesy of Steve Hinton.)

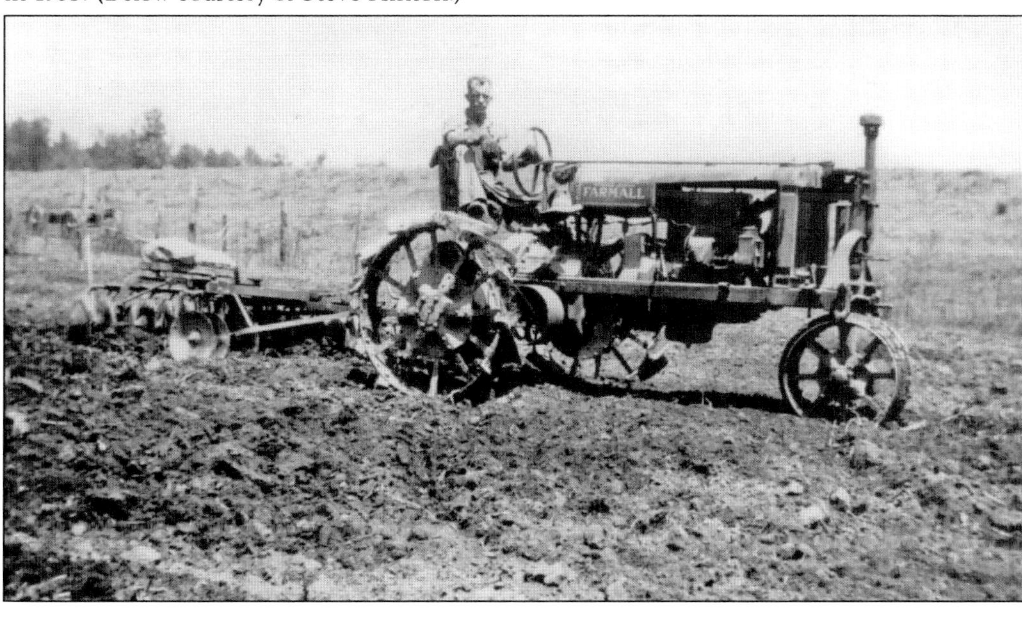

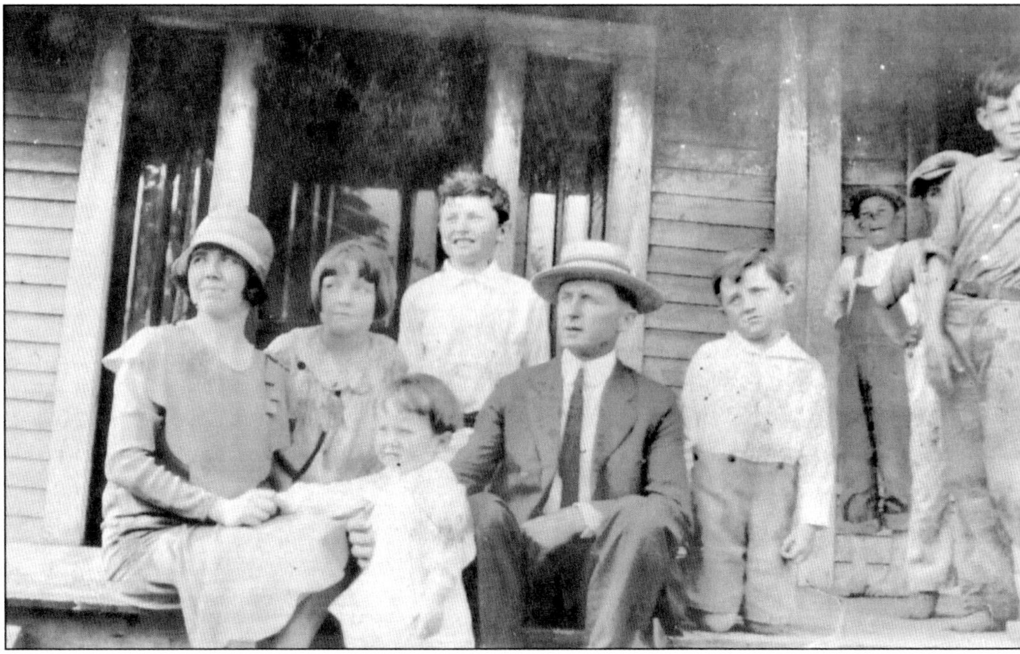

Presley Wiley Meacham, born in Tennessee in 1888, married Arkansas native Virginia Louise. Meacham was a traveling salesman when he arrived at Monroe by train in 1914. There was a new general store there where Meacham hoped to peddle his goods; however, the merchant declined to buy any of his wares. He learned the school needed a teacher, and being destitute, he accepted the position. After two years in Monroe, he fell back into his father's grace and with his help purchased area land for farming. At the time of Meacham's death, he was one of the largest landowners of the region. The photograph of the Meacham family above includes, from left to right, Virginia, Louise, Barbara (foreground), Cowan, Presley, Wiley, and Kirby. Below, from left to right, Virginia, Matthew, Wiley, Barbara, and Louise are pictured by a rice shock in June 1935. (Both courtesy of Wiley Meacham.)

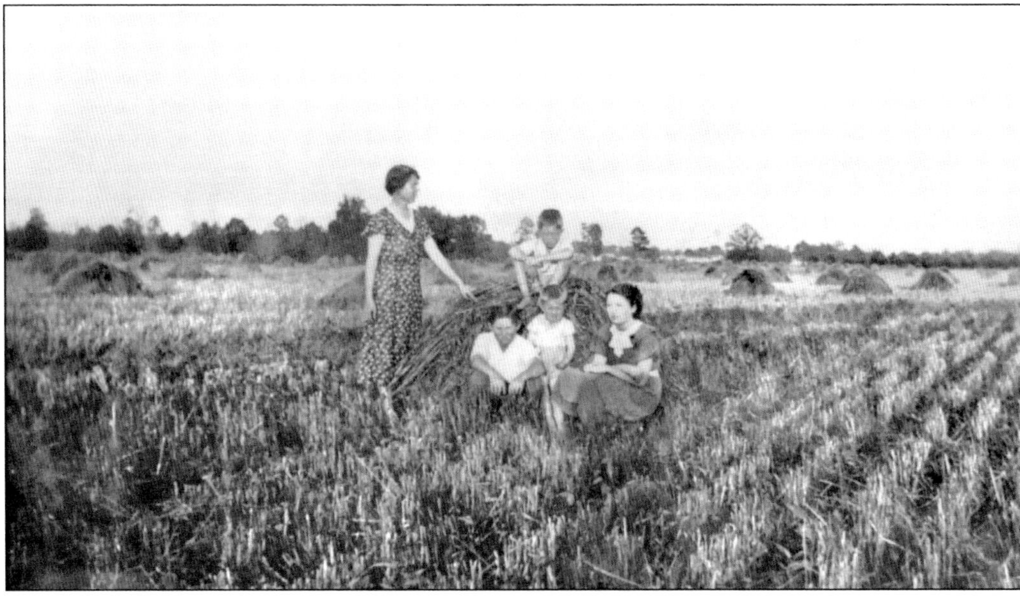

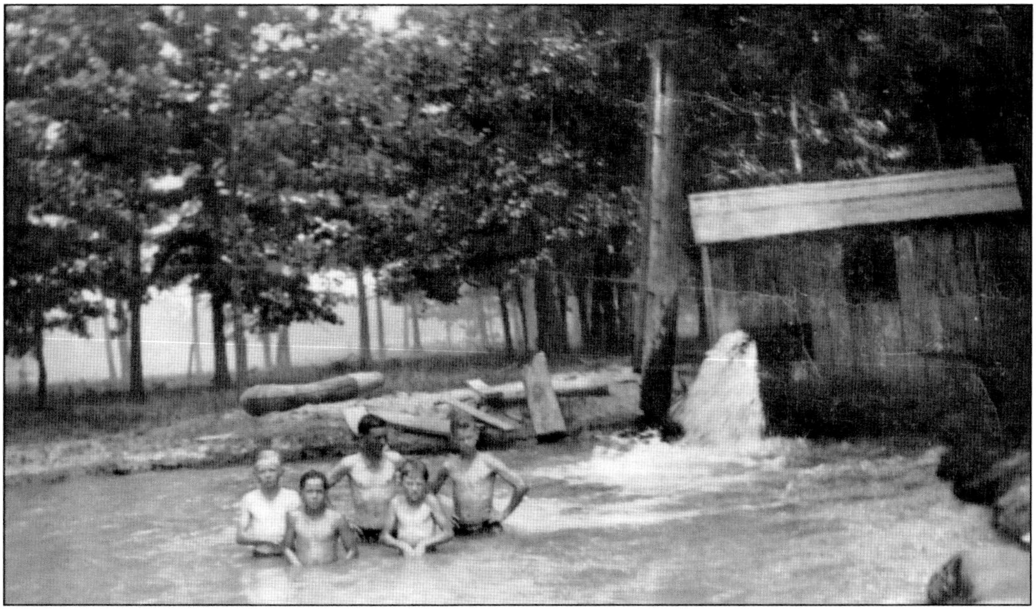

In 1940, the first rice well, powered by a one-cycle diesel engine, was installed on the Meacham farm. It was also a popular swimming hole for the Meacham children and their friends. From left to right are Billy Sebastian, Marvin Metts, Billy Morris, Wiley Meacham, and O'Neal Watts. (Courtesy of Wiley Meacham.)

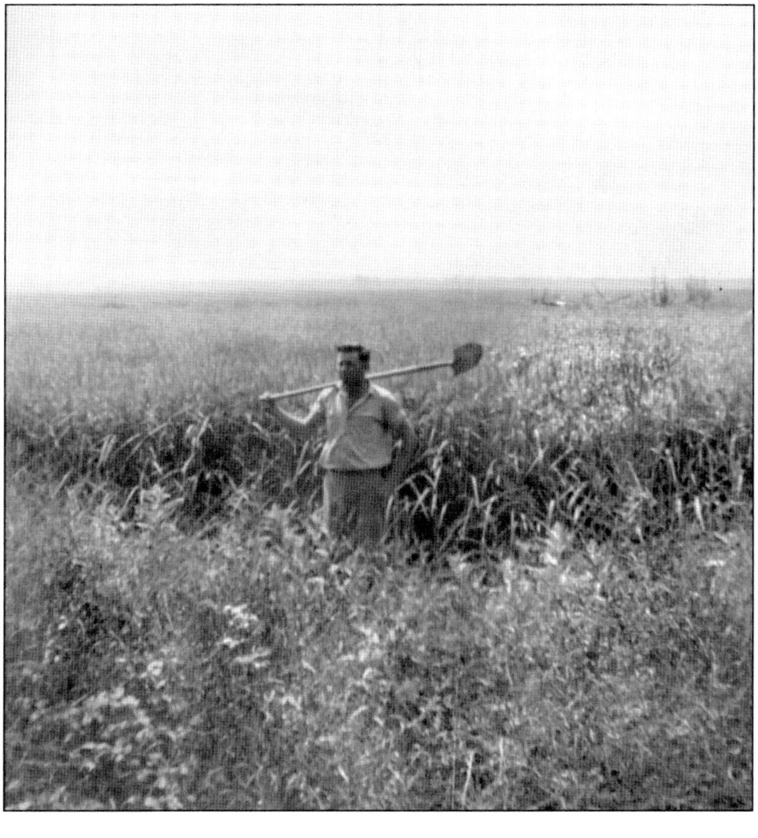

Wiley Meacham stands in his rice field in this 1956 photograph. His son, Steve, and family won the coveted title of Farm Family of the Year in 2008, continuing the long tradition of farming started by Presley Meacham in the mid-1900s. (Courtesy of Wiley Meacham.)

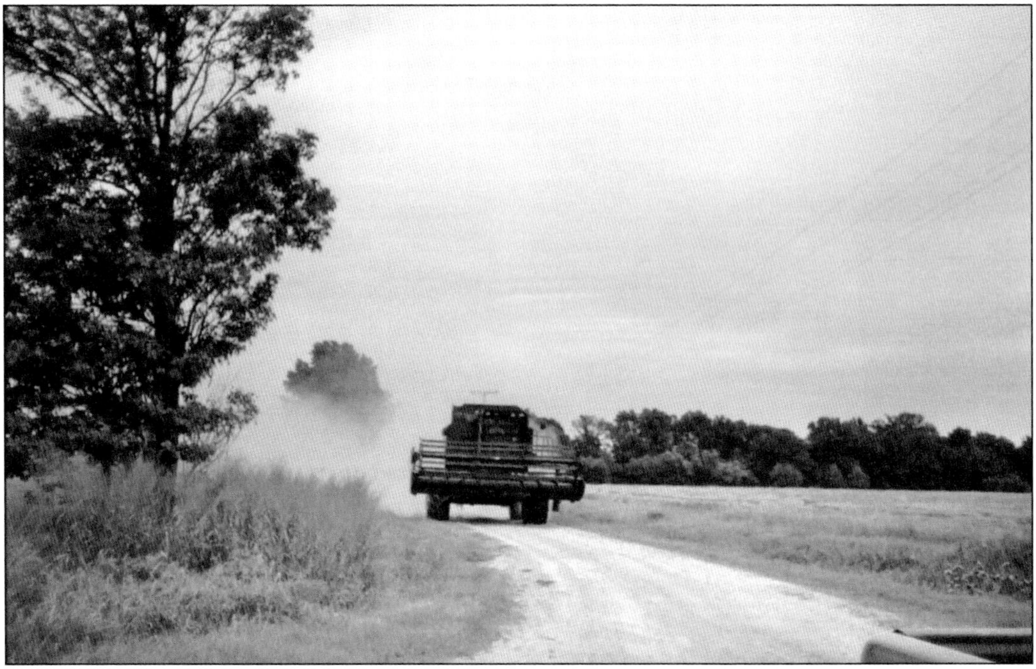

Agriculture has played a major role in Monroe County since territorial times, when farmers made up more than 90 percent of the population. For more than 150 years, agricultural practices had remained largely the same, using hand tools and draft animals. World War II transformed agriculture with the advent of machinery that turned what had been a lifestyle into a capitalist endeavor for the rural farmer. These *c.* 1960 photographs capture a combine on its way to the rice field for harvest. (Both courtesy of Billye Frein.)

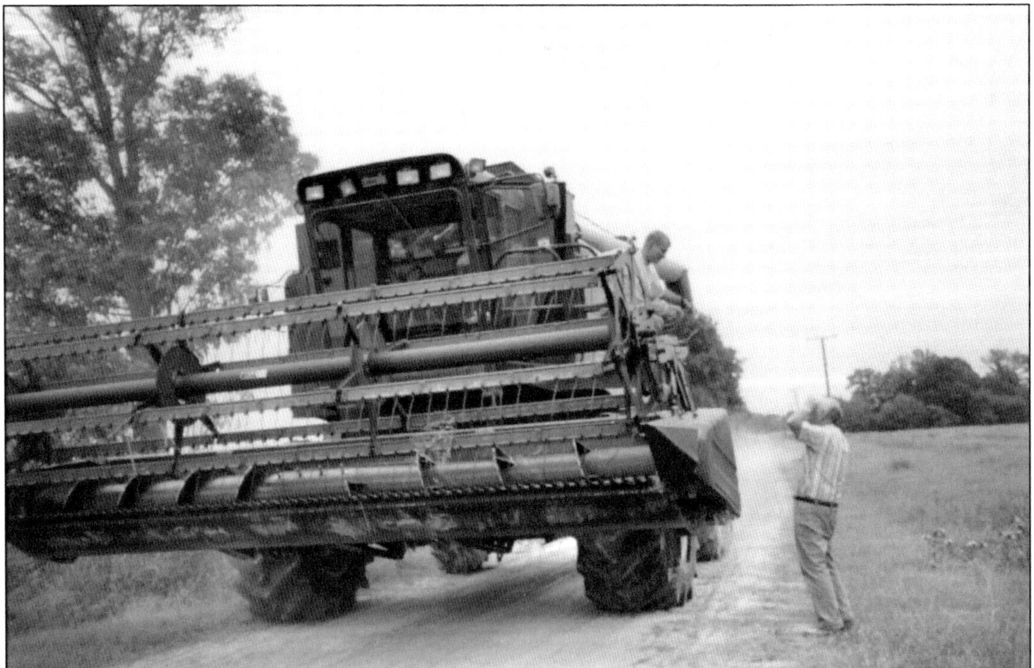

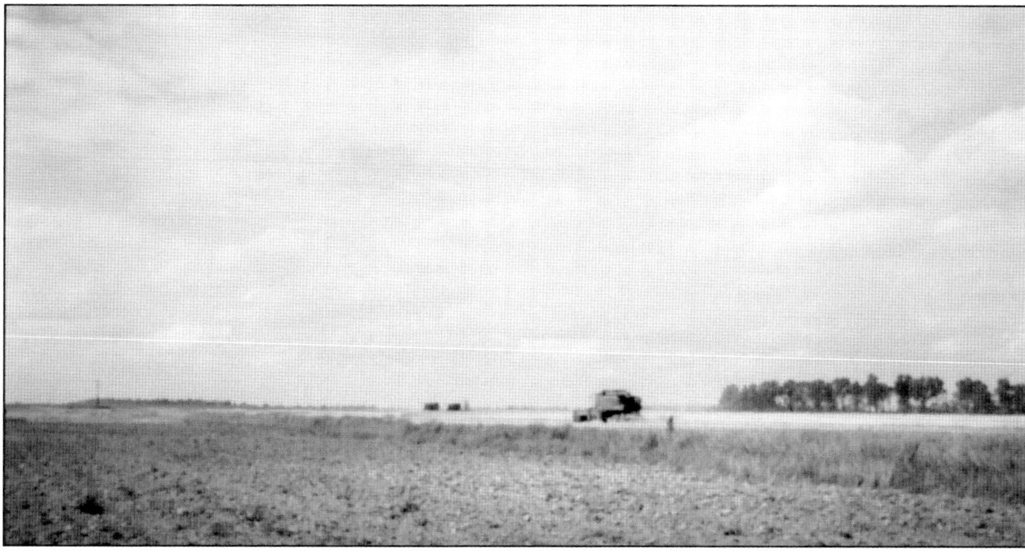

The need for labor in wartime industries drained rural Arkansas of farm workers in the 1940s, and most domestic laborers did not return after the war. Faced with a critical labor shortage, the nation turned to Mexico for workers. A treaty was signed between the United States and Mexico to formalize a plan called the Bracero Program. It brought thousands of immigrants to the fields of the delta and filled a vital need for field hands. These 1960s photographs are of a combine harvesting the rice (above) and quickly unloading its yield into a grain cart pulled by a tractor (below) so the combine can resume the harvest with little delay. (Both courtesy of Billye Frein.)

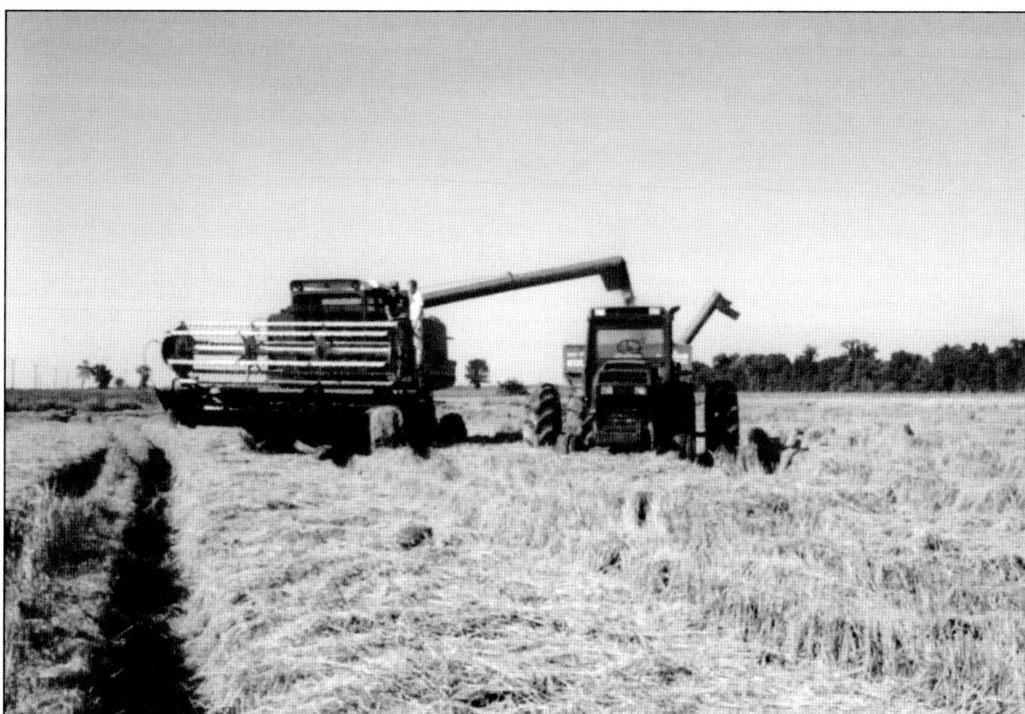

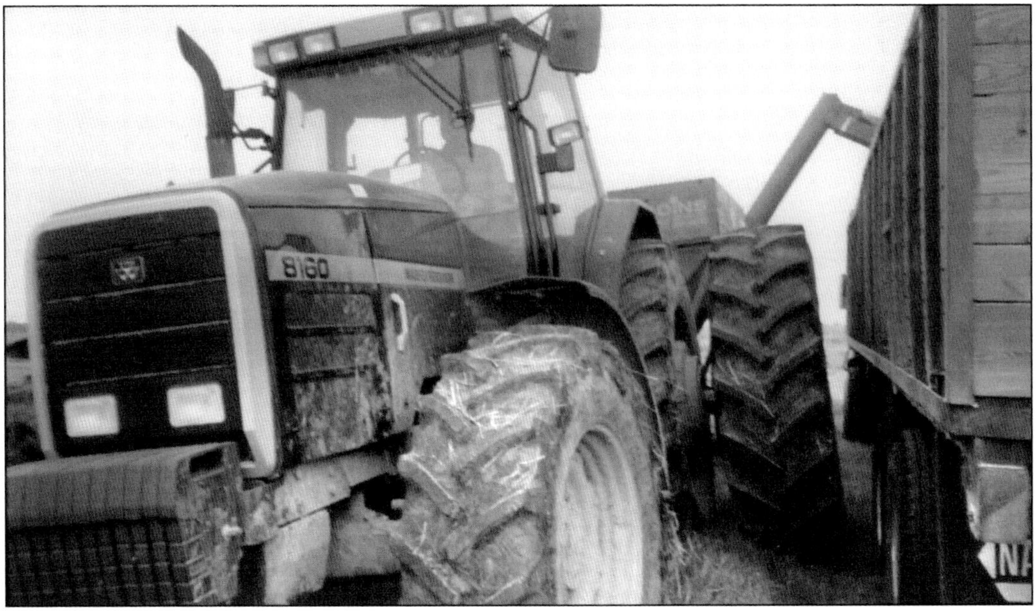

From the late 1930s through the 1950s, the delta experienced an agriculture boom. Hand labor farm production had been replaced by diversification, mechanization, and chemical and biological practices. Farmers had become a new minority and, at the same time, the new elite. The cost of machines and land that was priced at between $1,095 and $2,500 per acre had forced out all but the most skilled and daring farmers. They were heavily capitalized, with access to thousands, even millions of dollars. With greater investment comes greater risk, and between 1985 and 1995, some 11,000 farmers left the delta, victims of debt, low prices, and bankruptcy. From the 1960s through the 1990s, thousands of small farms in the area were absorbed by large corporate-owned agribusinesses, leaving small communities to stagnate. The farm hand on the tractor, above and below, is unloading his grain cart into the grain hauler for transport to the rice dryers in these 1960s photographs. (Both courtesy of Billye Frein.)

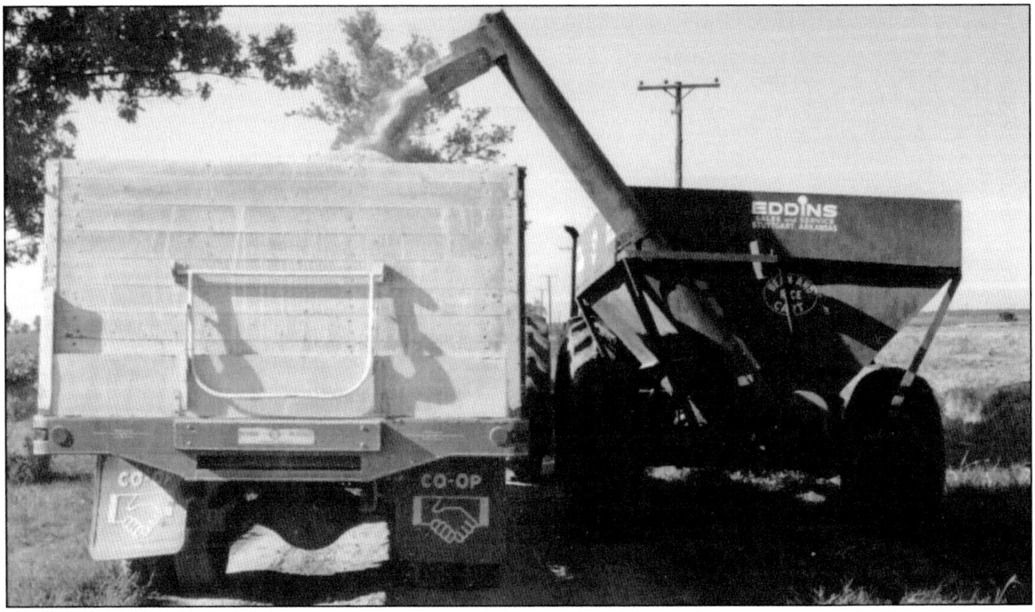

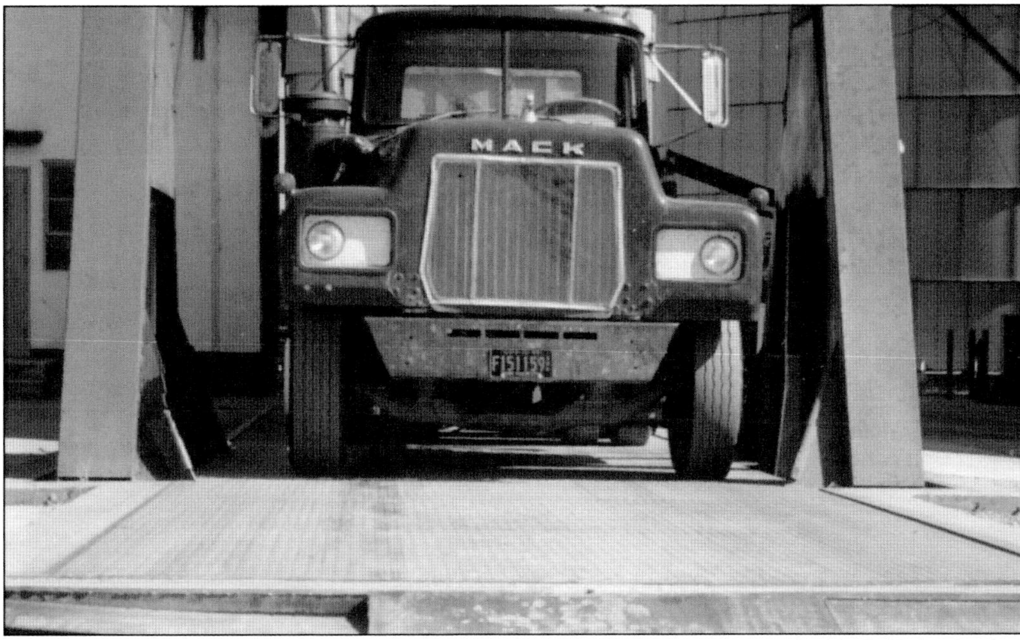

Arkansas is the largest rice-producing state in America, harvesting one-half of all the bushels produced nationwide. Rice is a high-cost crop for farmers, requiring high temperatures, plentiful water, a smooth land surface to facilitate uniform flooding and drainage, and a subsoil hardpan that inhibits the percolation of water. Planting begins in April, with harvest usually occurring from September through October. Arkansas rice is produced in irrigated fields and achieves the highest yields in the world. Rice is the world's third largest crop, with corn being first and wheat second. These 1960s photographs display a Mack truck grain hauler unloading rice into the dryer's storage bin and leaving to return to the rice field for another load. (Both courtesy of Billye Frein.)

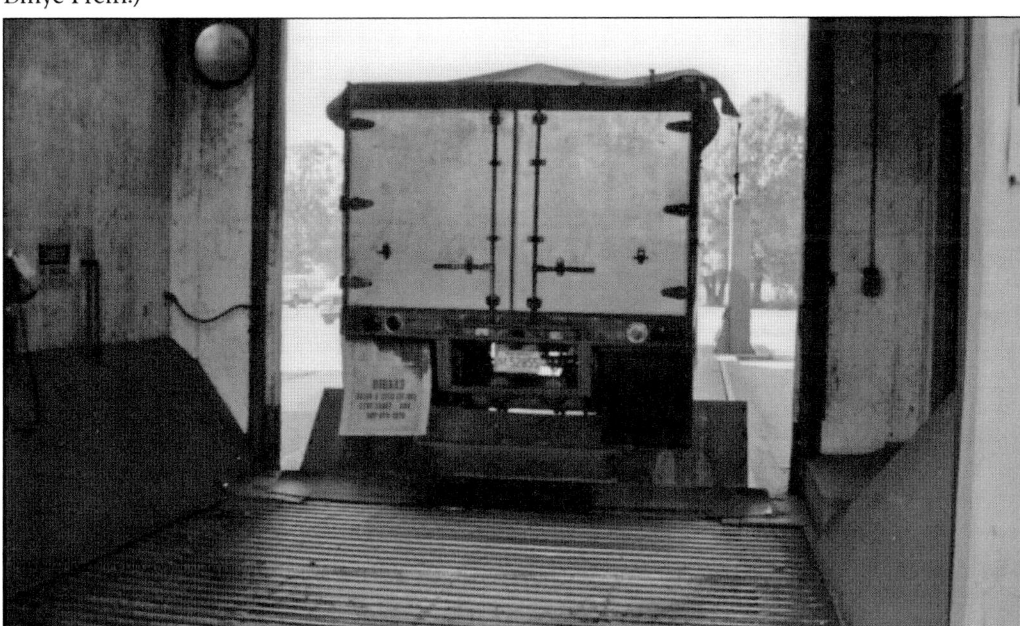

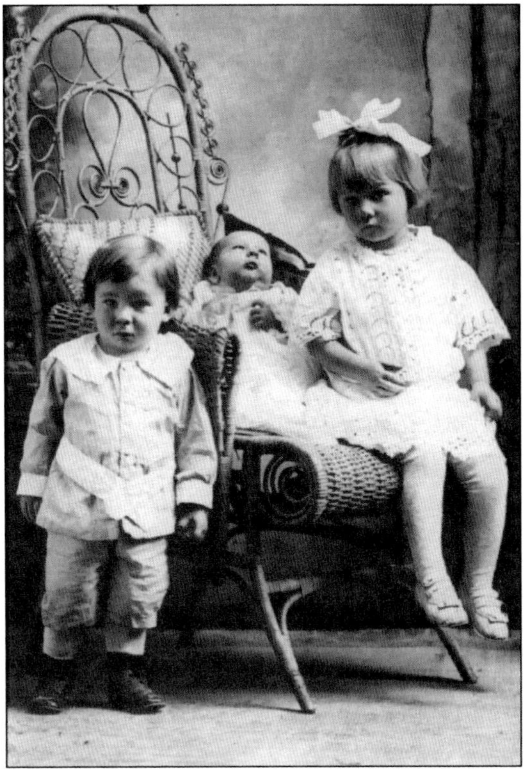

Pictured at left in this c. 1918 photograph are the children of prominent farmer and businessman Vernie Wesley Williams Sr. and Sarah Williams of Monroe. From left to right are Vernie Wesley Williams Jr., Elzie "Pete" Williams, and Stella Williams. (Courtesy of Sarah Williams McKnight.)

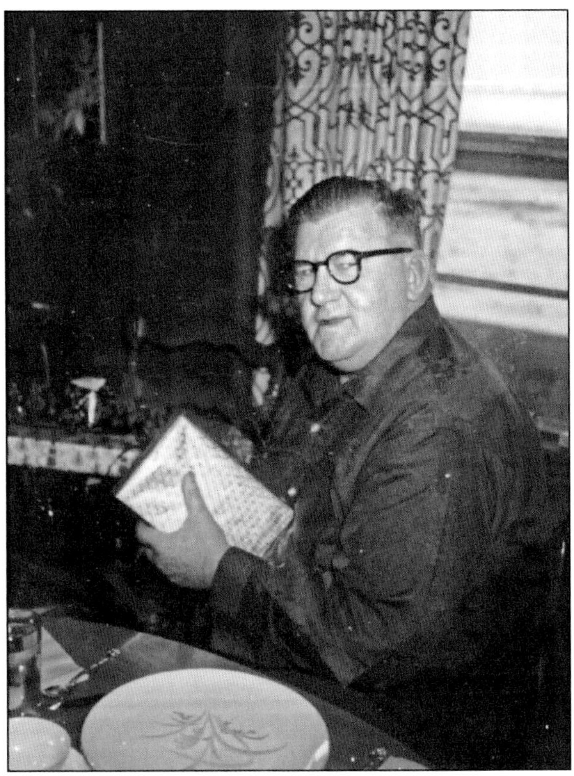

Vernie W. Williams Jr. (pictured at right in 1966) was an enterprising resident of Monroe. In addition to cultivating his 1,500-acre farm, he went into business with Dr. Valentine Pardo and his brother Pete, and began a cotton ginning business in the town. He also owned and operated a general store, a sawmill, and a cattle ranch. (Courtesy of Sarah Williams McKnight.)

Eight

LIFE ON THE BROADWAY

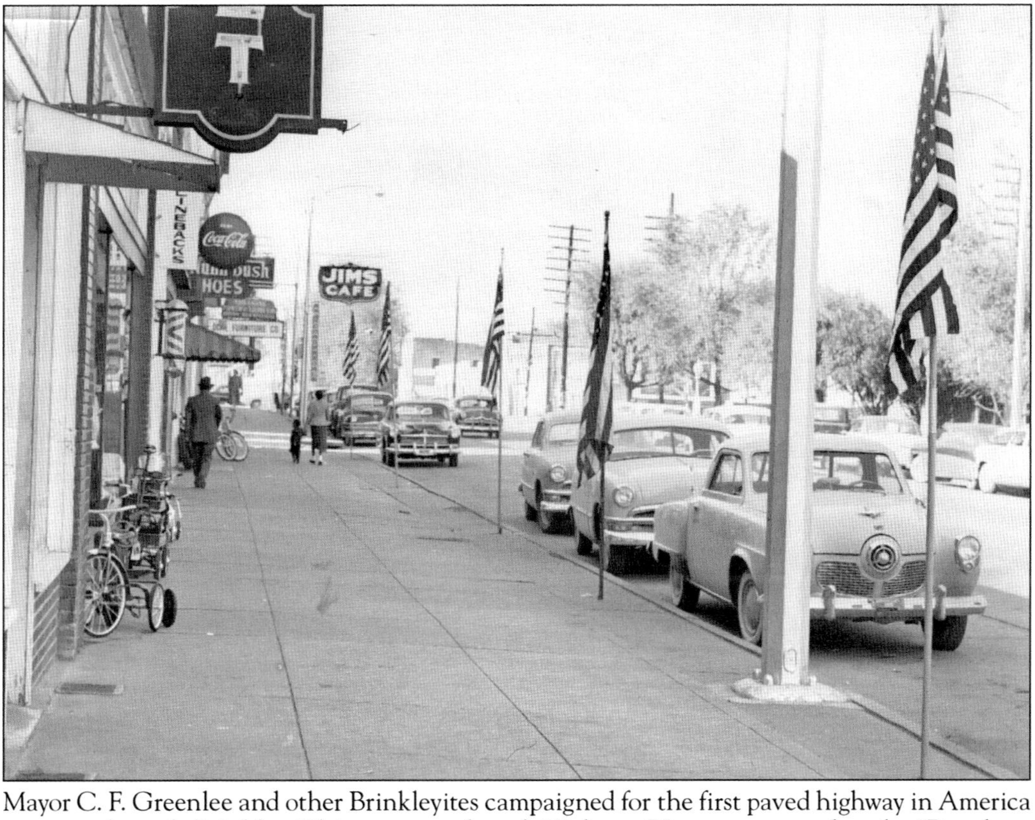

Mayor C. F. Greenlee and other Brinkleyites campaigned for the first paved highway in America to come through Brinkley. This new paved road, Highway 70, was promoted as the "Broadway of America" beginning in 1917 and was to extend from coast to coast. It was routed through Brinkley and, along with the railroad, brought tourists and boom days for the town. Businesses flourished until the end of railroad passenger service and the completion of Interstate 40, which runs parallel to Highway 70, both occurring in 1967. Cypress Street is part of Highway 70 and is shown here in the 1950s during its heyday.

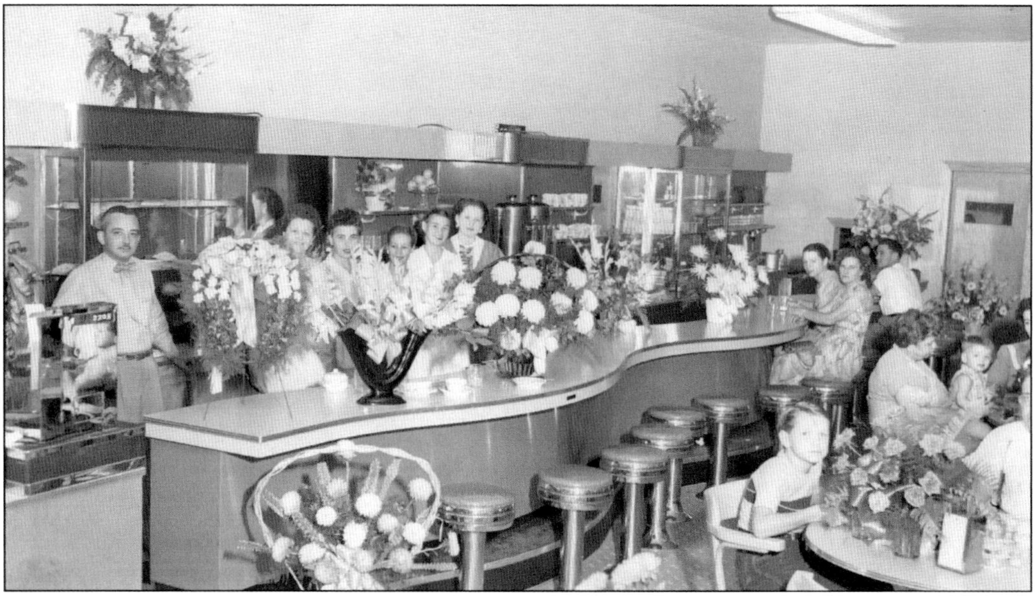

The Town House Café was owned and operated by Charles and Louisa Sands of Brinkley. It was located near the railroad tracks on Cypress Street, across from the Central Delta Depot Museum. Upon its opening in the 1950s, the *Brinkley Argus* reported, "The café equipment is something new in Brinkley, in fact in Arkansas, and those who have traveled far and wide, are stopping to marvel at the elegance and modernness of it all." Charles Sands stands to the far left with his staff at the grand opening. (Courtesy of Felecia Sands.)

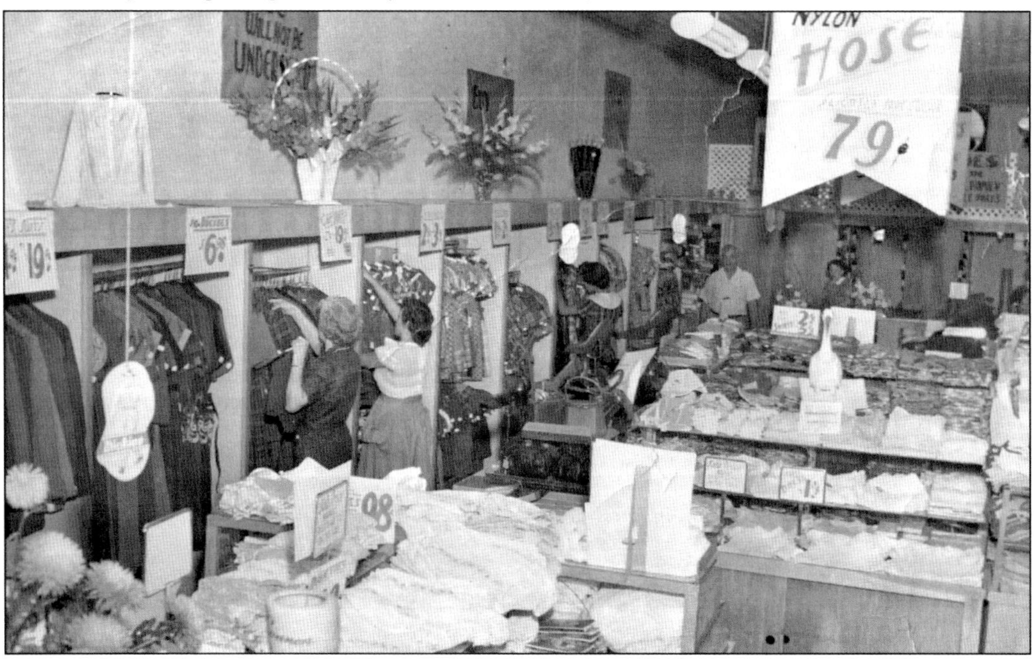

This 1950s photograph is a view of the grand opening of Shabans Store in Brinkley. The unidentified shoppers were part of a large crowd that gathered on the Friday morning of its opening, likely for the sale on ladies dresses priced at $2.49. The store was owned and operated by Joe Shaban and his wife, Alise Shaban.

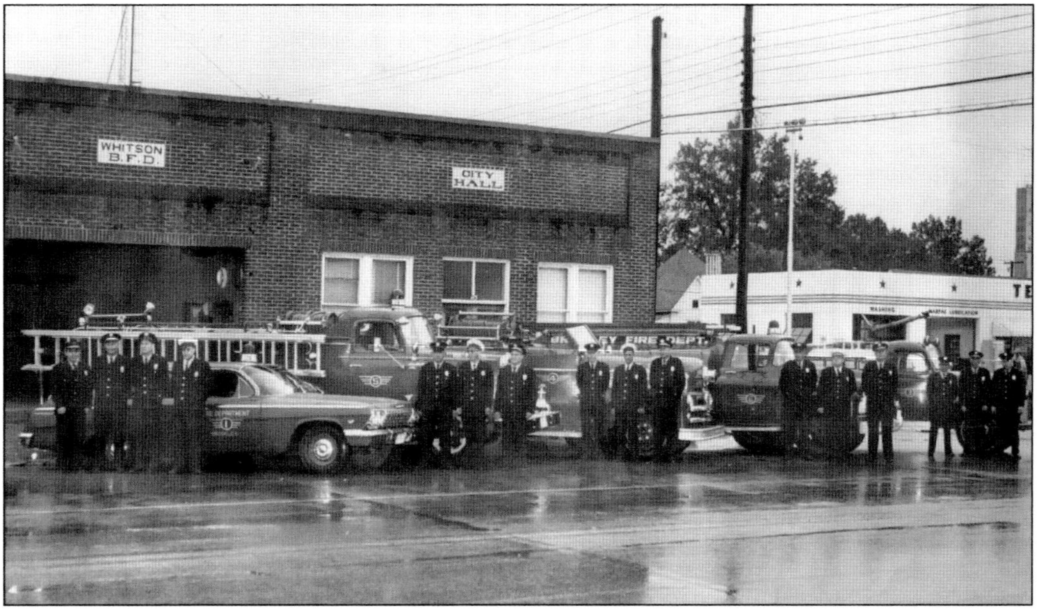

This photograph of the Brinkley Fire Department was taken on Sunday, September 27, 1964, in front of the old fire station. From left to right are Don McGarity, Charles O'Brian, Gene Roy, Johnny Holliday, Tom Miley, Bill Terhune, Bob Raney, Mike Sullivan, Tommy Thompson, John Glover, James Nutt, Bill Hickman, Ed Reiter, Raymond Bowerman, Don Baldwin, and Calvin Tefteller.

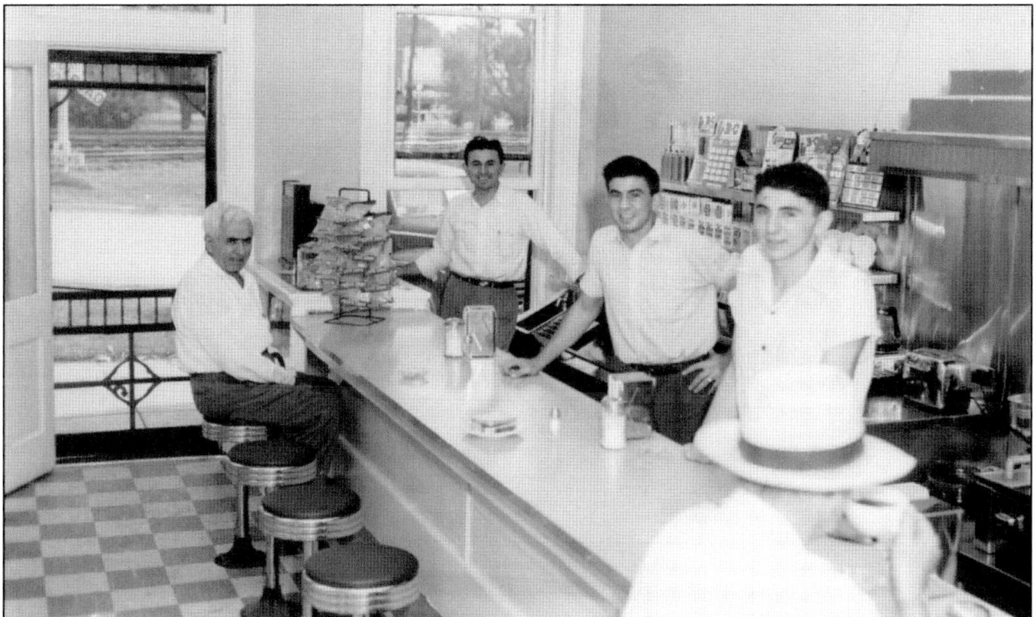

Joe Malham was from a village near Beirut, Lebanon, and came to America in 1902. He arrived in Brinkley sometime around 1913 and opened a grocery store on the corner of New Orleans Avenue and Walnut Street. In the 1930s, he purchased the Arlington Hotel from Gus Rusher and renamed it the Hotel Malham. It burned to the ground in 1977 and was never rebuilt. This 1950s photograph was taken inside the hotel grill. From left to right are (seated) Joe Malham and unidentified; (standing) Isaac Malham, Raymond "Zoom" Malham, and Charles B. Malham.

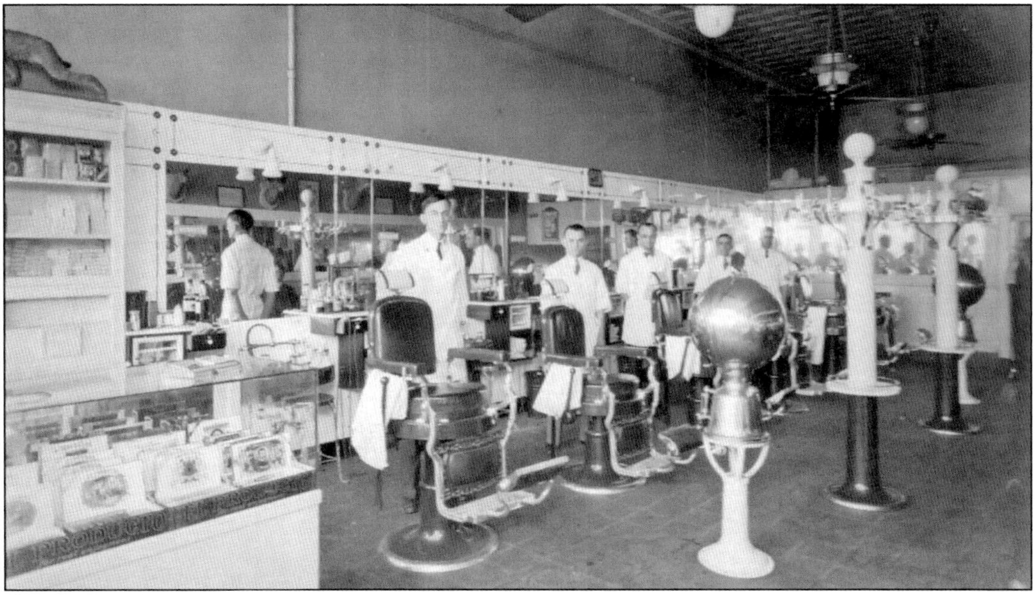

Six chairs, six barbers, was the advertisement patrons of Jack Lineback's barbershop remember. He was the most prominent barber of the region whose business was frequented by the socially elite. The photograph above shows his shop on Cypress Street, but later he moved to the building behind the Sharp and Sharp Law Firm. The two shiny globes in front of the barbers were used to keep towels warm and moist. Jack Lineback is pictured to the far left, and Alton Wilson is standing by the second chair next to him.

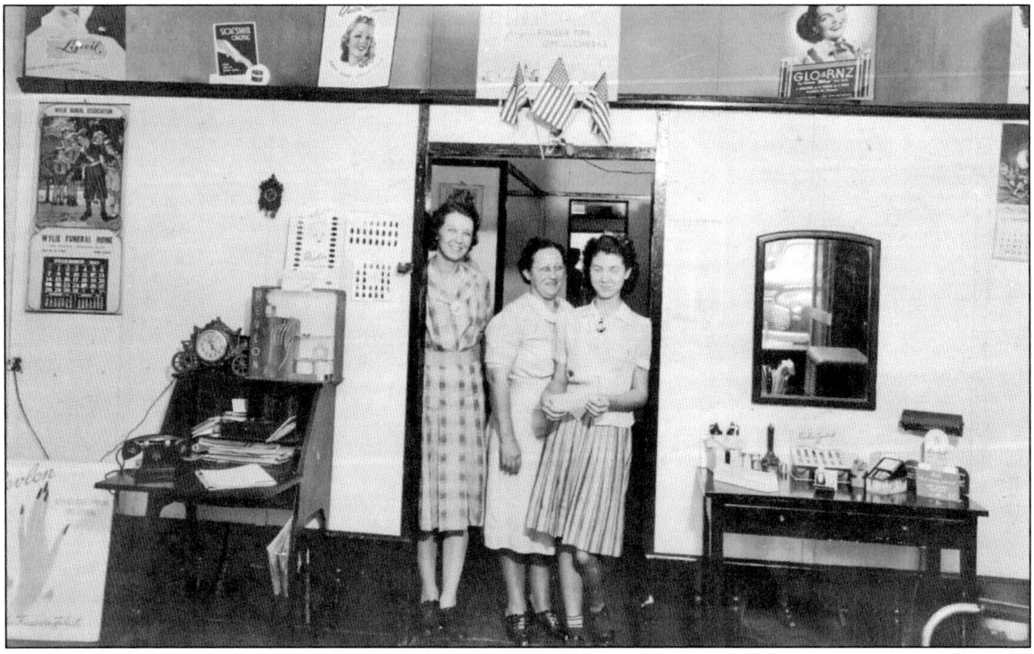

Pictured here are the beauticians of White Way's Beauty Shop, located on the second floor of the Gazzola building on the corner of Cypress Street and New Orleans Avenue. Leone Henard Wilson, wife of barber Alton Wilson, stands in the doorway to the left, and her sister, Louise Henard Parker, is pictured on the right. This third woman is unidentified.

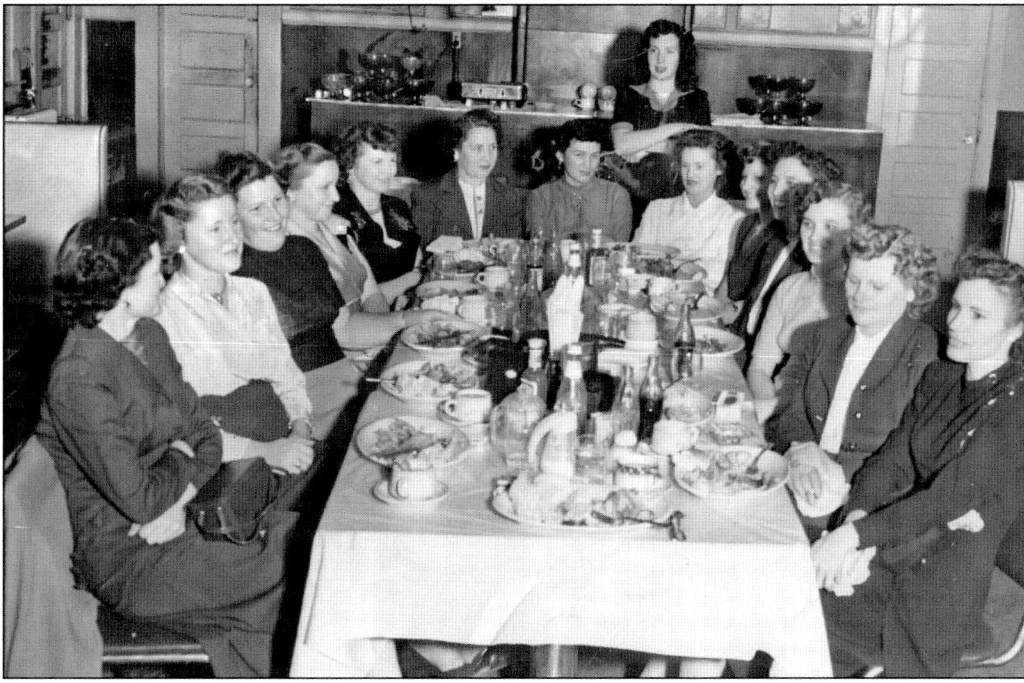

Pictured in the fall of 1952, the ladies of the Brinkley button factory enjoy some time together away from the factory. From left to right are "Toots" Redman, Bessie "Shoemar" McClellan, Virginia Ellis, Lelah O'Brian, Connie Clinton, Christene Cain, Floid "Clinton" Utley, Thelma Newbie (standing), Gussie "Clinton" King, Pearl Weatherly, ? Nylon, Gertrude Hagger, Clare Parker, and ? Long.

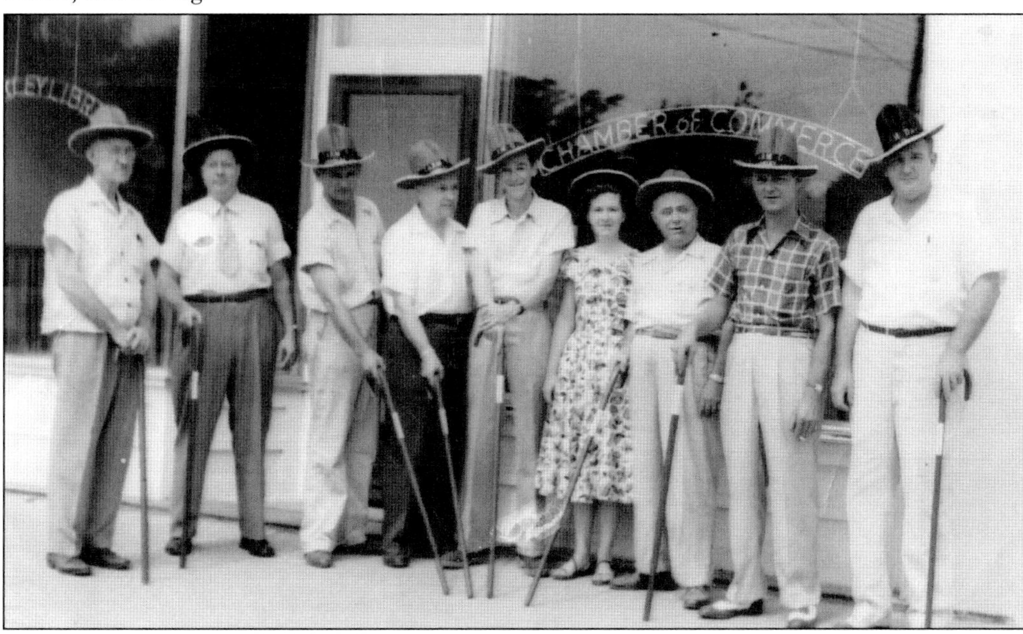

In the 1950s, members of the chamber of commerce pose in front of their office for this Brinkley Farm Days photograph. From left to right are Fred Simmons, Robert Ed McKnight, unidentified, Albert L. Rusher, Gus Elledge Jr., unidentified, Marion Satterfield, Bob Hawkins, and John Crow.

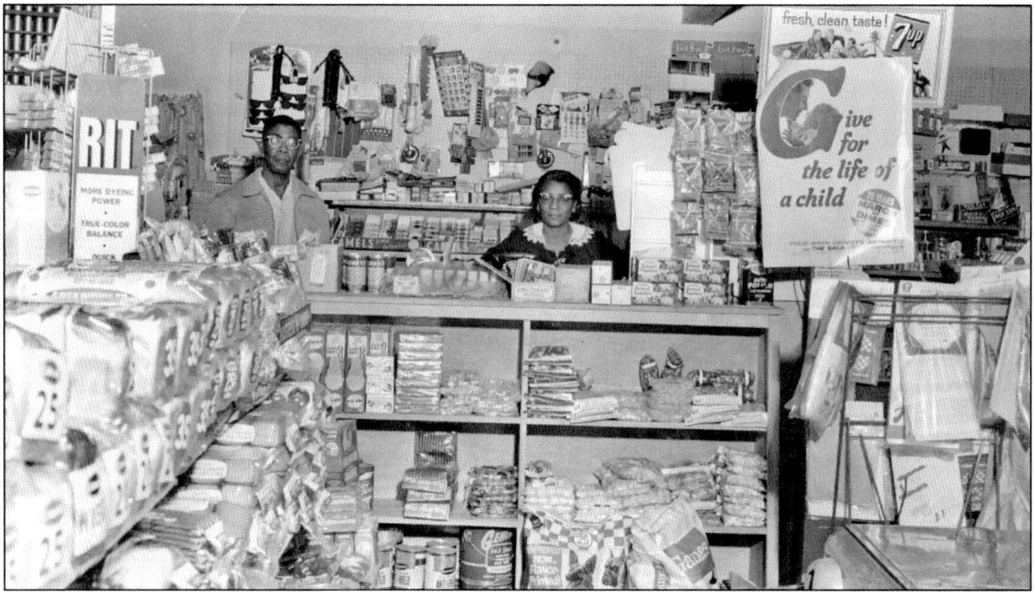

Booker T. Thomason Sr. and his wife, Ora Lee Thomason, opened Thomason's Grocery in 1947 on Main Street in Brinkley. She ran the store while he worked for the Cotton Belt Railroad as a stationary fireman. The couple met and became sweethearts at the Consolidated White River Academy, which was a boarding school in Brinkley. Booker was from McCrory, and Ora Lee was from Cotton Plant. Neither town possessed a high school for black children in the era of segregation, so they had to be sent to another town to finish high school. These photographs were taken in January 1963, the year their son, Harold Thomason, left the military to help his mother run the store because of her failing health. He continued running the family business after the passing of his parents until December 31, 2008. (Courtesy of Harold Thomason.)

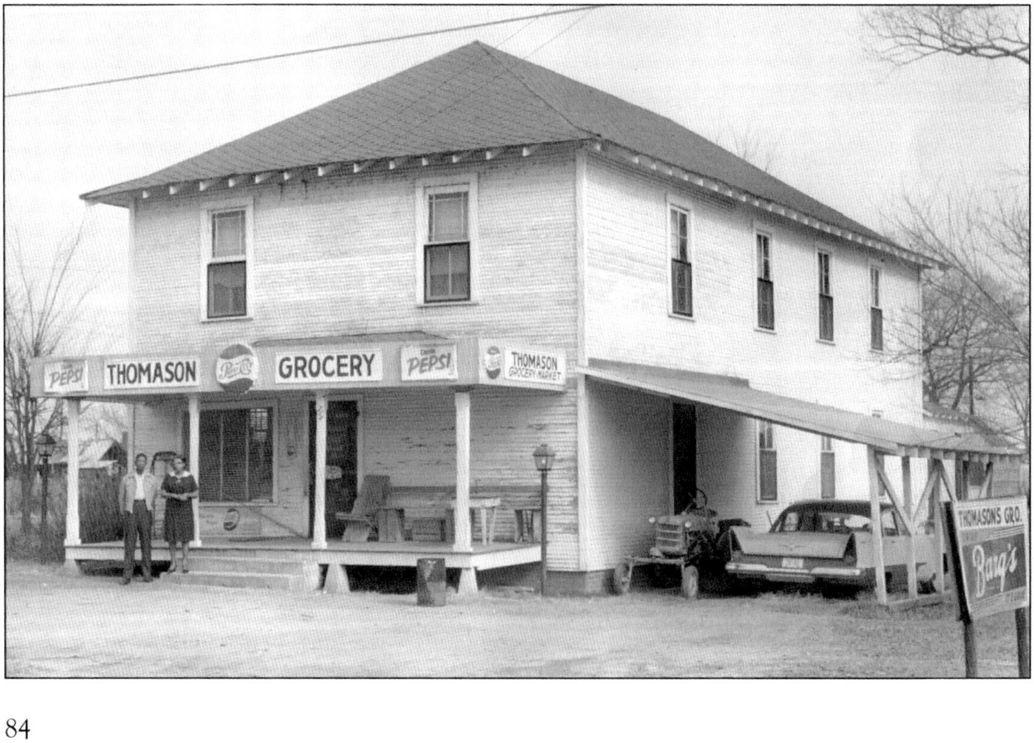

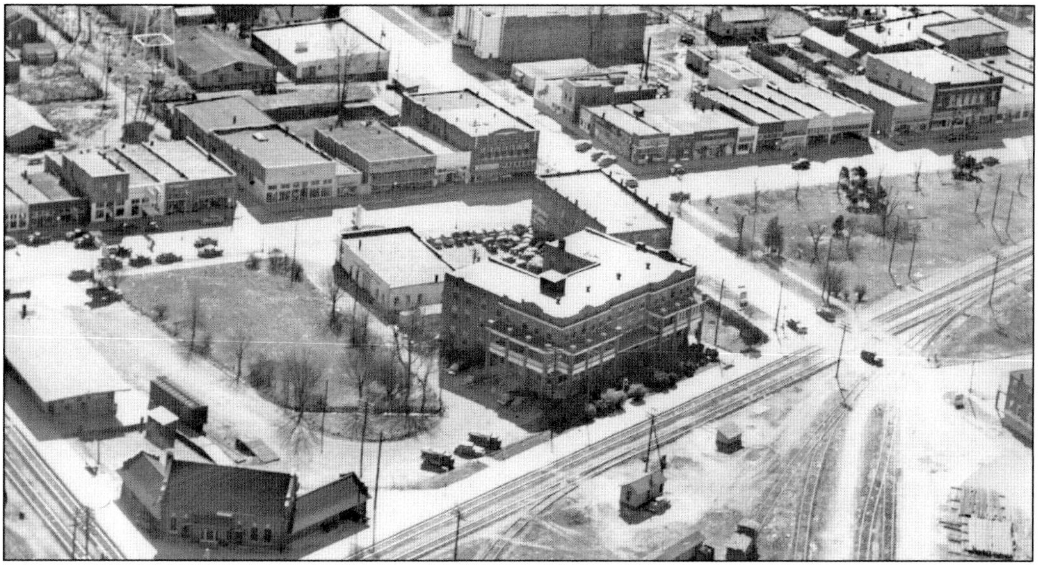

At the time this 1950s aerial photograph was taken of Brinkley, the town boasted more than 200 businesses. There was 1 hospital, 2 nursing homes, 4 motels, 1 hotel, 2 bus lines, 5 funeral homes, 4 florists, 1 veterinarian, 3 pharmacies, 1 ice company, 1 wholesale grocer, 1 theater, 1 skating rink, 30 service stations, 16 restaurants, beauty shops, retail merchants, ladies and men's ready-to-wear merchants, petroleum product bulk plants, building supply companies, farm equipment dealers, 2 banks, 2 newspapers, 1 radio station, 3 aircraft services, 2 major railroads servicing passengers, 17 churches, and 1 public library.

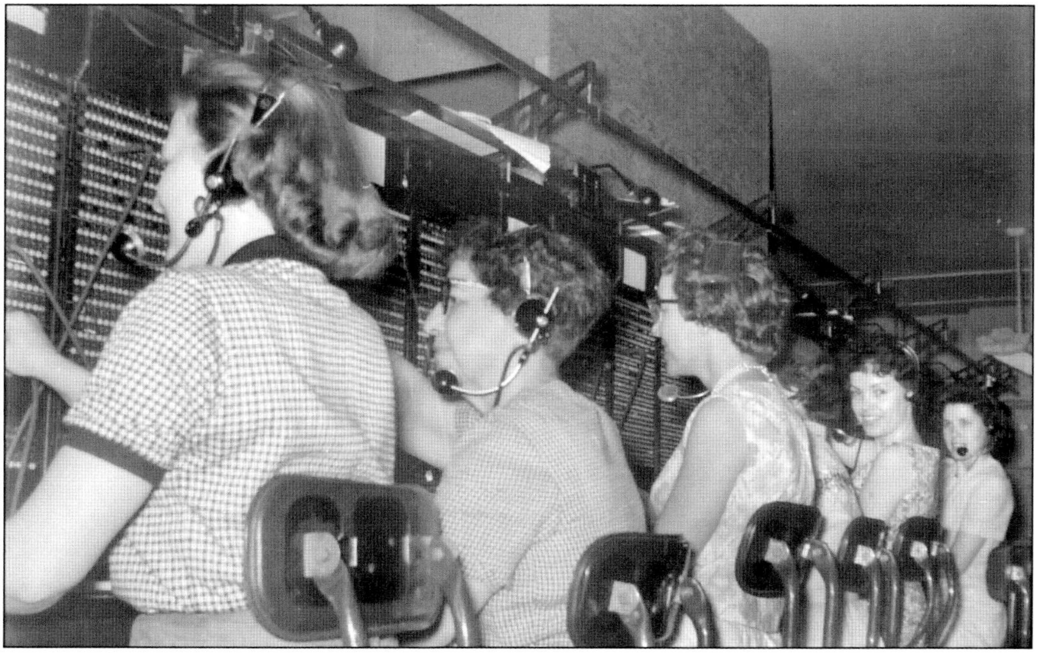

The telephone office employed many local women of the community as switchboard operators. Brinkley converted to dial in 1963, making the switchboard obsolete, which left these women to look for other means of support. Pictured above from left to right are Angela Hinton, Mozelle Osborn, Anna Lee Rigdon, unidentified, Nellie Brown, and unidentified. (Courtesy of Steve Hinton.)

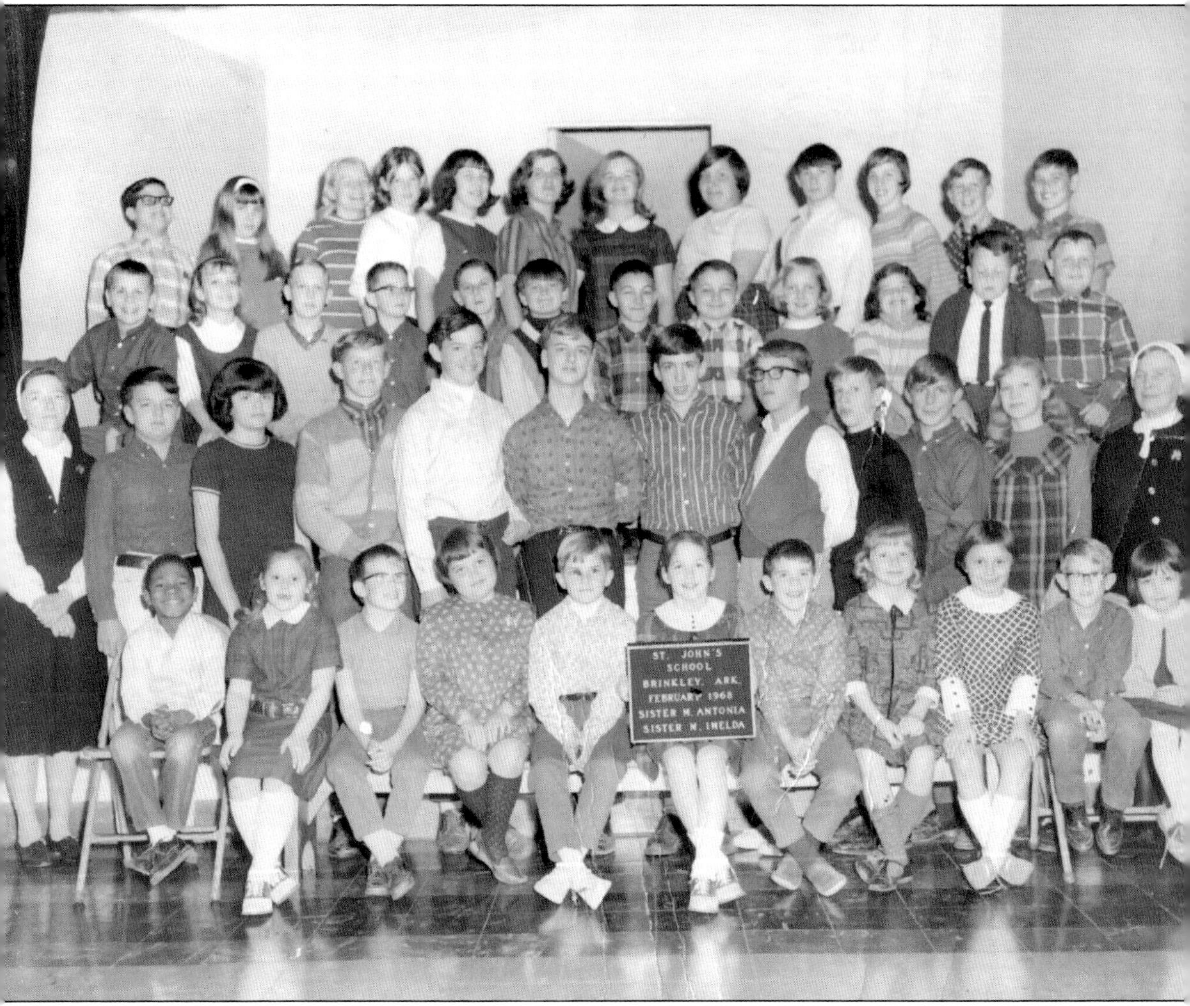

The last class of St. John's Catholic School is pictured in their 1968 class photograph. From left to right are (first row) unidentified, Lee Ann Frein, unidentified, April Holiday, Kevin Smith, Colleen Farrell, Michael Potthast, Mary Frein, Rosemary Terrice, unidentified, and Monica Bauer; (second row) Sister Antonia, ? Siler, ? Siler, Lendon Hinton, Jon Smith, Henry Farrell, Ricky Clifton, Gary Smith, Hank Farrell, Albert Snelson, Judy Frein, and Sister Imelda; (third row) unidentified, Edith Frein, Tom Frein, Michael Tehan, Larry Frein, Fred Sands, Tony Terrice, Johnny Terrice, Jane Warblow, Linda Malham, unidentified, and Charles Holmes; (fourth row) Robert Malham, unidentified, Rasia Hale, Paulette Smith, Tamra Baird, Nancy Snelson, Madeline Sharp, unidentified, Chris Smith, Margaret Farrell, Pat Farrell, and Billy Rattas Potthast. (Courtesy of Billye Frein.)

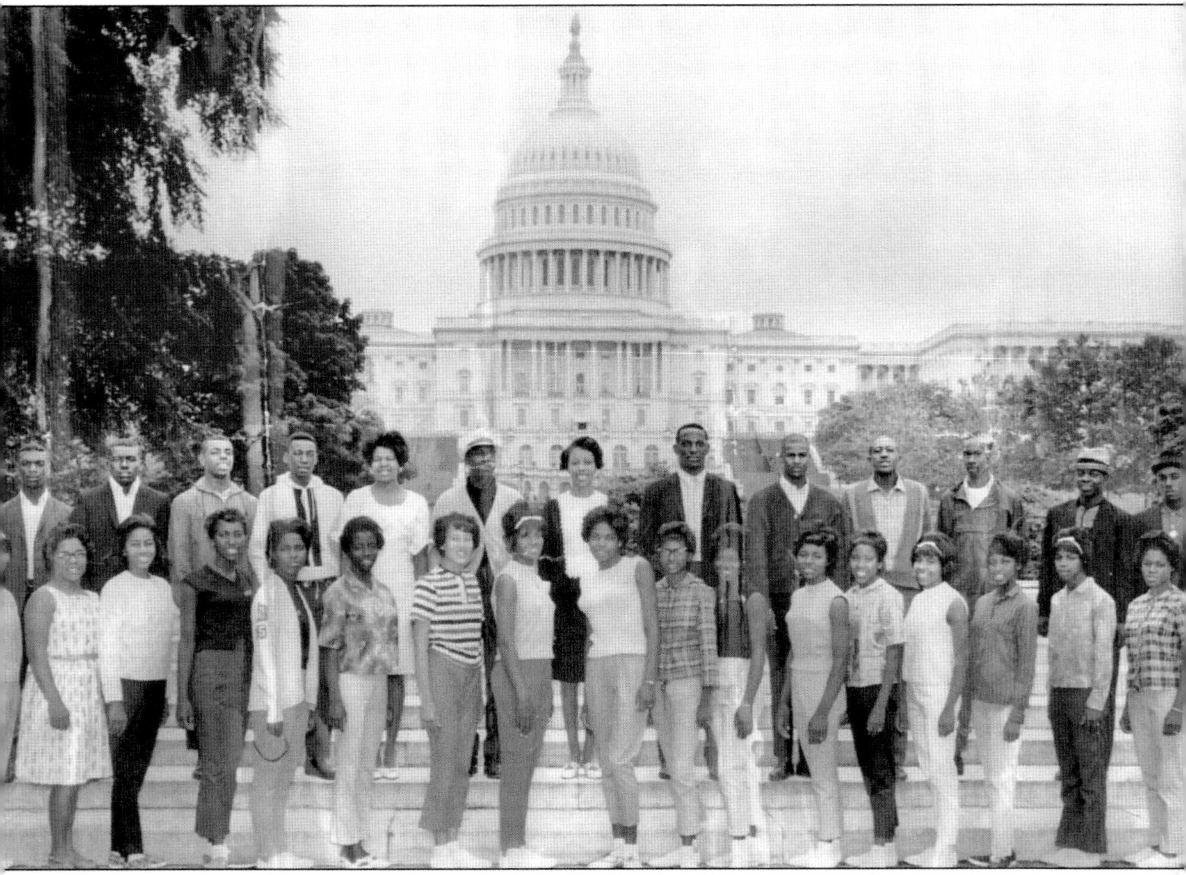

In 1966, the senior class of Marion Anderson High School made a trip to Washington, D.C. From left to right are (first row) Thelma McKissick, Lillie Johnson, Mable Tyler, Virginia Banks, Minnie Bowe, Vasti Halliburton, Jeanette Myers, Georgia Weekly, Dot Swanigan, Sandra Hudson, Myrna Clayton, Mary Gray, Eva Myers, Eva McKissick, Mary Moore, Shirley Dorsey, and Lanell Thomas; (second row) Ervin Smith, Raymond Clay, Damon McMillion, Erbie Jenning, Roger Marshall, Reba Thomason (sponsor), R. V. Person (sponsor), Lois Collins (sponsor), Samuel Dillard, Wallace Miller, Paul Hollister, Warren Foster, Robert Lenair, and John Bean. (Courtesy of Dot Swanigan Young and Damon McMillion.)

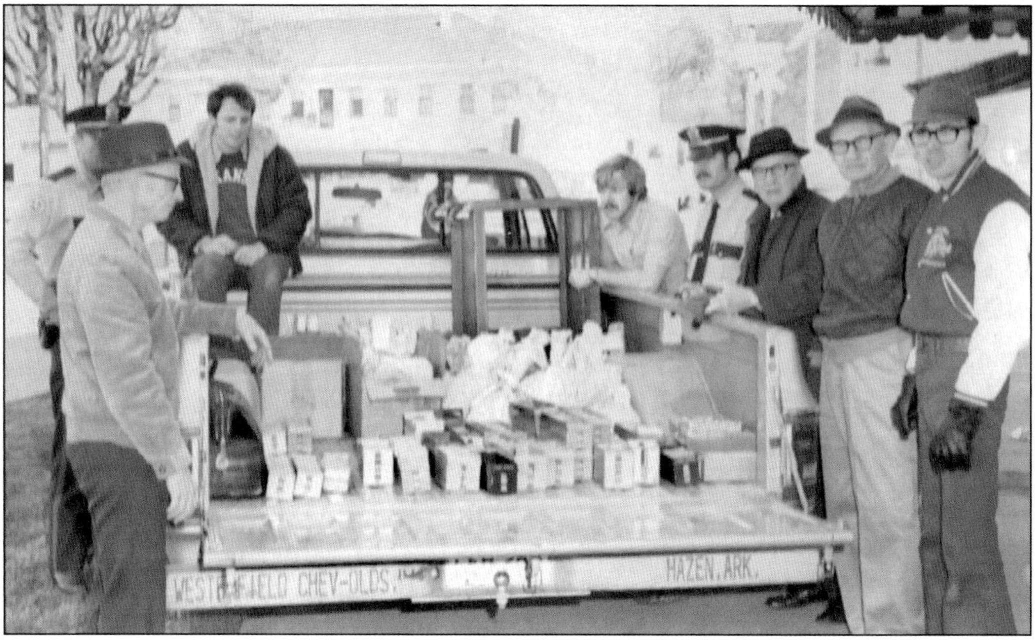

The Bank of Brinkley built a new half-million-dollar facility on the corner of Ash Street and New Orleans Avenue, and on the 72nd year of its existence, its new doors officially opened at 9:30 a.m. on February 25, 1974. The officers and employees were quick to point out that it was built for its customers and to meet their needs in a growing community, featuring two of the latest modern drive-in windows. Pictured above is the transportation of cash from the vault of the old bank to the new one. Below, a large crowd is gathered with a camera crew for the grand opening ceremony. (Both courtesy of Albert H. Rusher.)

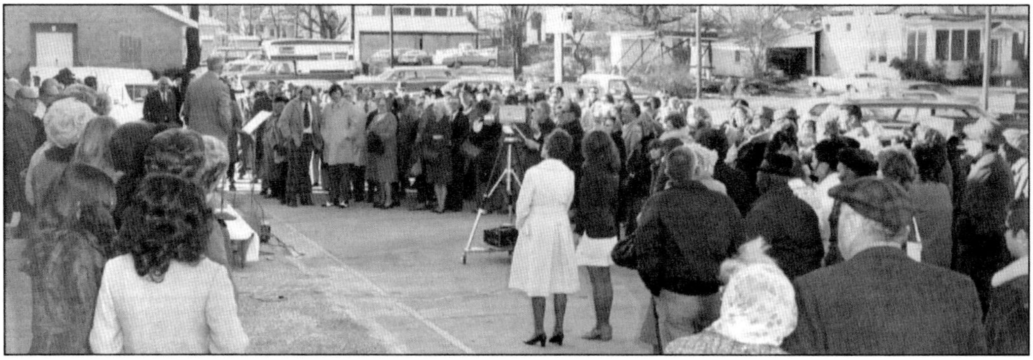

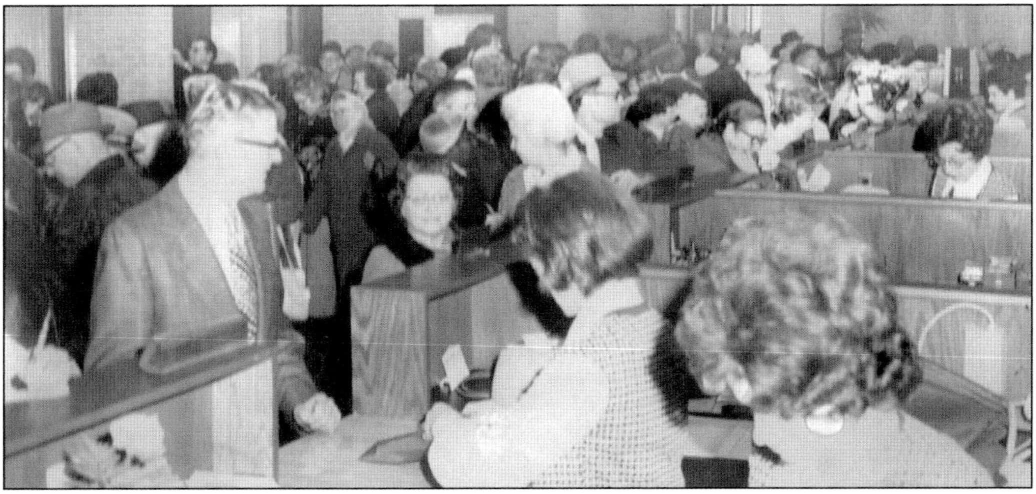

The Thursday, February 21, 1974, issue of the *Brinkley Argus* featured an article on the upcoming opening of the Bank of Brinkley, stating, "The bank will be open until 4:30 Monday afternoon, and everyone is cordially invited to come by to visit the new building, receive a souvenir gift and register for some very nice Grand Opening prizes which will be given away. These prizes include a cash ribbon, savings account, barbecue grill, electronic radar oven and a console color TV." In the photograph below, Charlie Sands (right) is shaking hands with John Cole (left), executive vice president of the bank, after winning a new television courtesy of the Bank of Brinkley. (Both courtesy of Albert H. Rusher.)

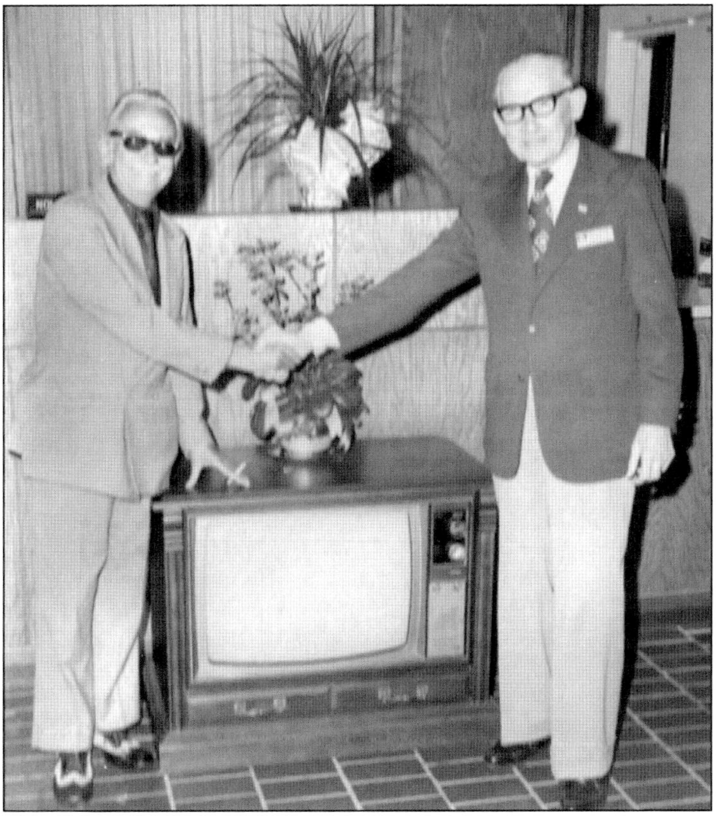

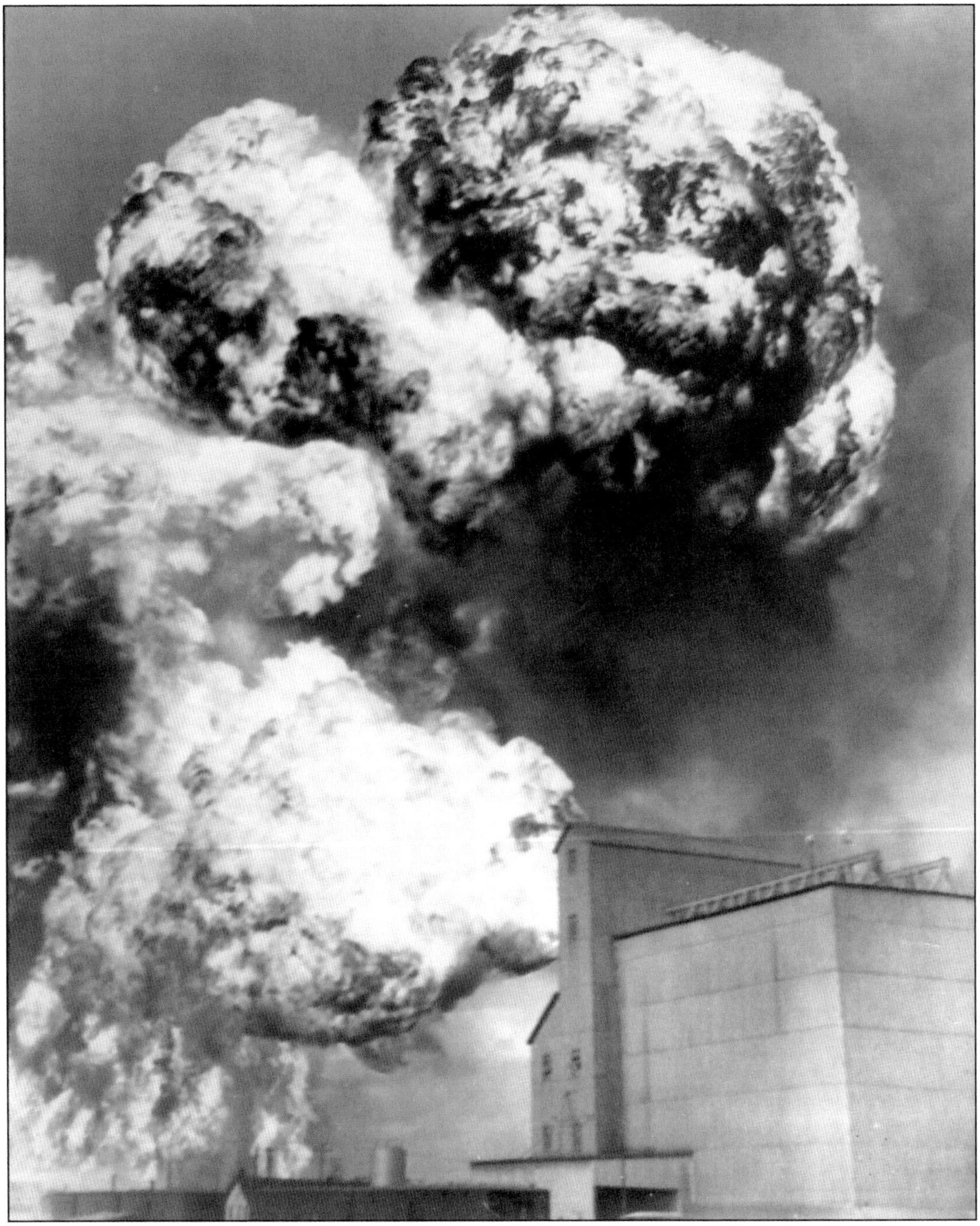

On the afternoon of March 12, 1959, butane tanks at the Weis Butane Gas Company on Cypress Street in Brinkley erupted in flames. The magnitude of the explosions was seen 20 miles away as the orange and black clouds billowed hundreds of feet into the sky. Fire trucks from Forrest City, Marianna, Wynne, Clarendon, Cotton Plant, Hazen, Carlisle, Stuttgart, Lonoke, and North Little Rock lined the streets for two or three blocks to fight the blaze that lasted nearly three hours. The Weis family was among the first to thank the firemen in the aftermath in both contribution and a public thank-you that stated, "We are hurt in material value, but the damage to property of others and injury to persons (firemen especially) is much more regrettable than our own plant loss. This we regret very much." A new plant was later built on South Grand Avenue, far from the downtown.

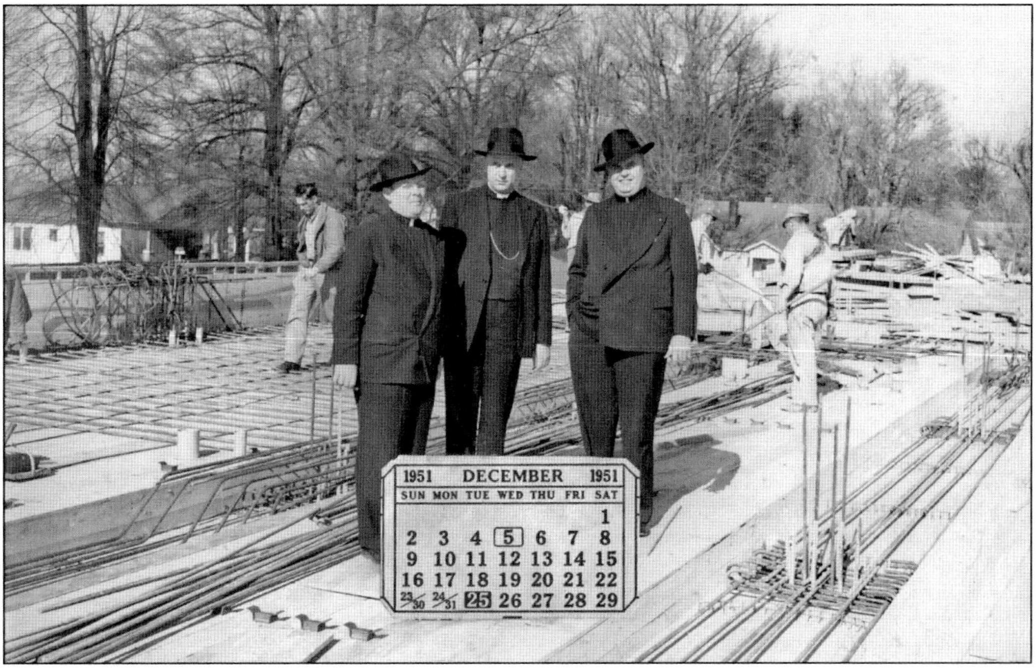

Upon the passing of Brinkley's millionaire, John Gazzola, on October 9, 1937, his will contained every detail for the construction, maintenance, and supervision of a hospital to be located in Brinkley. Due to legal technicalities, the estate was not settled until the beginning of World War II. By that time, prices and shortages of materials had so advanced that the sum bequeathed by Gazzola was inadequate. At the conclusion of the war, the chamber of commerce raised additional funds for the hospital's construction. Gazzola had left $100,000 for this purpose and directed it be operated under the supervision of the Sisters of Mercy. The dedication for the Mercy Hospital–Gazzola Memorial was held on February 21, 1953. The hospital was eventually closed in 1986.

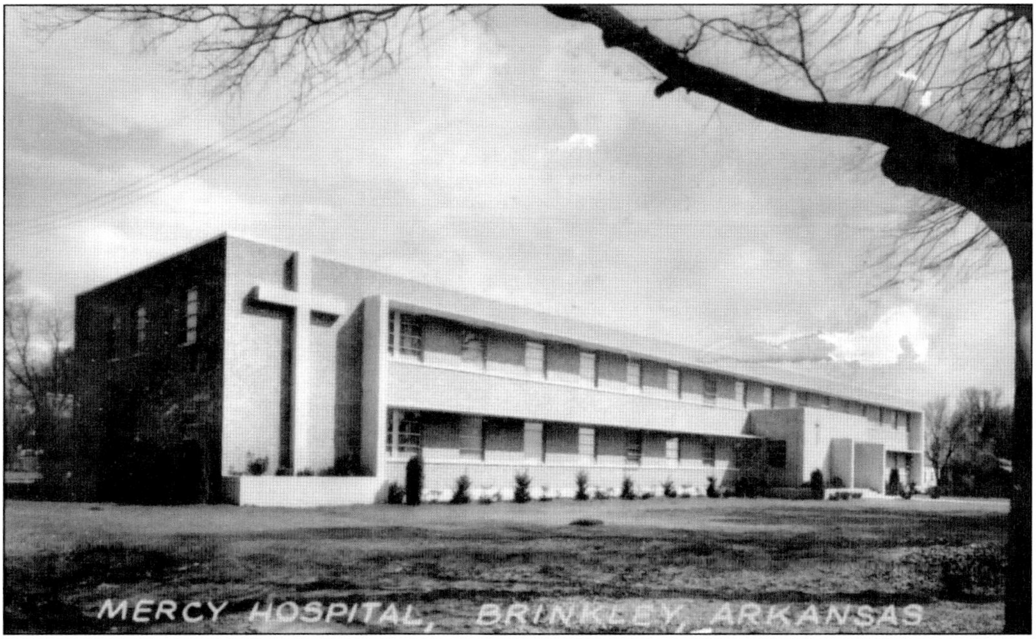

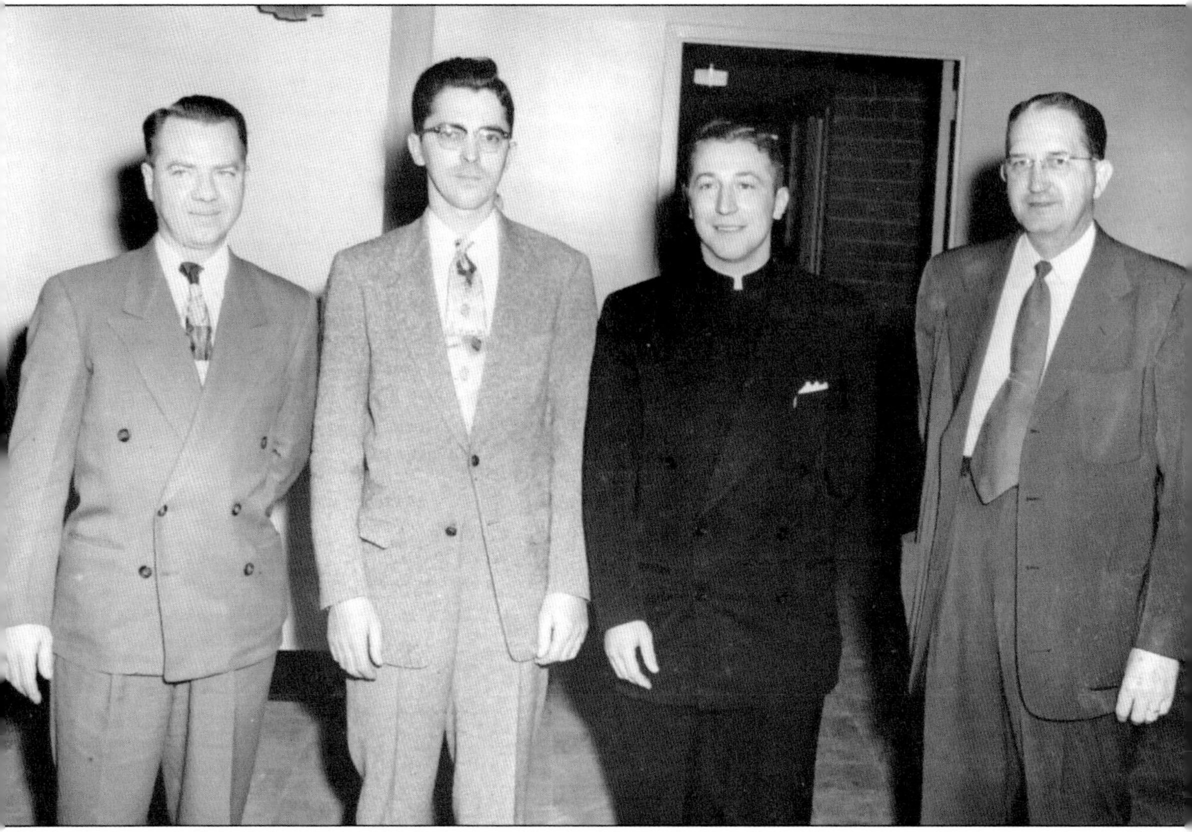

From left to right are Dr. Walter L. Walker, vice chief of staff; Dr. James P. Williams, secretary of staff; the Reverend John Kordsmeir, head of all Catholic hospitals in Arkansas; and Dr. Marvin L. Dalton, chief of staff, on a tour of the newly completed Mercy Hospital. St. Joseph Nursing Home was added to the hospital in 1968 and was staffed by the Olivetan Benedictine Sisters.

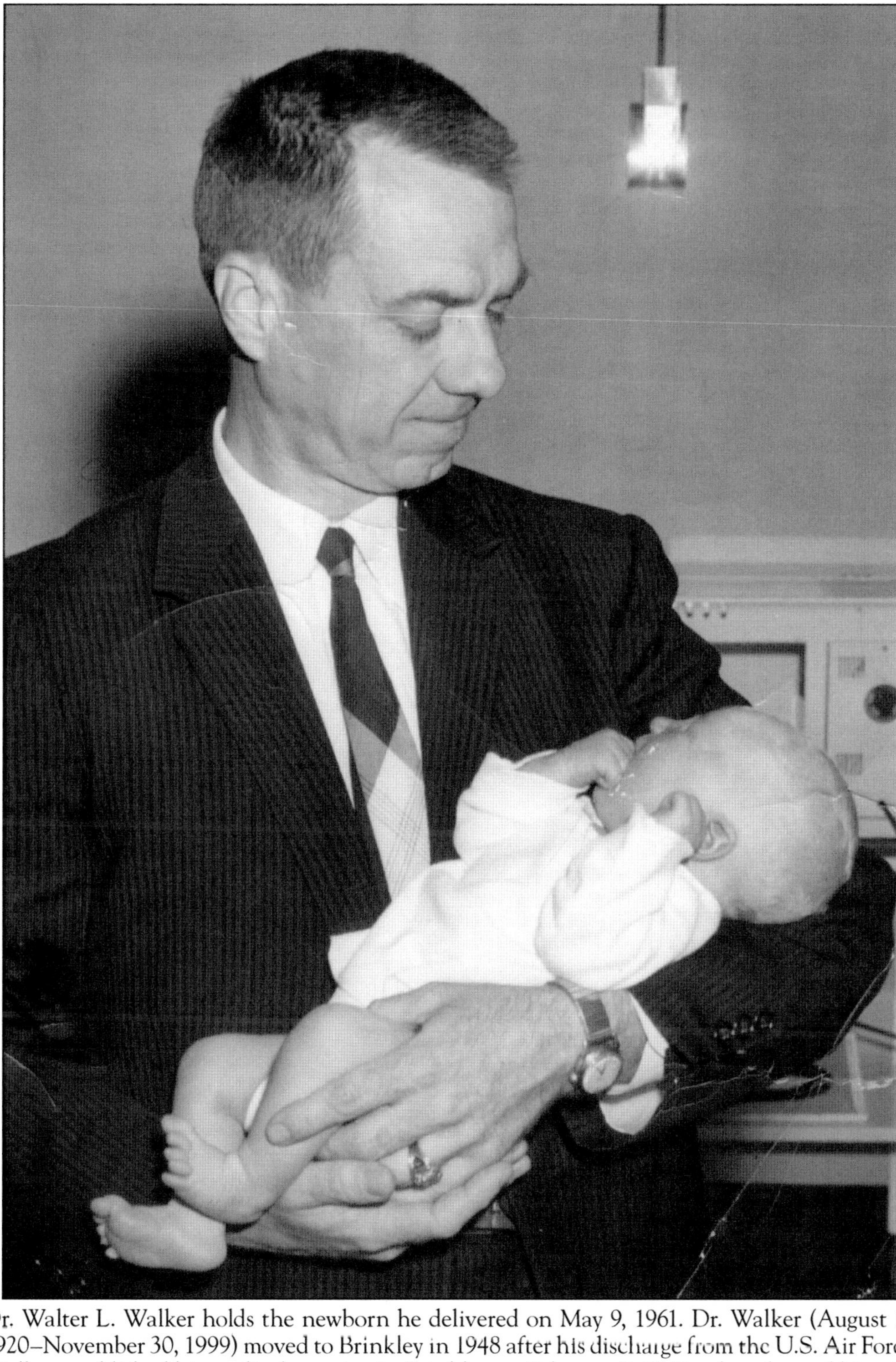

Dr. Walter L. Walker holds the newborn he delivered on May 9, 1961. Dr. Walker (August 17, 1920–November 30, 1999) moved to Brinkley in 1948 after his discharge from the U.S. Air Force. Walker established his medical practice in Brinkley on February 8, 1948, where he and his wife, Freddie, worked together until his retirement on April 28, 1992.

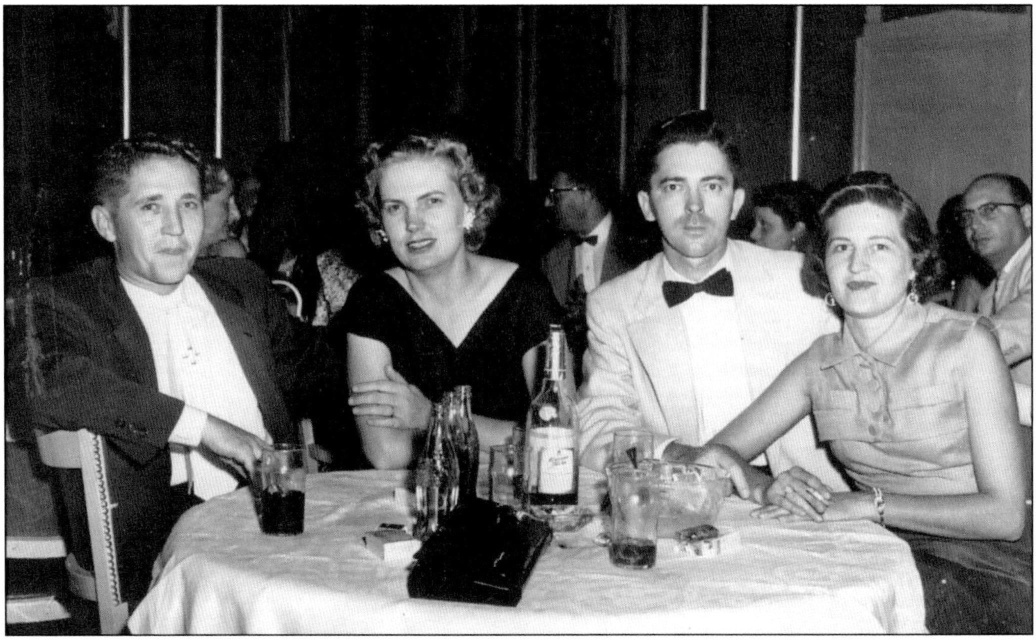

Dr. James P. Williams Jr. (above, third from left), born October 19, 1920, attended the University of Tennessee Medical School and practiced medicine in Brinkley from 1949 until his death in 1987. Below is his new examining room in the Walker Clinic in Brinkley. In his lifetime, he was a member of the Monroe County Medical Society, the American Academy of Family Physicians, the American Medical Association, and the College of Emergency Room Physicians. He was secretary of staff at Mercy Hospital, Monroe County deputy coroner, and a member of the Air Force Medical Corp during World War II. He passed away on November 6, 1987. (Both courtesy of Laura Beth Williams Bussell.)

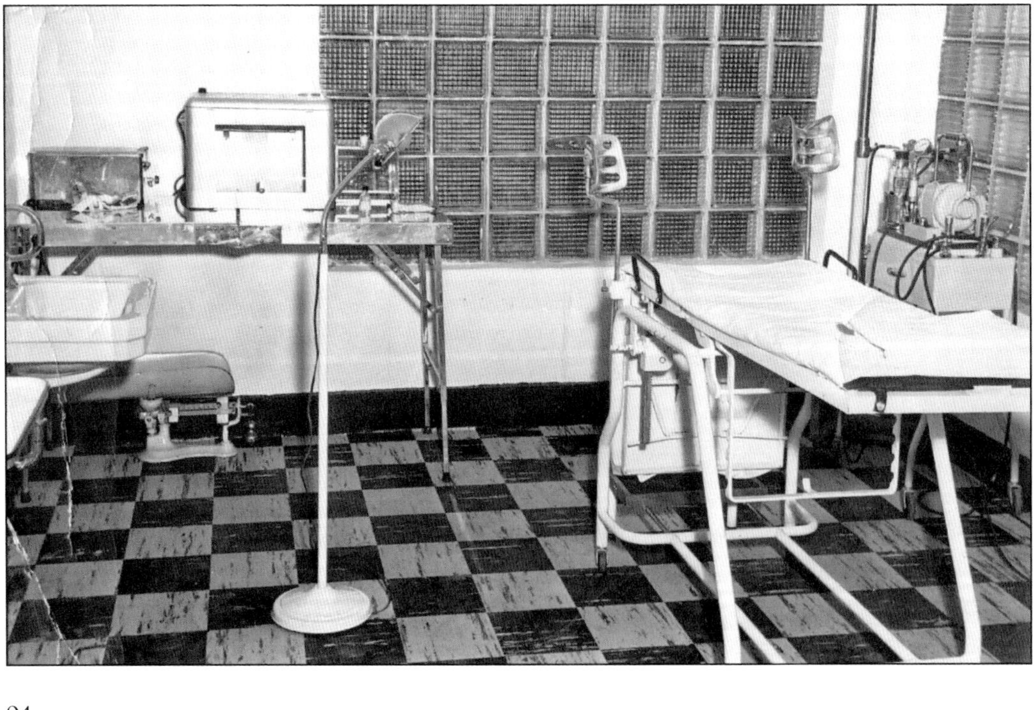

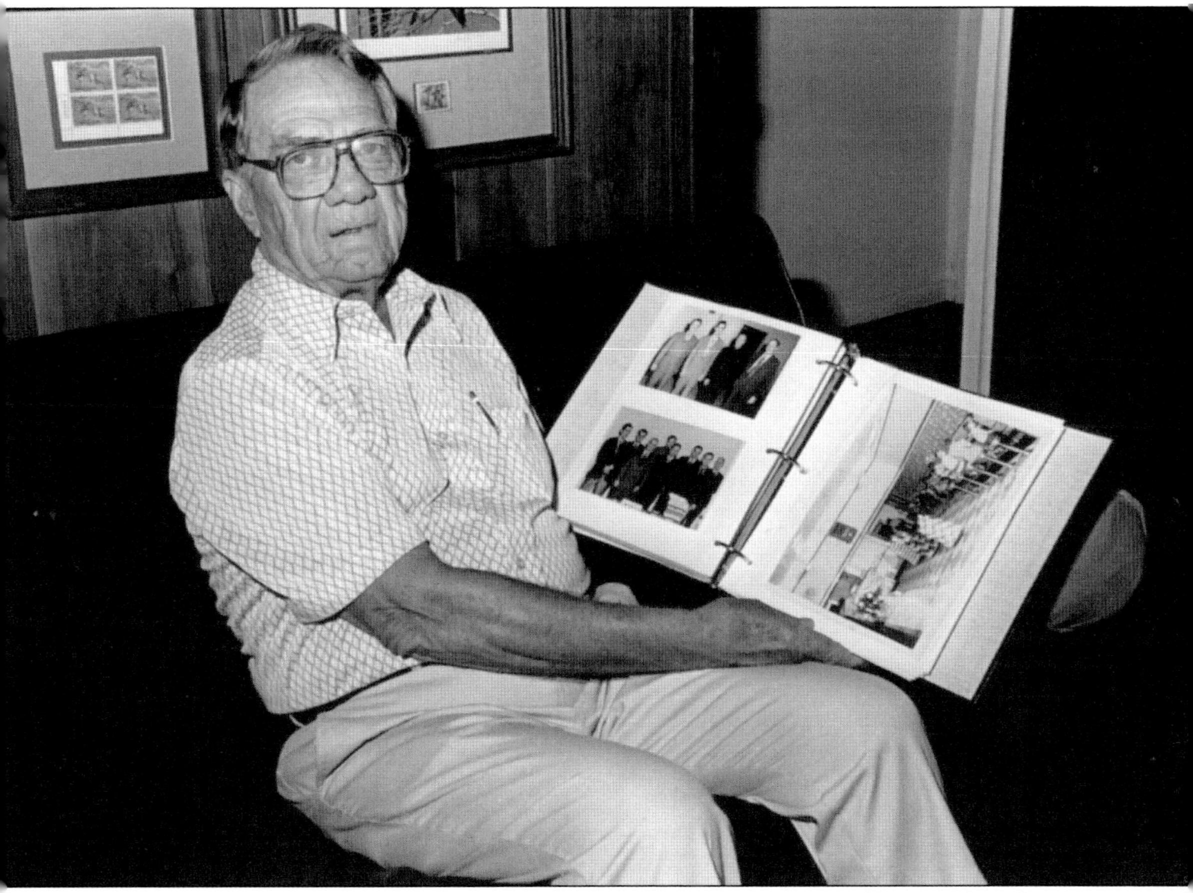

After suffering a stroke on April 27, 1992, Brinkley's beloved Dr. W. L. Walker was forced into retirement. In an outpouring of love and concern, the community contributed their photographs and letters to compile a friendship album in his honor. Several of the pictures in this book came from that album. Romey Short wrote, "Although I have had minimal contact with you since your unfortunate illness removed you from your daily rounds of looking after our health needs, I have kept up with your progress through reports from your many, many friends and Mike. I have never seen as much concern shown for anyone before. This has been an outpouring of love from your friends and patients that you have cared for these many years. . . . I look forward to your complete recovery enabling you to enjoy life to its fullest. You and Freddie have earned a rest." Dr. Walker is shown above with the friendship album.

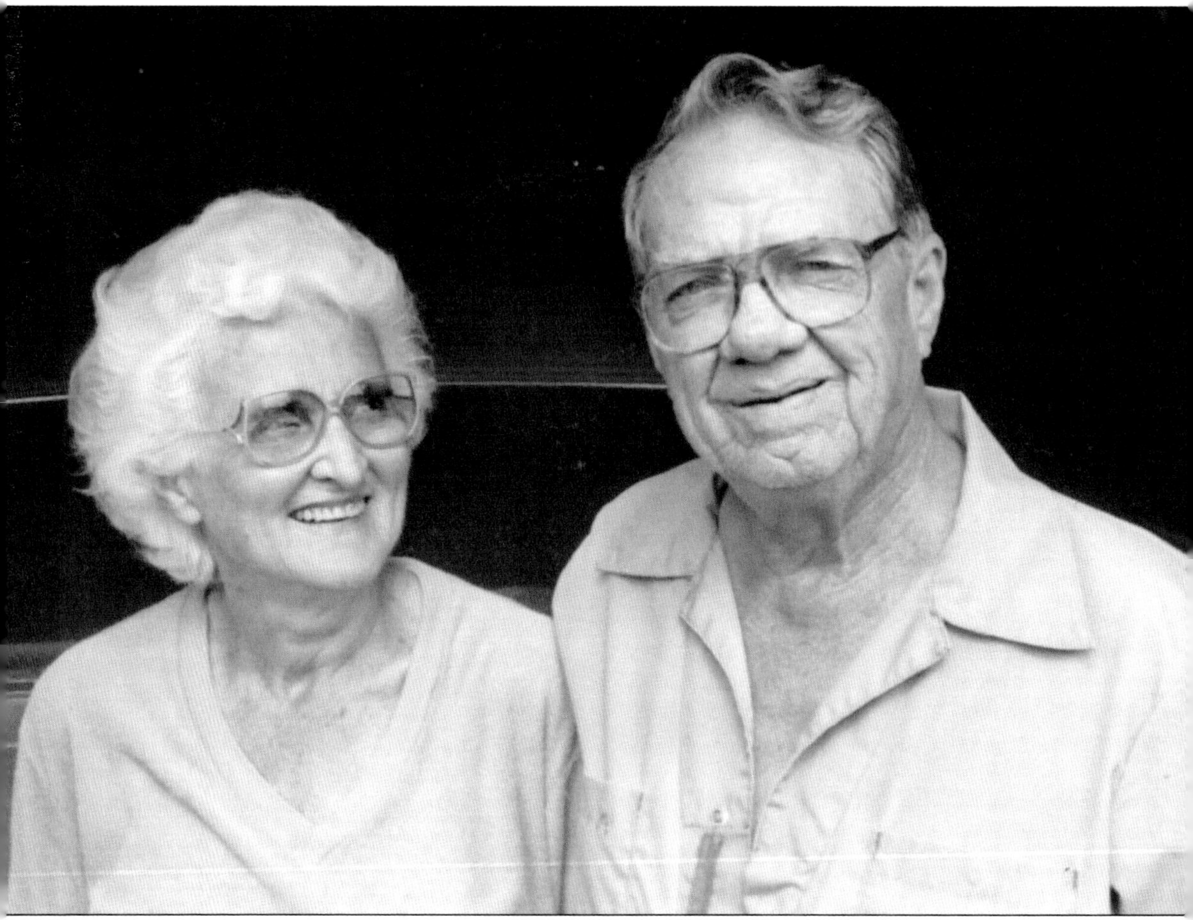

Dr. W. L. Walker is shown above with his wife, Freddie.

Nine

Social Affairs

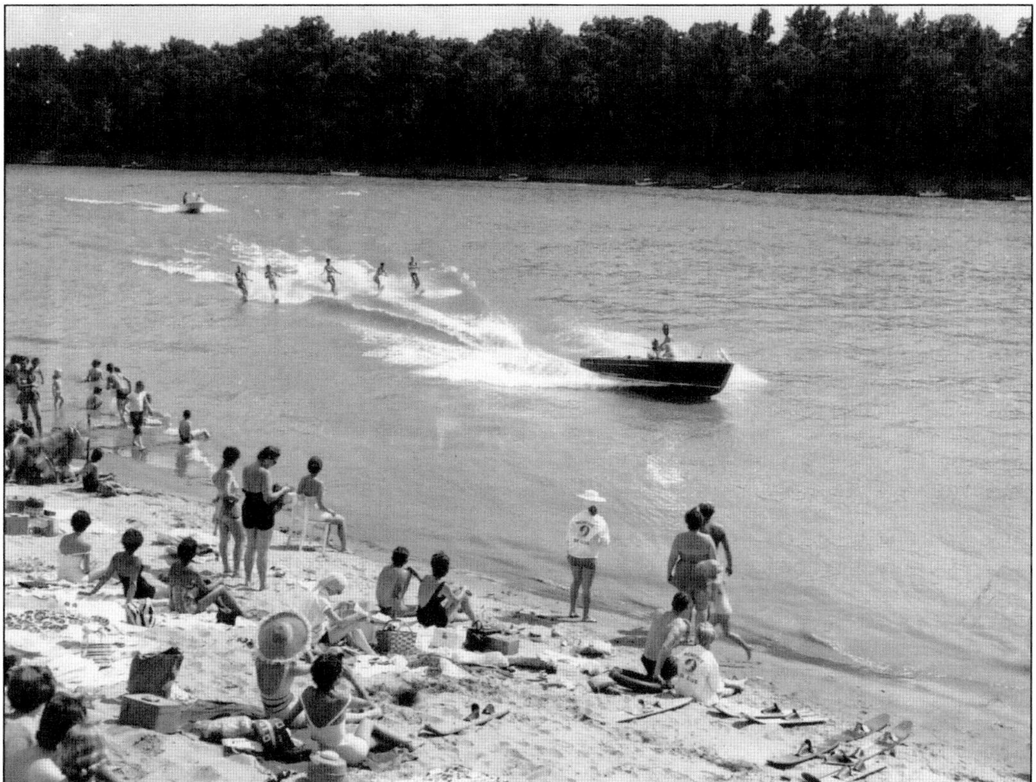

Pictured above is a ski show on Clarendon Beach on the White River in June 1954. Just south of Clarendon, the beach was a popular place in the 1950s and 1960s. On the Fourth of July each year, it was not unusual to see more than 3,000 people enjoying skiing and sky diving exhibits. In 1959, bathhouses and restrooms were built, along with concrete picnic tables. Vandalism led to the closing of the beach in the 1970s. (Photograph by ? Phelps, courtesy of the Arkansas Publicity and Parks Commission.)

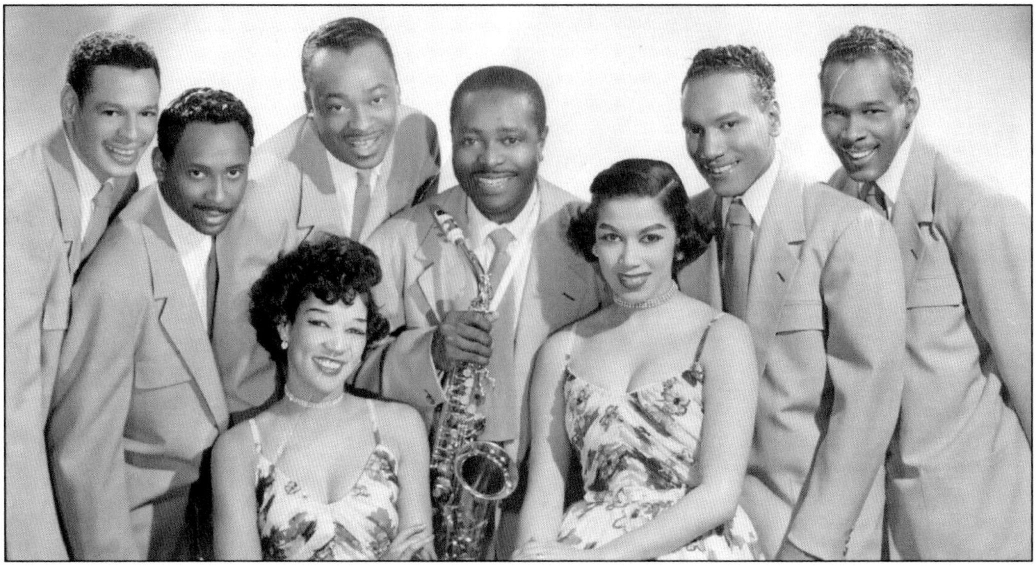

Born in Brinkley on July 8, 1908, bandleader Louis Jordan pioneered a wildly popular amalgam of jazzy blues with salty jive-talking humor. The music played by Jordan and his band, the Tympany Five, served as precursor to rhythm and blues and the rock and roll of the 1950s. The photograph above was a publicity picture Jordan sent to his father that had written on the back, "Hey Pop, this is my band." From left to right are (first row) Elaine Robinson and Ann Bailey; (second row) Jimmy Peterson—piano, Charles Rice—drums, Bob Mitchell—trumpet, Louis Jordan—saxophone, Bert Payne—guitar, and Bob Bushnell—bass. (Courtesy of Harold Thomason.)

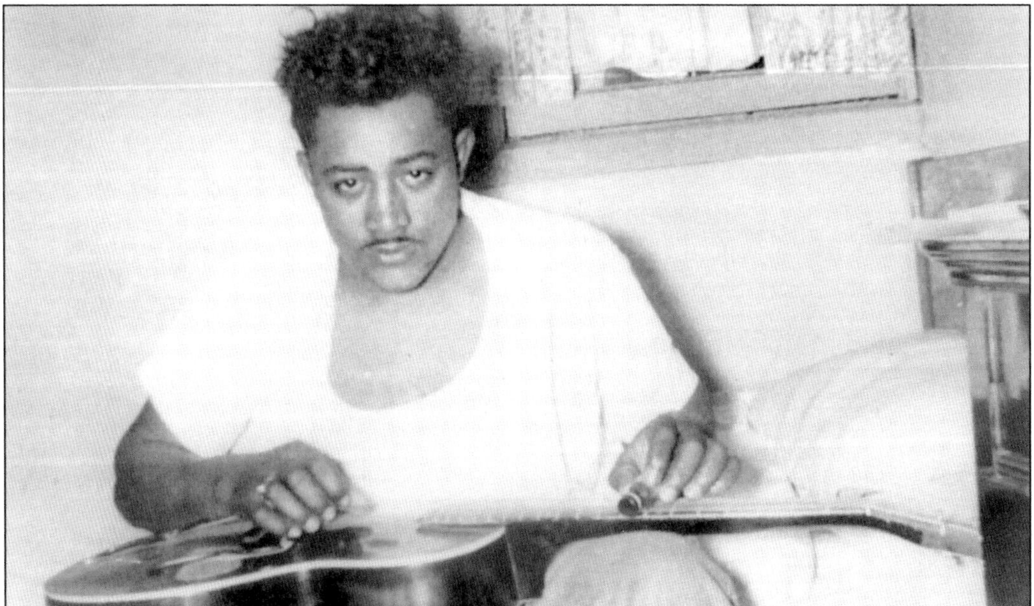

At the age of 29, John Weston (photographed above) bought a guitar with his brother-in-law. Born in 1927, he served his country during World War II and later operated a store/cafe and pool hall in Smale from 1967 to 1992. It was not until the 1980s that the award-winning entertainer began performing before audiences, booking engagements in Canada and Europe as well as the United States. (Courtesy of Bill Sayger.)

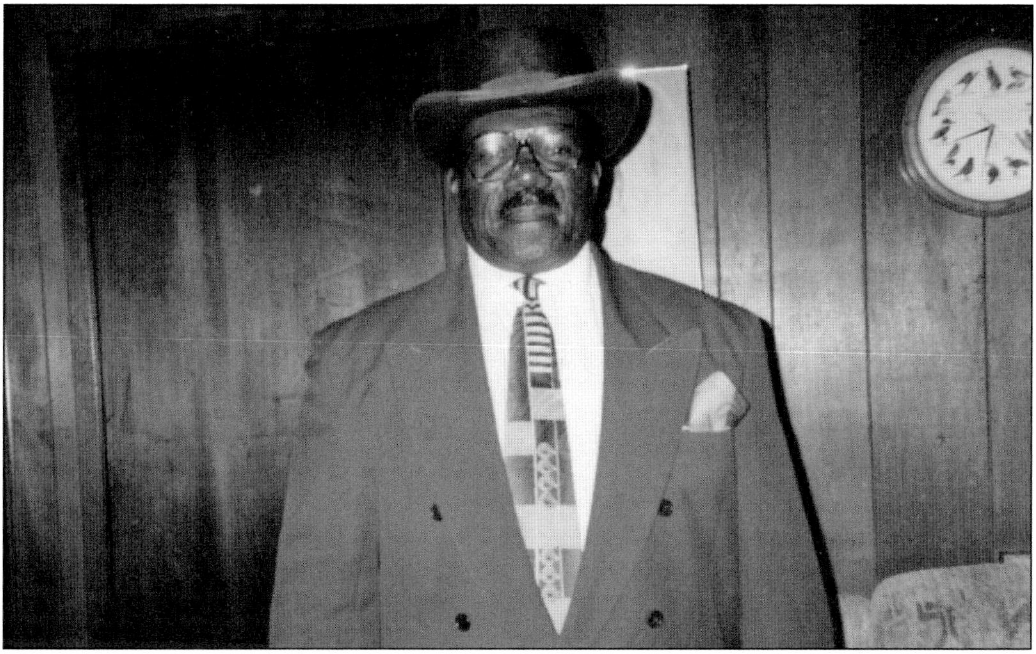

Born in Clarendon on May 29, 1942, Ivory Lee Mitchell started performing guitar blues at the age of 24 in 1965. He and his band, the Brothers of Soul, played for audiences in Memphis, Mississippi, and Arkansas. He later began to sing gospel music, which he has played for the past 35 years with his band, the Gospel Wonders. Mitchell grew up the son of a sharecropper on the Carroll farm on Swamp Poodle Road. (Courtesy of Ivory Lee Mitchell.)

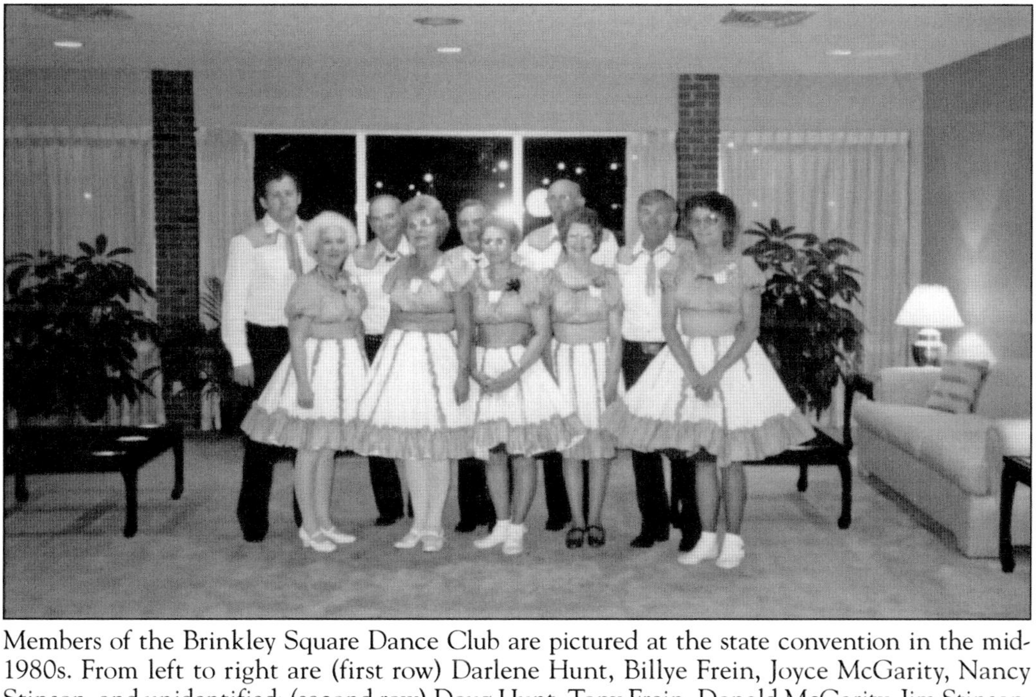

Members of the Brinkley Square Dance Club are pictured at the state convention in the mid-1980s. From left to right are (first row) Darlene Hunt, Billye Frein, Joyce McGarity, Nancy Stinson, and unidentified; (second row) Doug Hunt, Tony Frein, Donald McGarity, Jim Stinson, and unidentified. (Courtesy of Billye Frein.)

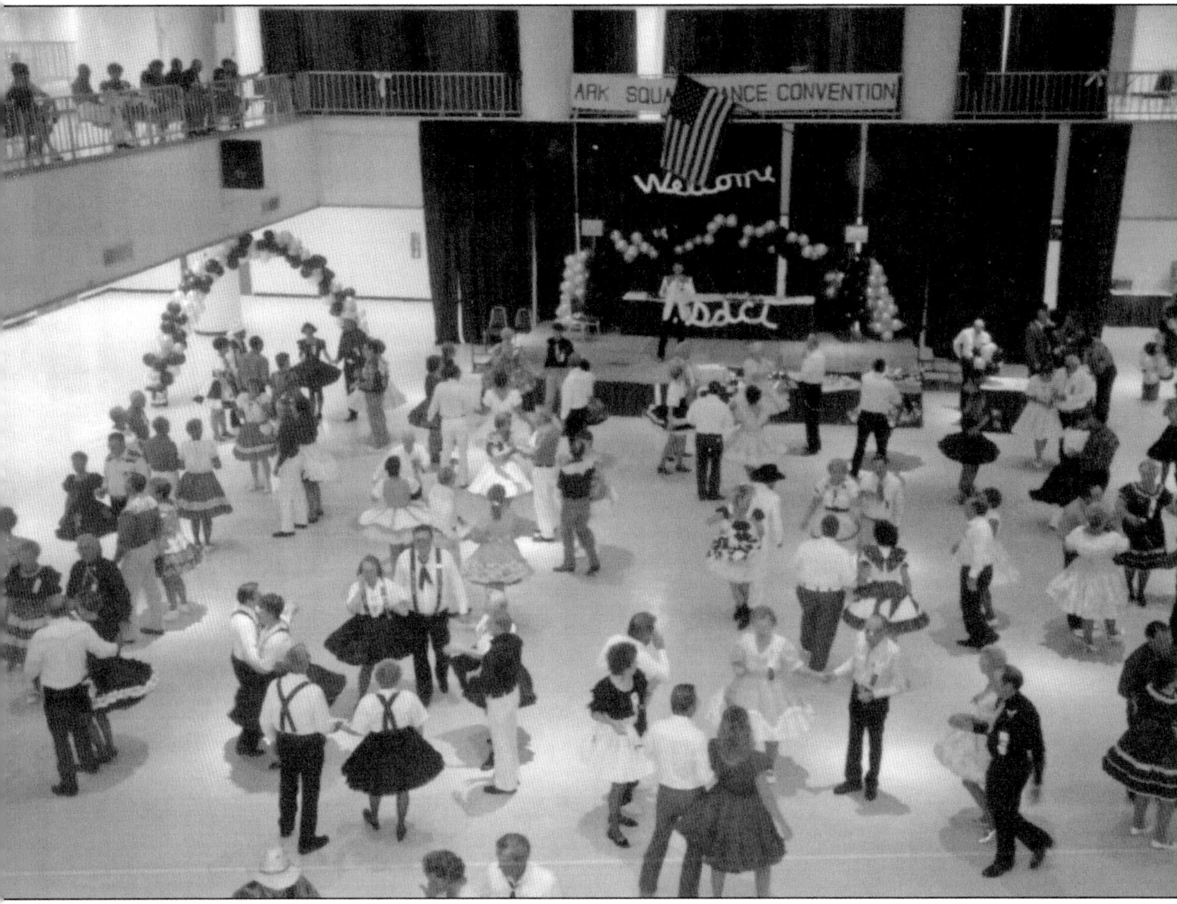

Brinkley square dancers went twice a year to participate at the convention held by the Arkansas Square Dance Federation in Little Rock. Square dancing dates back to the 19th century in Europe, Mexico, and the United States. Its popularity started waning in the 1980s, and the clubs that comprised the federation have slowly declined in number. (Courtesy of Billye Frein.)

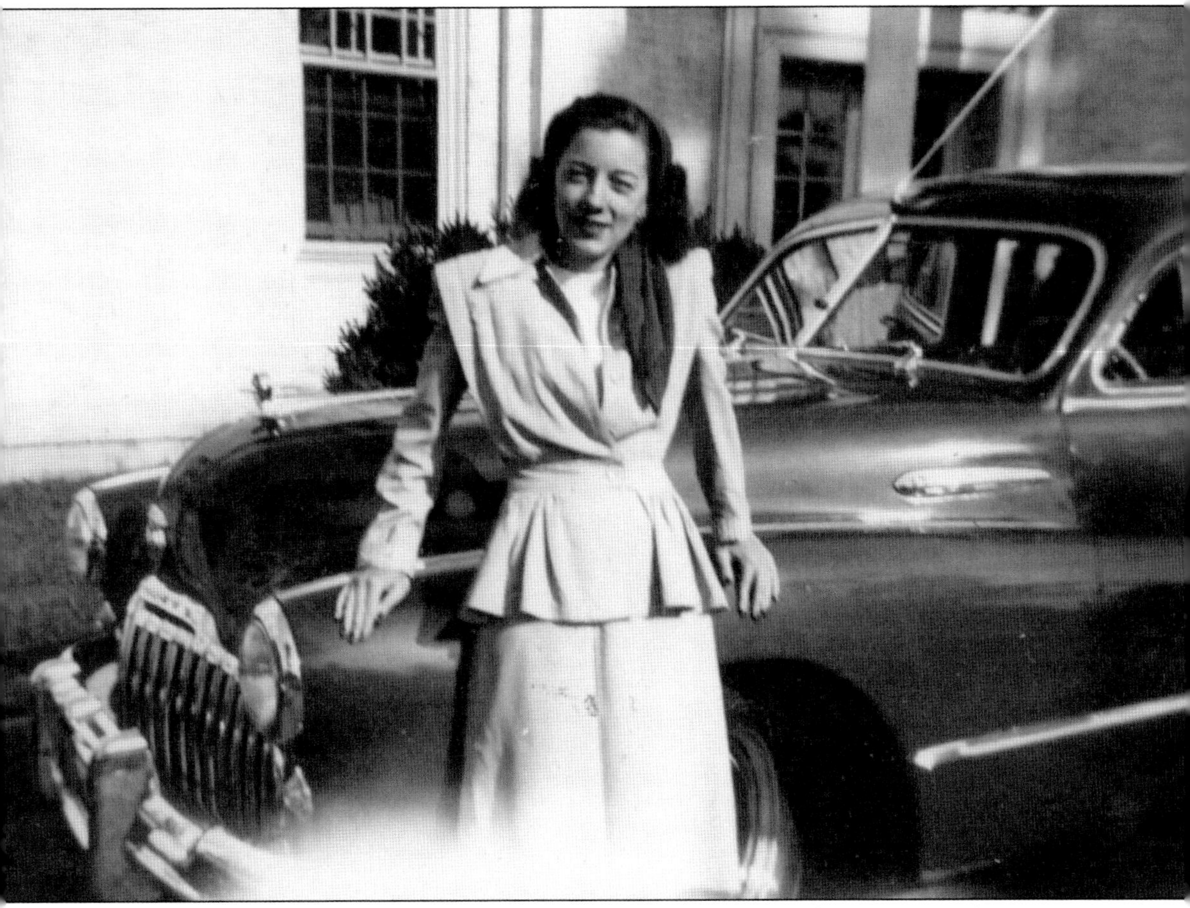

Brinkley's beloved Betty Rusher, wife of Albert H. Rusher, smiles for the camera in this 1940s photograph. Her father was the highly respected physician Dr. C. H. "Howard" McKnight of Brinkley. (Courtesy of Albert H. Rusher.)

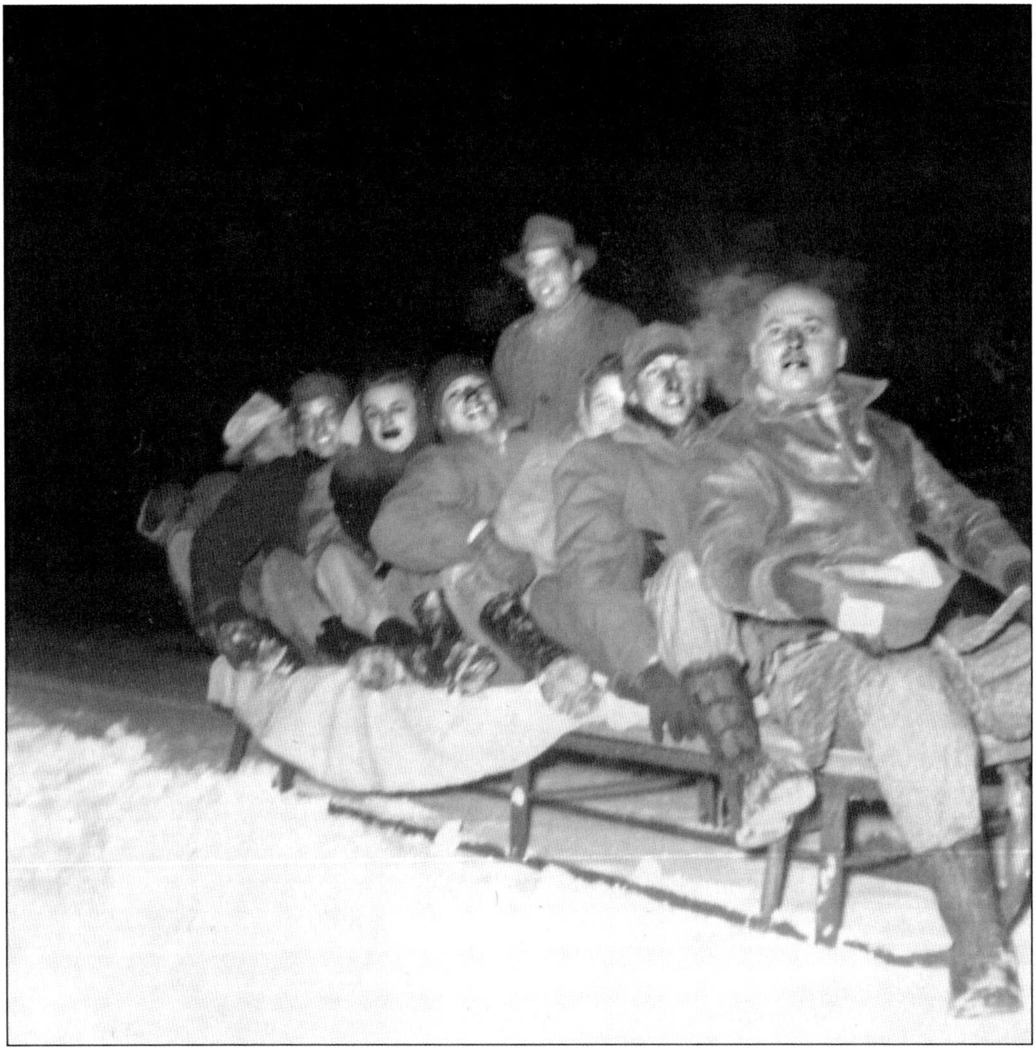

Snow in the delta rarely amounts to anything one can build a snowman with, or take a sleigh ride on, so this 1950s photograph of merry sleigh-riders is a rare sight. Having a sleigh in this area is a far rarer sight. From front to back are Joe Roberts, Dick Weis, Betty Rusher, Albert H. Rusher, Jeanne Roberts, Frances Weis, and unidentified. Standing by the sleigh is Louis Salinger. (Courtesy of Albert H. Rusher.)

Albert H. Rusher and his lovely wife, Betty (at right), and his parents, Albert L. Rusher with his wife, Dorcas (below), pose in these silly photographs, making fun of the way couples posed for photographs in the early days. The Rushers have a long history in Brinkley, from innkeepers to bankers. In 1924, John Gazzola, the largest stockholder in the Bank of Brinkley, sold out his entire holdings to Gus Roescher. After Gus's death on February 7, 1925, his son Albert Louis Rusher joined the board of directors of the bank and served as president from 1955 to 1969. In 1965, Albert Holly Rusher was elected to the board of directors and on October 14, 1969, was promoted to president. The Bank of Brinkley is still in operation under the ownership of the Signature Bank of Fayetteville. (Both courtesy of Albert H. Rusher.)

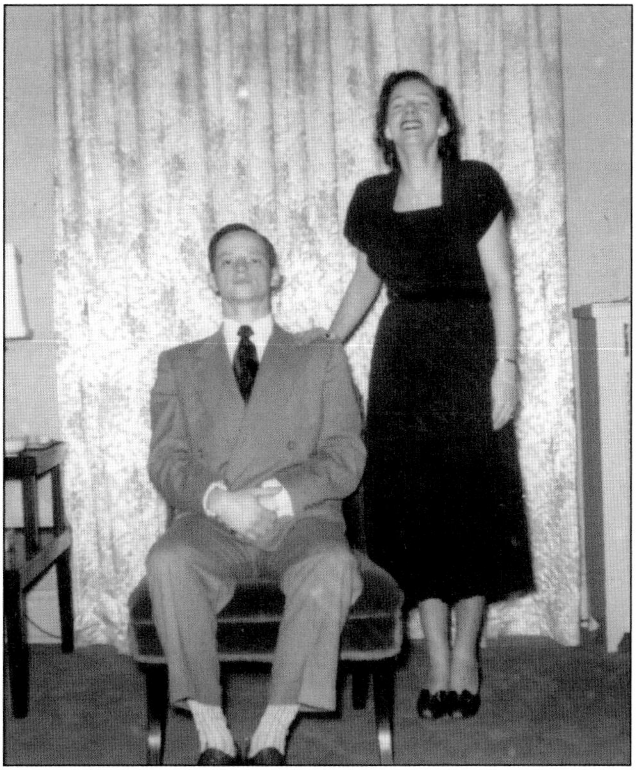

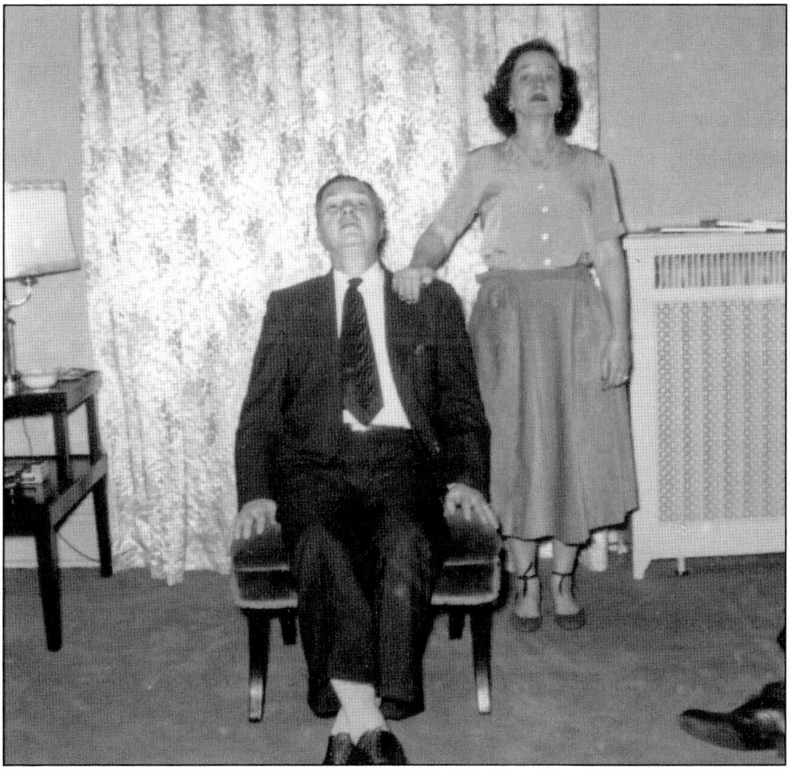

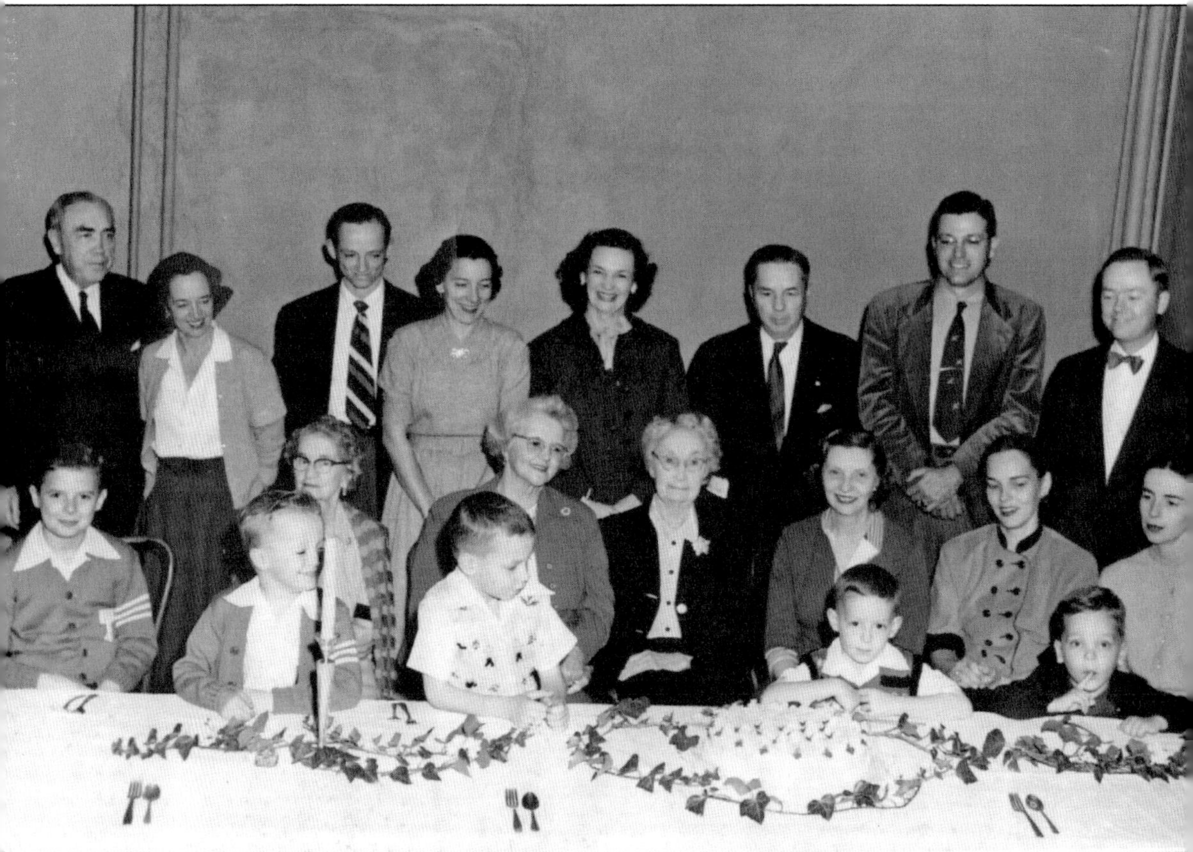

Brinkley's leading citizens are photographed above at a Christmas party in 1955. From left to right are (first row) "Sonny" Flynn, Fred Flynn, Buck Rusher, Gus Rusher, and Burton Moore; (second row) Lily Kessell, Mrs. Fred (Blanche) Rusher, Jennie Rusher, Carrie Sharp, Jennie V. Moore, and Anne Sharp; (third row) Wilson Sharp, Dorcas Rusher, Albert H. Rusher, Betty Rusher, Bernice Rusher Flynn, Albert L. Rusher, John B. Moore, and James B. Sharp. (Courtesy of Albert H. Rusher.)

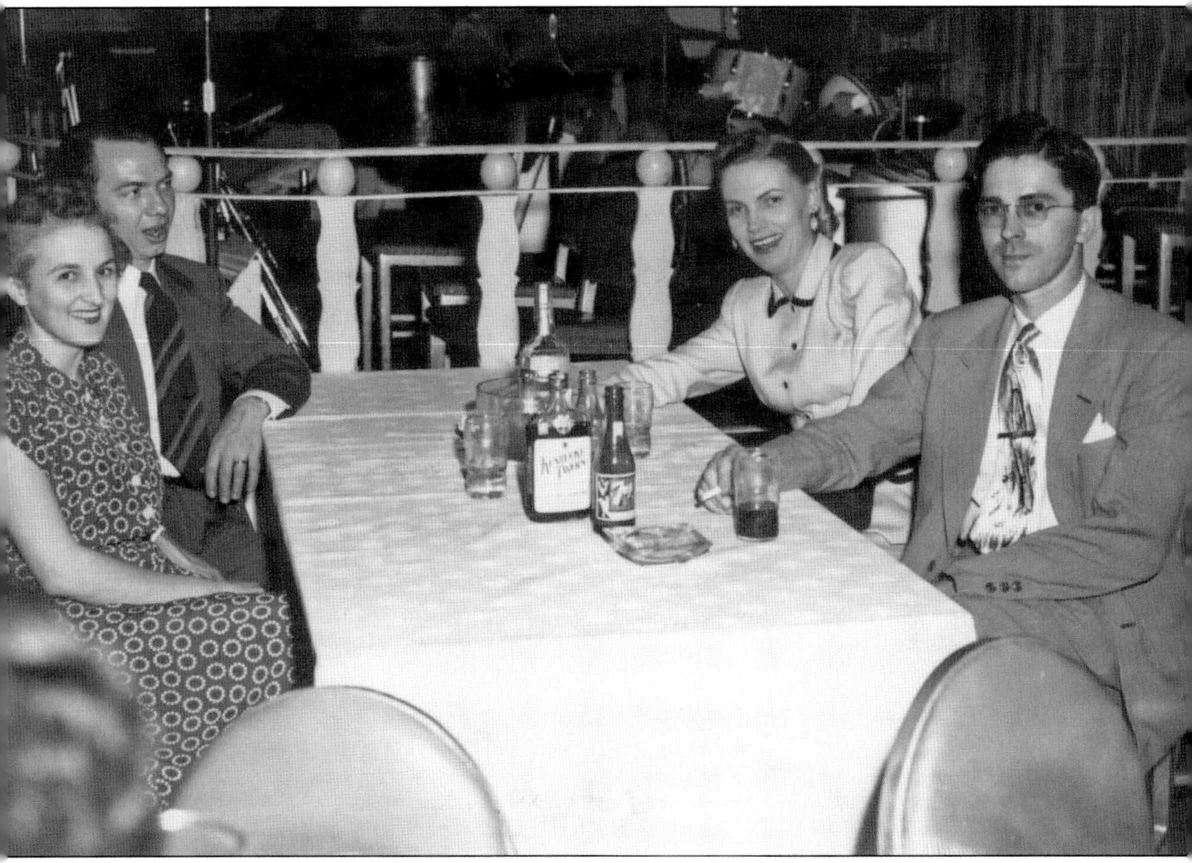

Dr. W. L. Walker and his wife, Freddie, (on the left) are enjoying a night out with Dr. James P. Williams Jr. and his wife, Rosemary, at the Exotic Balinese Room and Magnolia Roof Garden of the Hotel Claridge in Memphis, Tennessee, in 1951. Both men were longtime physicians of Brinkley.

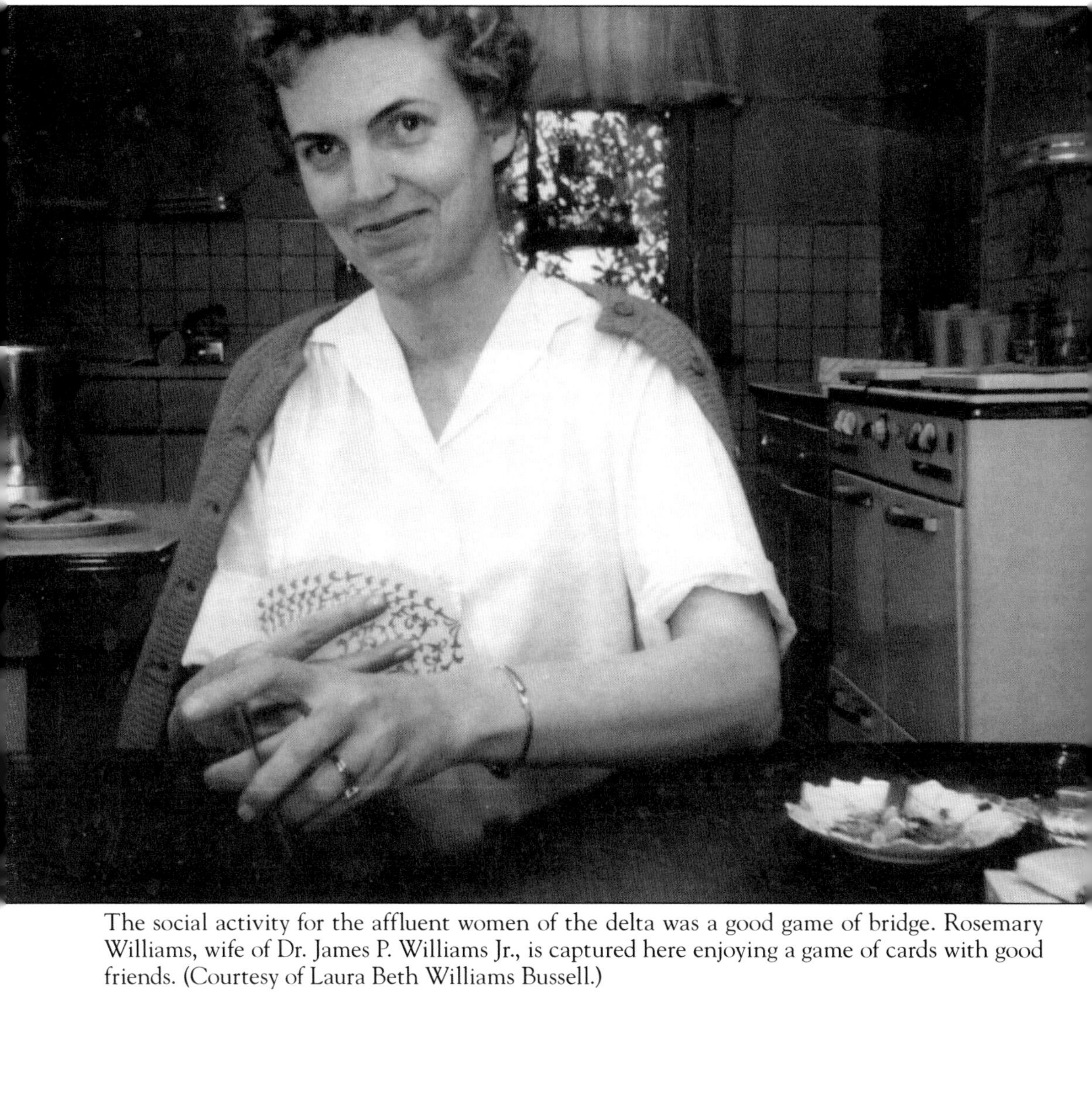

The social activity for the affluent women of the delta was a good game of bridge. Rosemary Williams, wife of Dr. James P. Williams Jr., is captured here enjoying a game of cards with good friends. (Courtesy of Laura Beth Williams Bussell.)

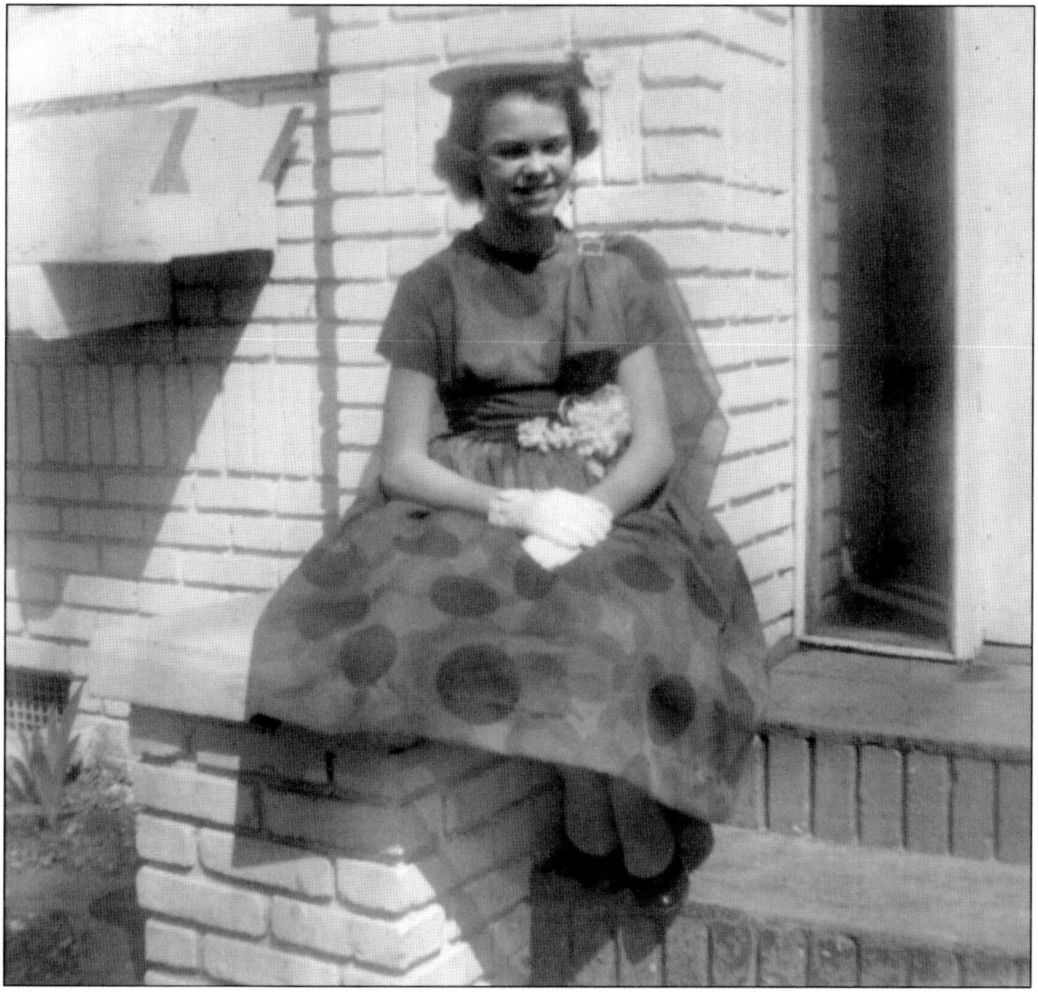

What is more special in any young girl's memory than going to church on Easter Sunday in a pretty new dress? Laura Beth Williams is captured above on Easter Sunday in her pretty new dress on the front porch of the Williamses' home. (Courtesy of Laura Beth Williams Bussell.)

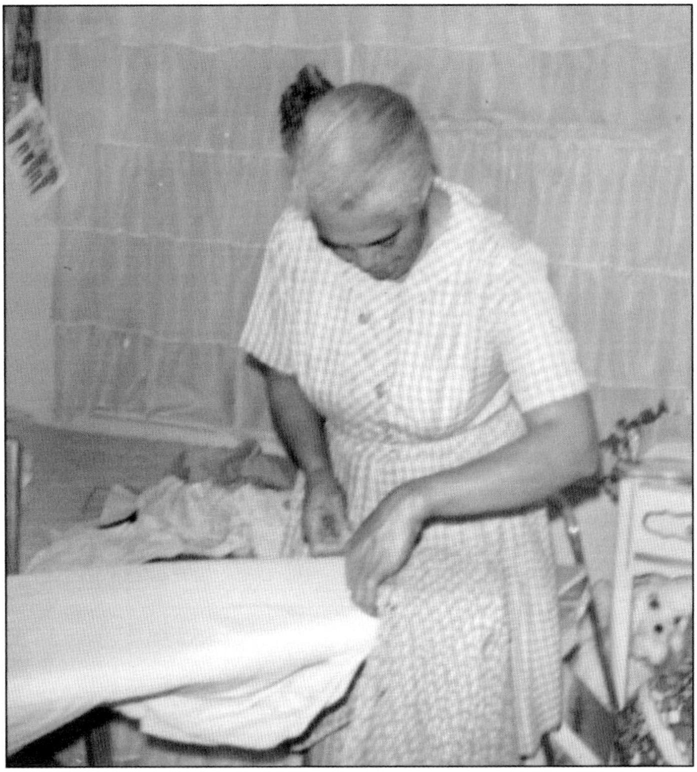

In a time now past, it was common practice for families of higher stature to employ a black nanny to raise their children and fulfill the duties of a housekeeper. The nanny, oftentimes, was viewed by the children as the one who raised them, to whom their affection never waned. Leola "Wowo" Coleman, in these photographs, was nanny to the children of Dr. James P. Williams Jr. of Brinkley. When asked why Laura Beth Williams Bussell called her Wowo, she said it was because they could not say Leola when they were little. That was the affectionate title the Williams children called her until her passing. (Both courtesy of Laura Beth Williams Bussell.)

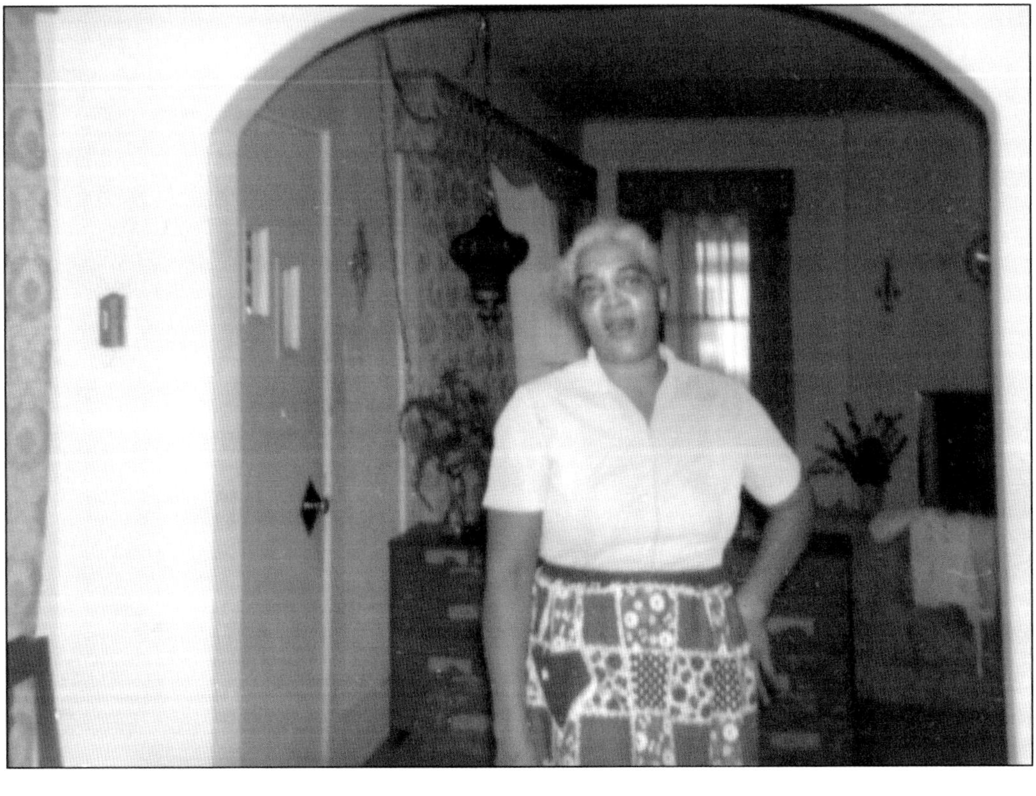

Helen Williams Farrell and Clarence "Buster" Farrell pose in this mid-1940s photograph. Helen was the sister of V. W. Williams Jr., who farmed the family's 1,500-acre Monroe farm and owned several business ventures in the area. Buster Farrell and his brothers owned and operated the Farrell Construction Company, Inc. Their company built dams, ocean ship locks, power plants, super highways, and bridges. They also ran the Farrell Mining Company, a coal and strip mining business in Tennessee, Alabama, and Arkansas, in addition to their Brinkley businesses. (Courtesy of Sarah Williams McKnight.)

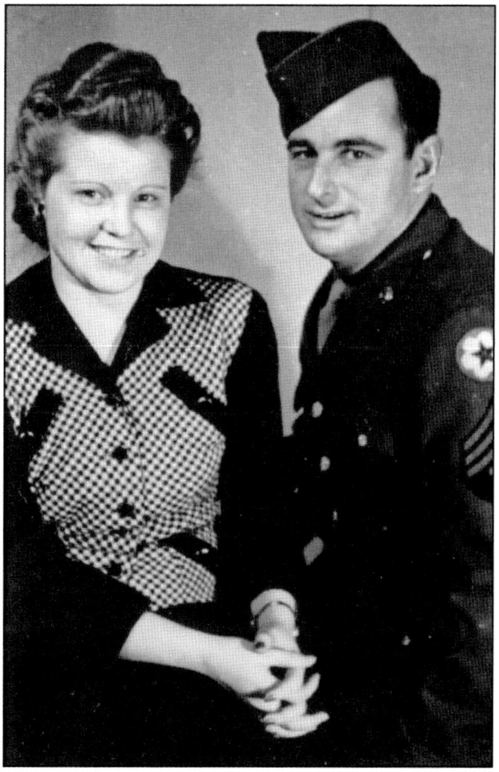

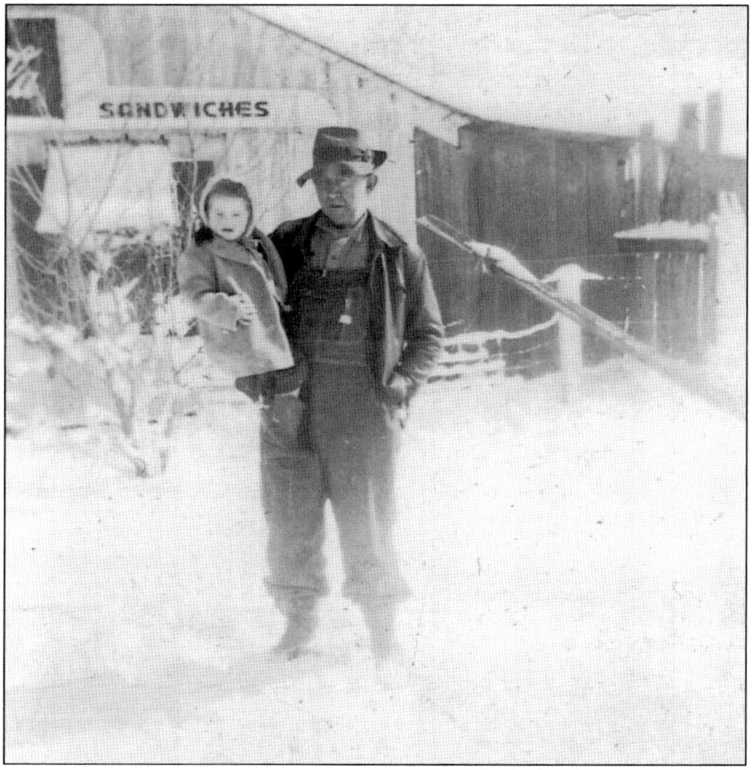

Vernie Wesley Williams Sr. poses with his granddaughter, Dianne, in front of an old Monroe store in the mid-1940s after a rare snowfall. He and his family moved to Monroe in the early 1910s with little to their name. He began selling tobacco and soon acquired land in the area, which he farmed and used for collateral to start other business ventures in the town. Upon his death, he was a wealthy and well-respected man of Monroe. (Courtesy of Sarah Williams McKnight.)

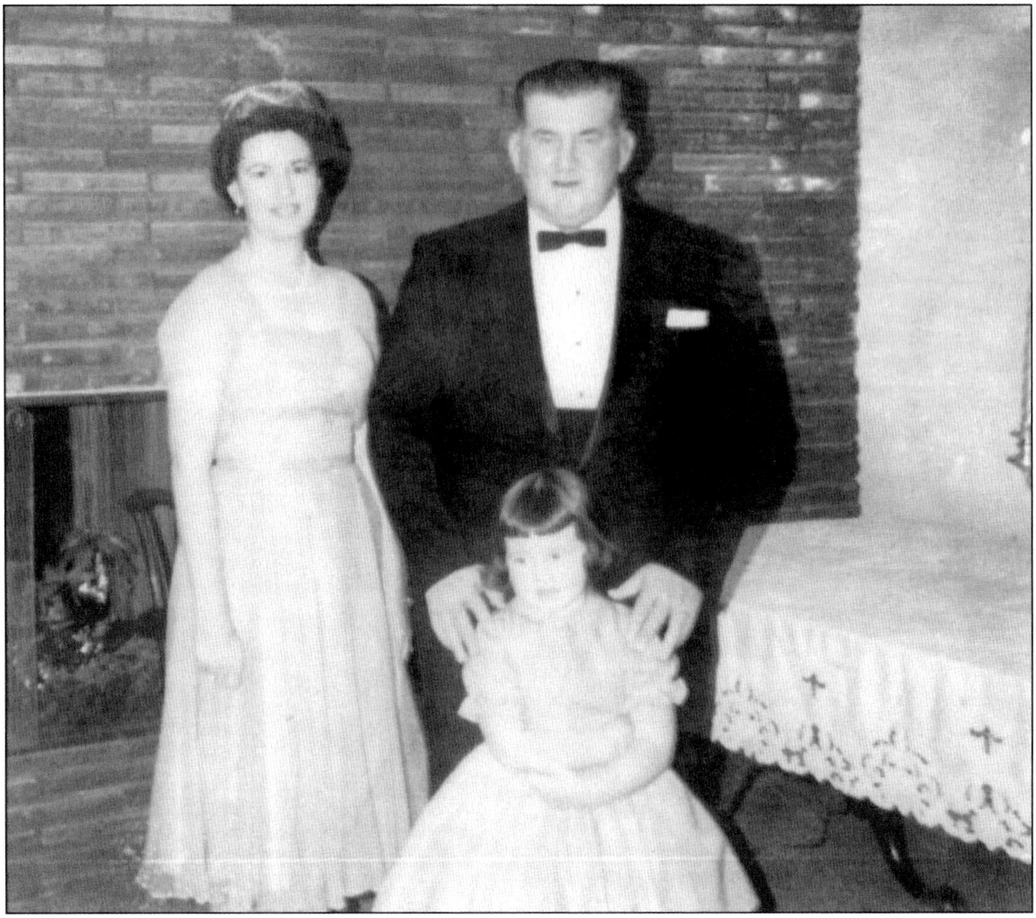

Sarah Williams McKnight, Vernie W. Williams Jr., and Kathy Williams Frein (in front) of Monroe are captured above on Christmas 1964 at the wedding of Dianne Williams. Sarah Williams McKnight is a longtime member of the Central Delta Historical Society and is currently serving on the board of directors. (Courtesy of Sarah Williams McKnight.)

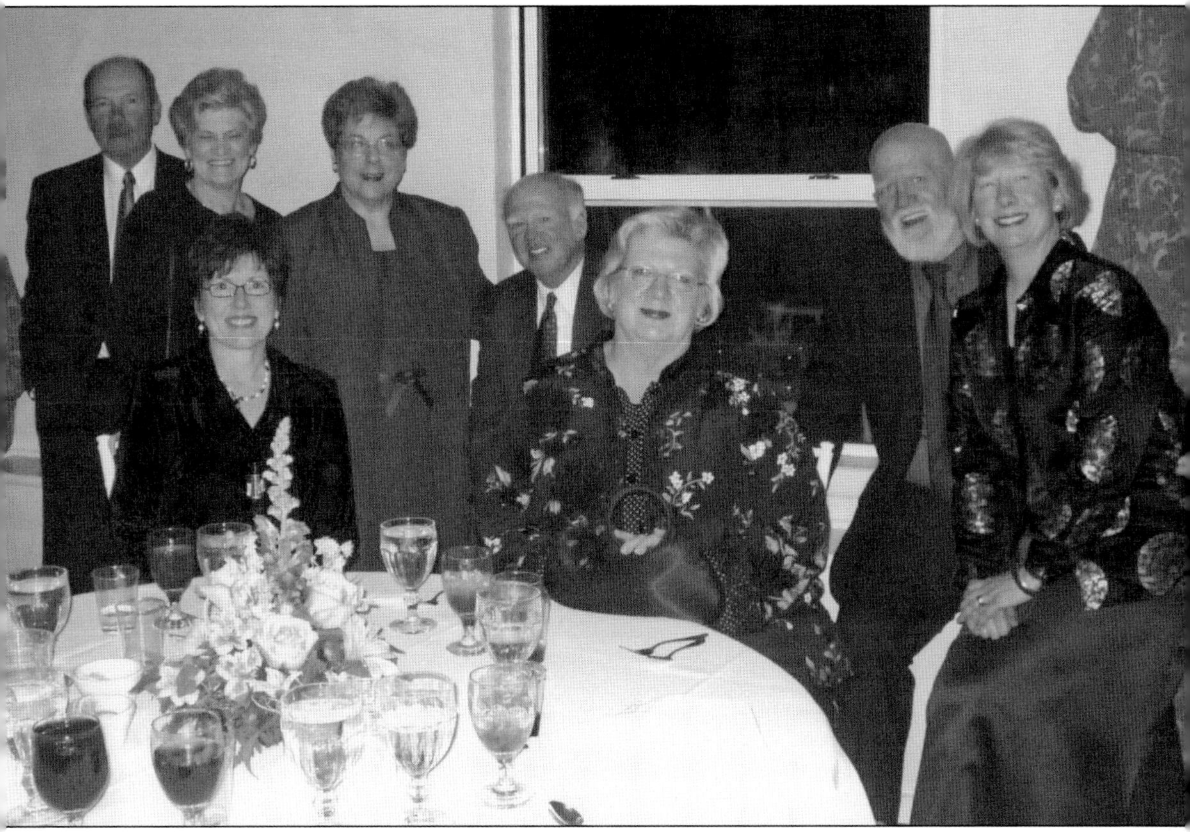

The children of V. W. Williams Jr., Elzie "Pete" Williams, and Maritha Williams Harvey are pictured at the wedding of a younger Vernie Williams. From left to right are (first row) Kathy Williams Frein (V. W.) and Betty Williams (Pete); (second row) Wesley Harvey (Maritha), Dianne Williams Langley (V. W.), Jane Williams Ritchie (Pete), Darrell Ritchie, Vernan Wayne Williams (V. W.), and Julia Williams Fletcher (Pete). (Courtesy of Sarah Williams McKnight.)

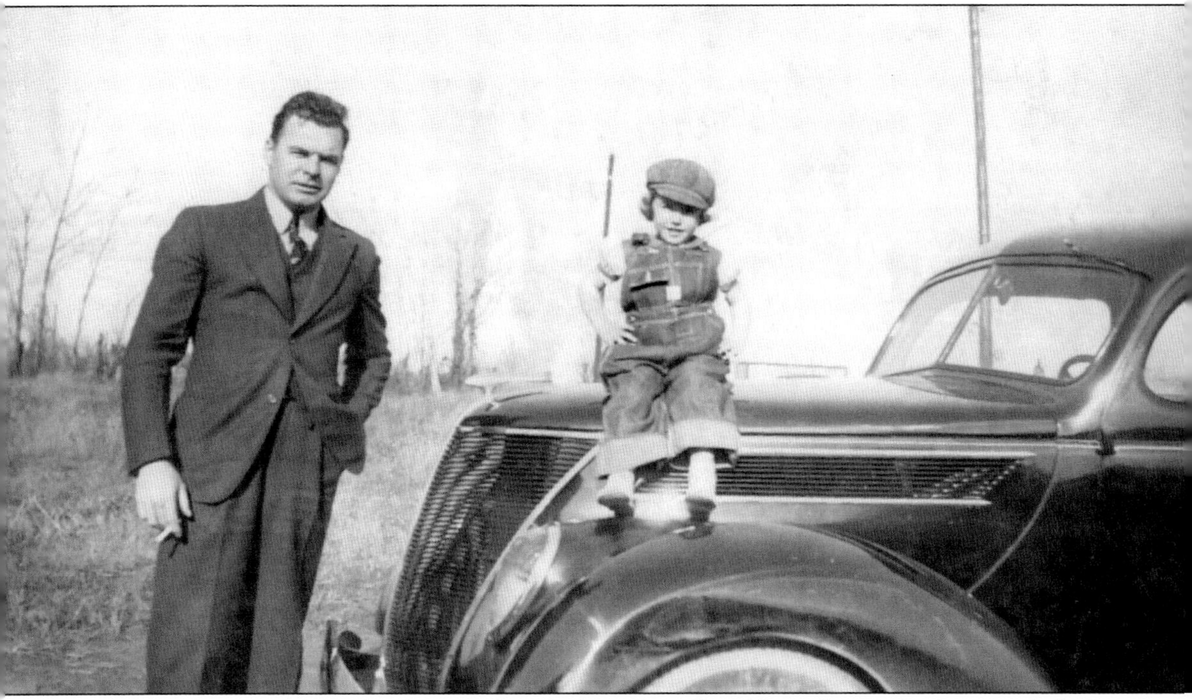

Jolly Jackson is with his daughter, Barbara Jackson Bussell Wolfe, in this 1940s photograph. Jackson was a hardworking man who was employed by Farrell-Cooper Lumber Company of Brinkley. The lumber mill was destroyed by fire on August 10, 1955, but was quickly rebuilt and opened again for business on June 14, 1956. (Courtesy of Laura Beth Bussell.)

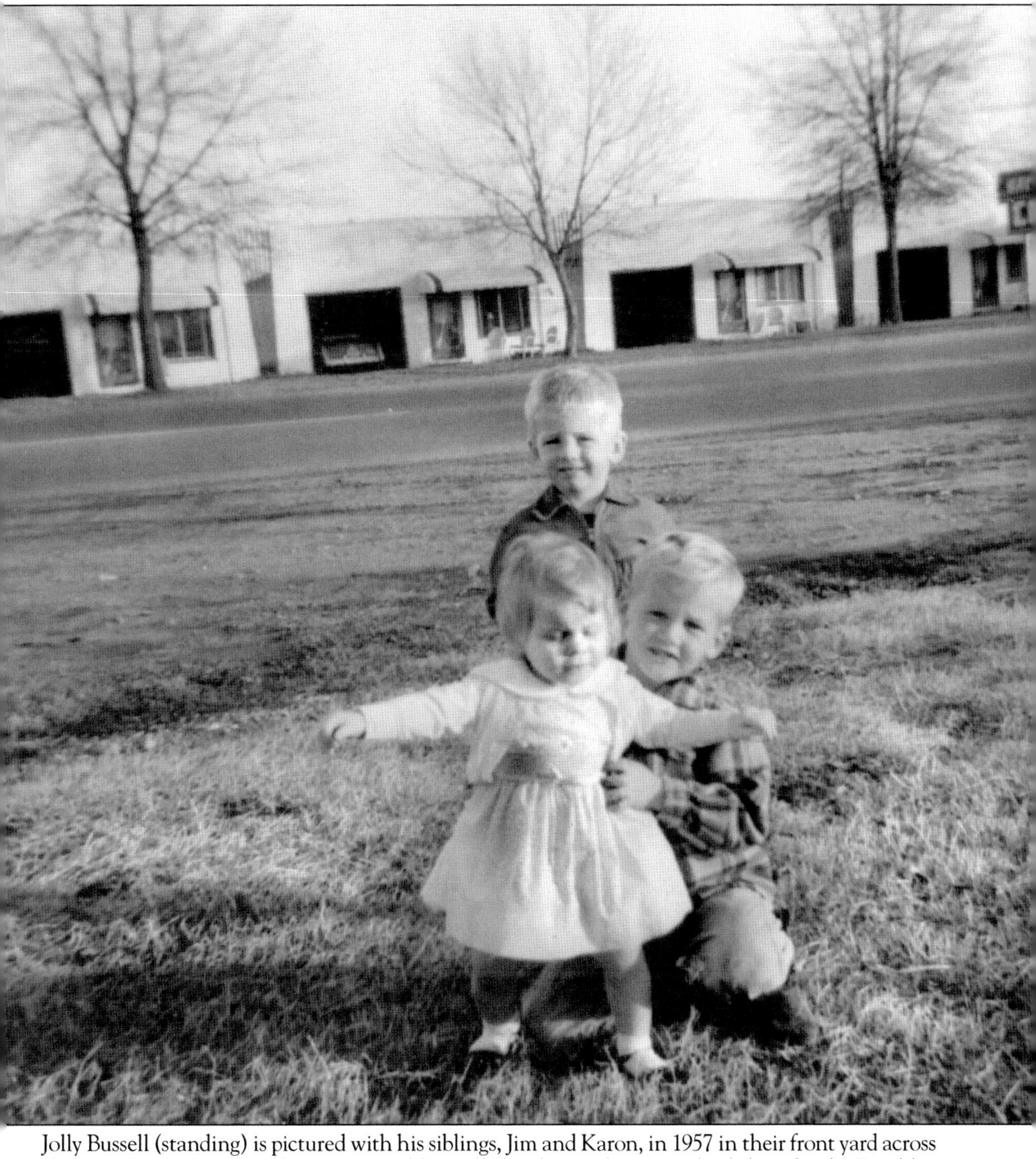

Jolly Bussell (standing) is pictured with his siblings, Jim and Karon, in 1957 in their front yard across the street from the Wayside Inn in Brinkley. Jolly has been a longtime firefighter for the Brinkley Fire Department and was recently appointed as fire chief. (Courtesy of Laura Beth Bussell.)

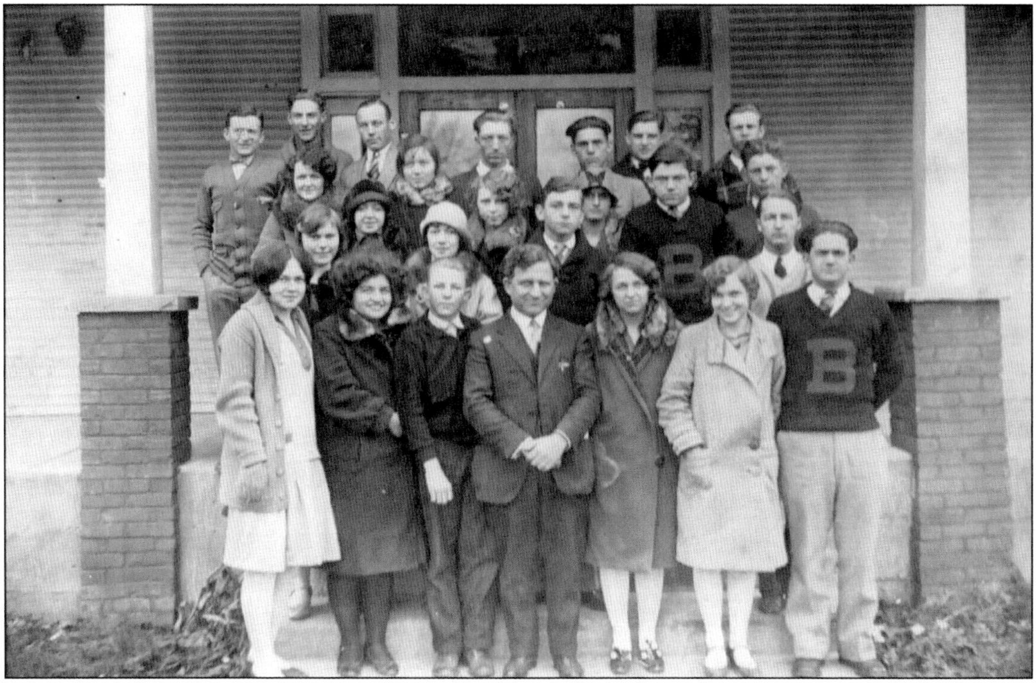

The Brinkley High School class of 1927 proudly poses for the camera. This photograph is from the high school memory book of Mildred Crowley Dickson. She was a longtime employee of the Bank of Brinkley, who was loved and respected by all who knew her.

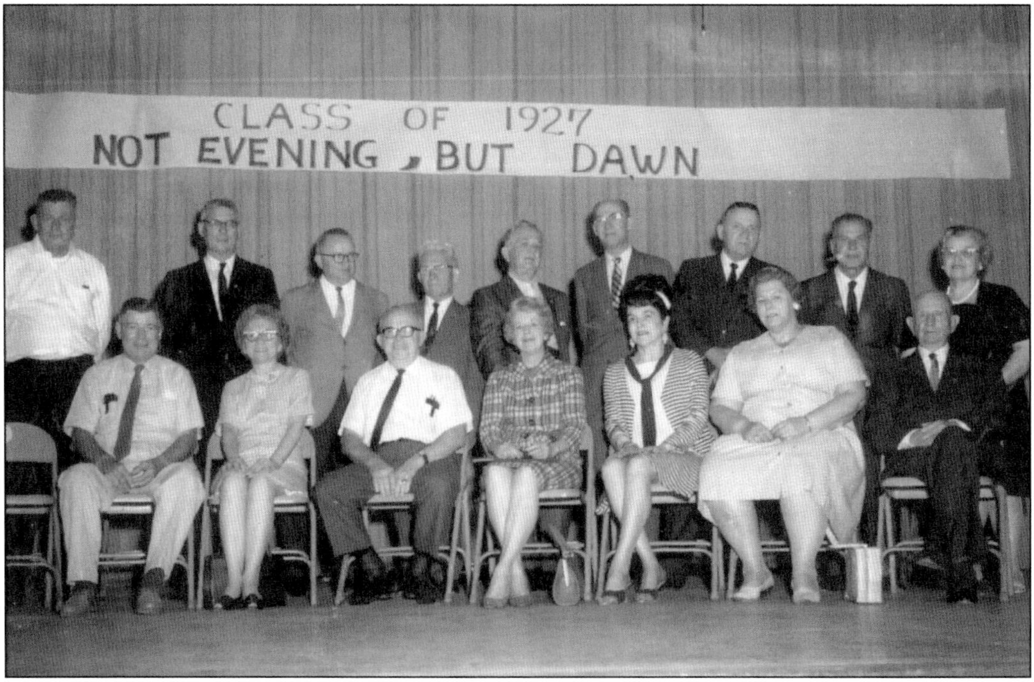

Above is the high school reunion of Brinkley High School's class of 1927, whose motto was "Not Evening, but Dawn." The always elegant Mildred Dickson is pictured fifth from the left in the first row of this undated photograph.

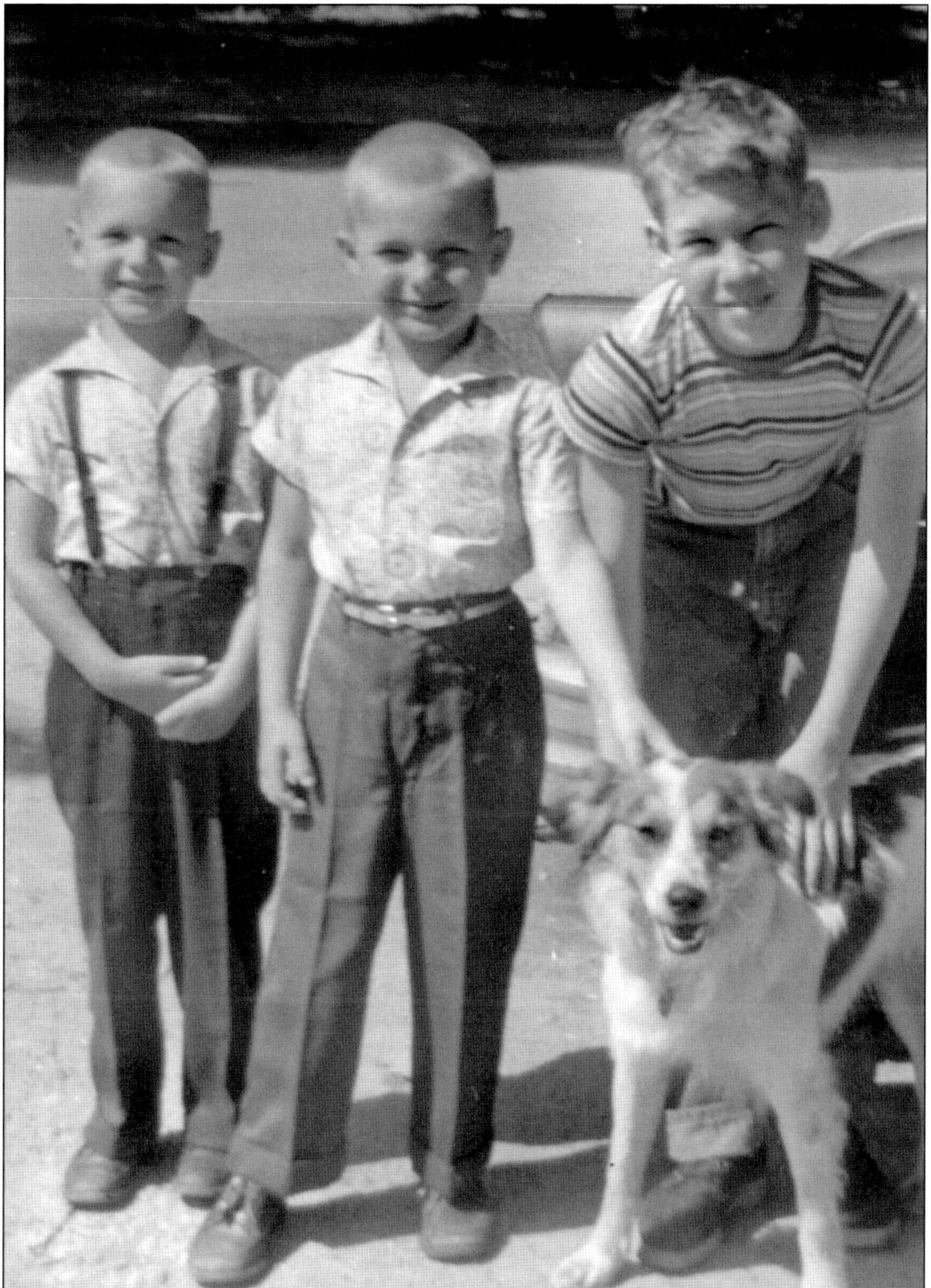

Rick Elledge (left) and Steve Elledge (center), the sons of newspaper proprietors Franklin and Flora Jean Elledge, along with their uncle, Buddy Clifton, are immortalized in this 1950s photograph with their faithful dog Floppy.

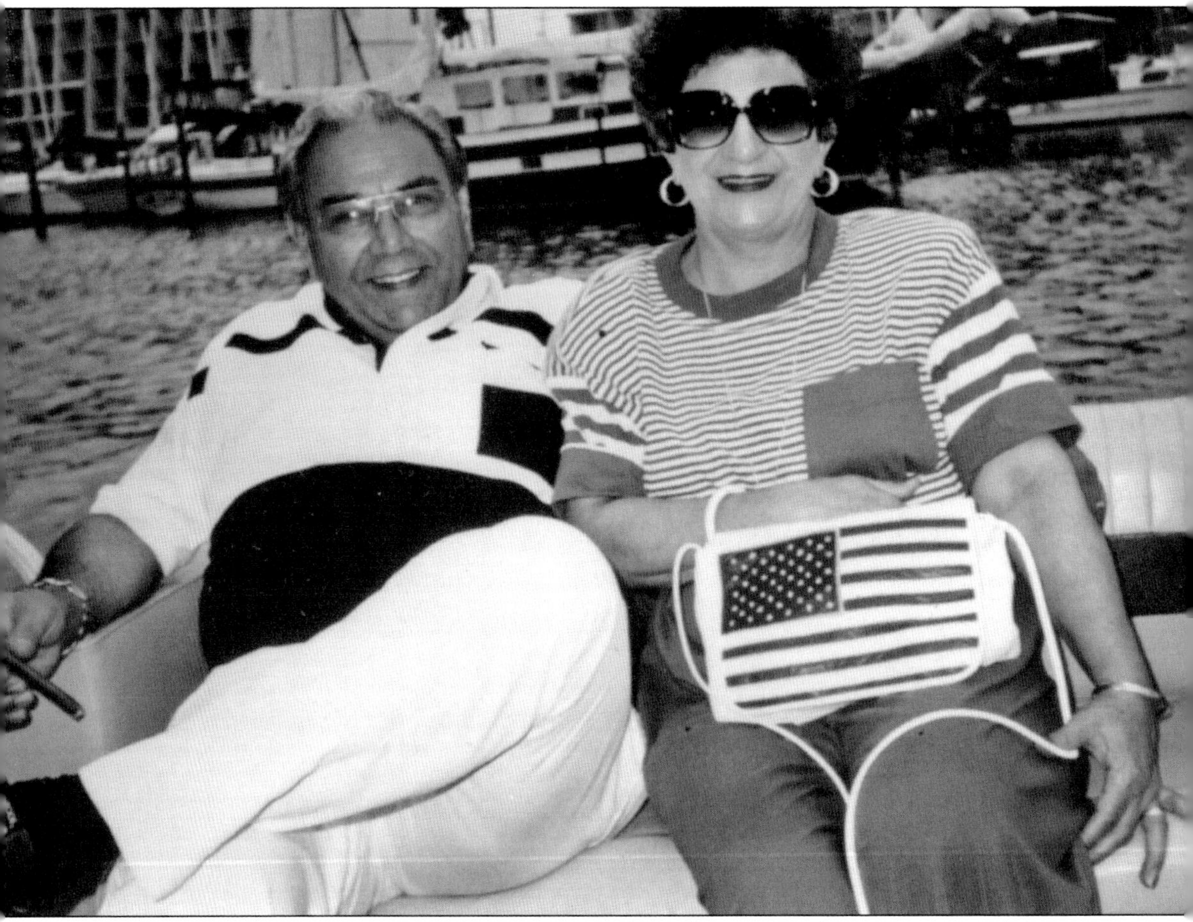

Arnold Malham was a prominent businessman and merchant in Brinkley. He pioneered the concept of a bent tubular frame carport with a sheet metal cover, which is popular in this area since it is portable. He was also a member of the Knights of Columbus, and no one in the community could say no when he went about the task of selling pancake tickets for the September festival. He is pictured above with his wife, Sada, on one of their many travels.

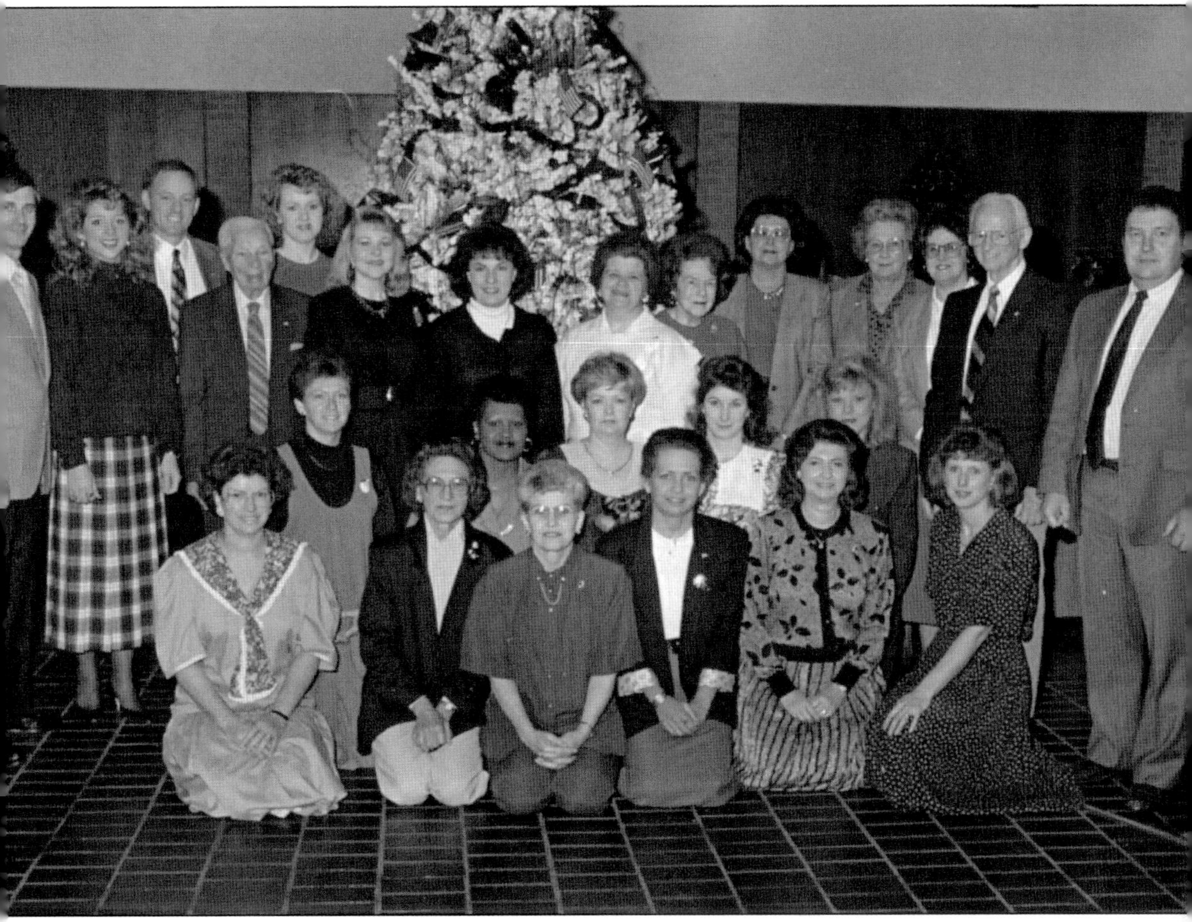

Officers and employees of the Bank of Brinkley are gathered in front of the Christmas tree in this 1980s photograph. From left to right are (first row) Gladys Churchwell, Kitty Smith, Virginia Simpson, Delma Gross, Maxine Thomas, and Terry Geisler; (second row) Margie Erwin, Alma Camper, Mary Ann Dorman, Rachelle Thompson, and Beverly Banks; (third row) Harold Hardwick, Jana Malloy Lee, Gus Rusher, Albert L. Rusher, Sharon Green, Jennifer Martin, Ruth Ann Singleterry, Linda Penn, Mildred Dickson, Jean Duke, Margaret Cooper, Gloria McMontgomery, Albert H. Rusher, and Terry Singleterry. (Courtesy of Gladys Churchwell.)

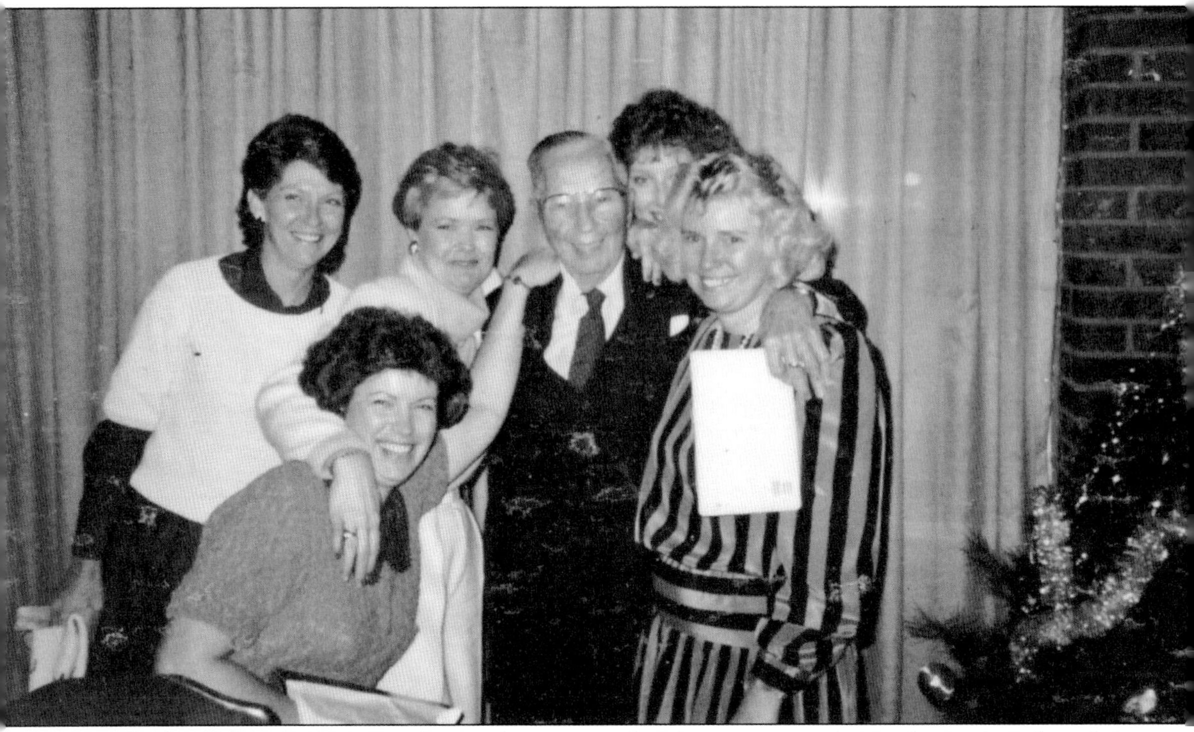

The late Albert L. Rusher smiles for the camera while being surrounded by the lovely ladies of the Bank of Brinkley at one of the bank Christmas parties. From left to right are (first row) Gladys Churchwell; (second row) Margie Ervin, Mary Ann Dorman, Albert L. Rusher, Tina Riggs, and Janie Nicholson. (Courtesy of Gladys Churchwell.)

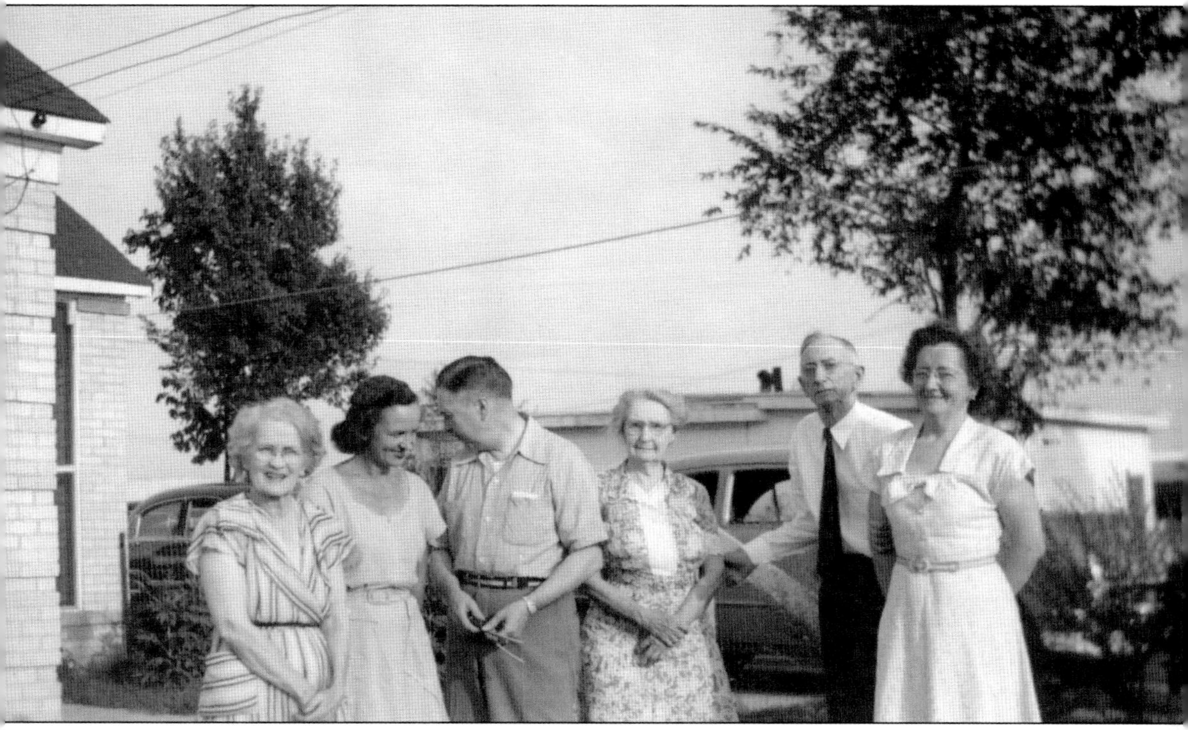

Dr. Howard McKnight was a longtime physician in Brinkley. He was stricken with crippling arthritis in later years yet still continued to see patients from his bed. From left to right are Lily Kessell, Dorcas Rusher, Albert L. Rusher, Jennie Rusher, Dr. C. H. "Howard" McKnight, and Mrs. C. H. (Dott) McKnight. (Courtesy of Betty Rusher.)

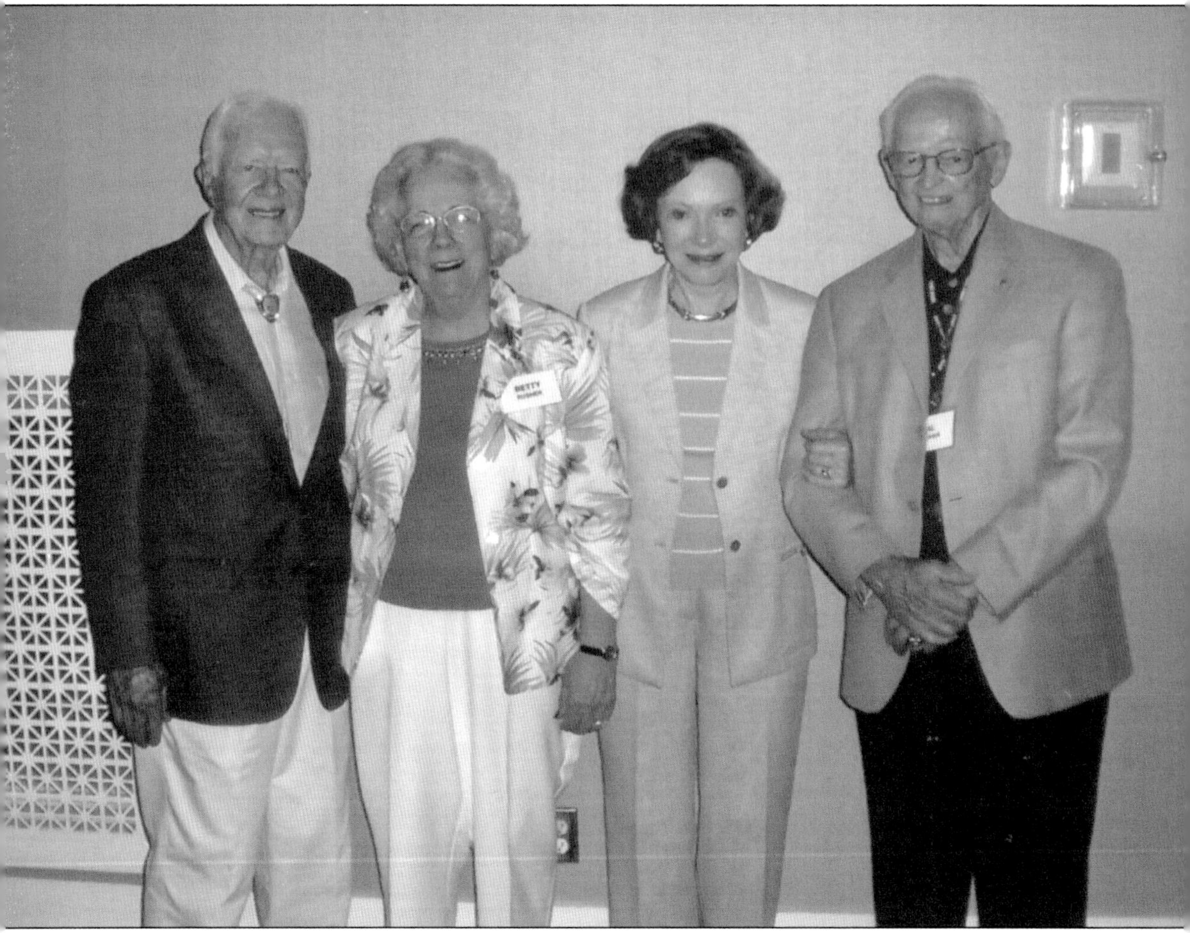

Albert H. Rusher of Brinkley and former president Jimmy Carter were roommates at the U.S. Naval Academy for a time during World War II. They have been lifelong friends since that time and continue to stay in touch with regular visits. From left to right are Jimmy Carter, Betty Rusher, Rosalyn Carter, and Albert H. Rusher.

Ten

Religion in the Bible Belt

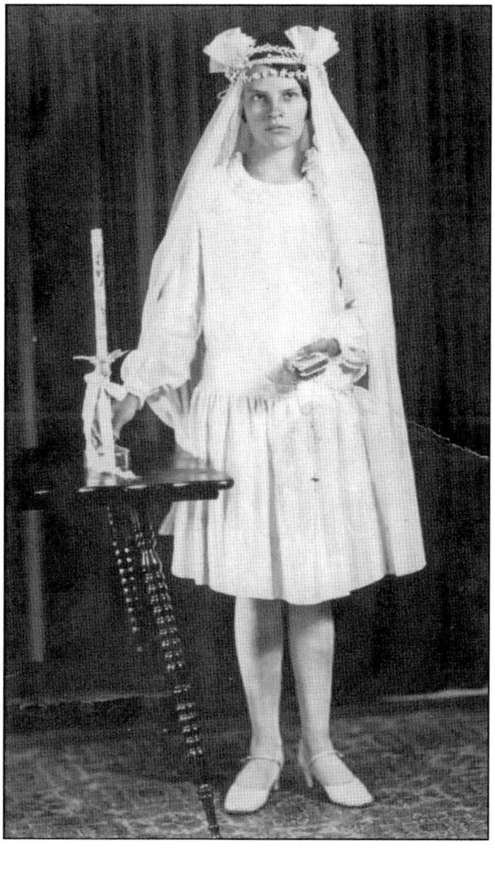

Emma Gaisbauer, born in Poland in 1867, stands at right during her solemn communion at St. John's Catholic Church on June 17, 1928. The church was built in 1875 through the efforts of the Reverend D. A. Quinn, who had stated it was "chiefly erected through the munificence of Messrs Gunn and Black." It was the only church in Brinkley to survive the 1909 tornado. (Courtesy of Steve Hinton.)

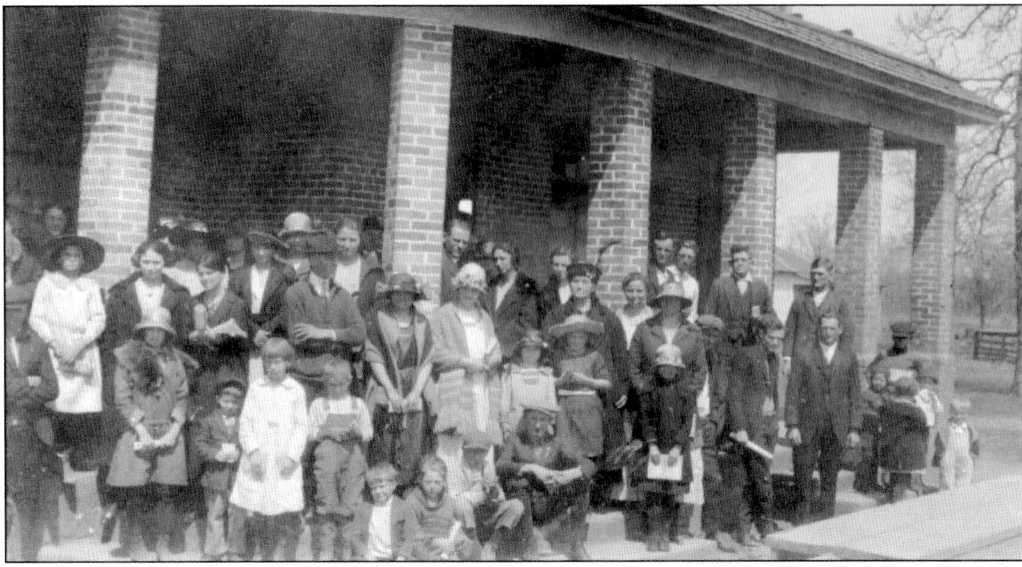

Both of these photographs were taken in Allendale at the church after Sunday school, the lower one in 1943. Religion has played a major role in rural Arkansas, bringing people together through good times and bad, and offering a social outlet, which can readily be seen in these pictures. In addition to its church, Allendale was privileged to have an excellent school that went from grades 1 through 12. This would be a tribute to the members of the small community that valued a good education for its youth to empower them with a better future.

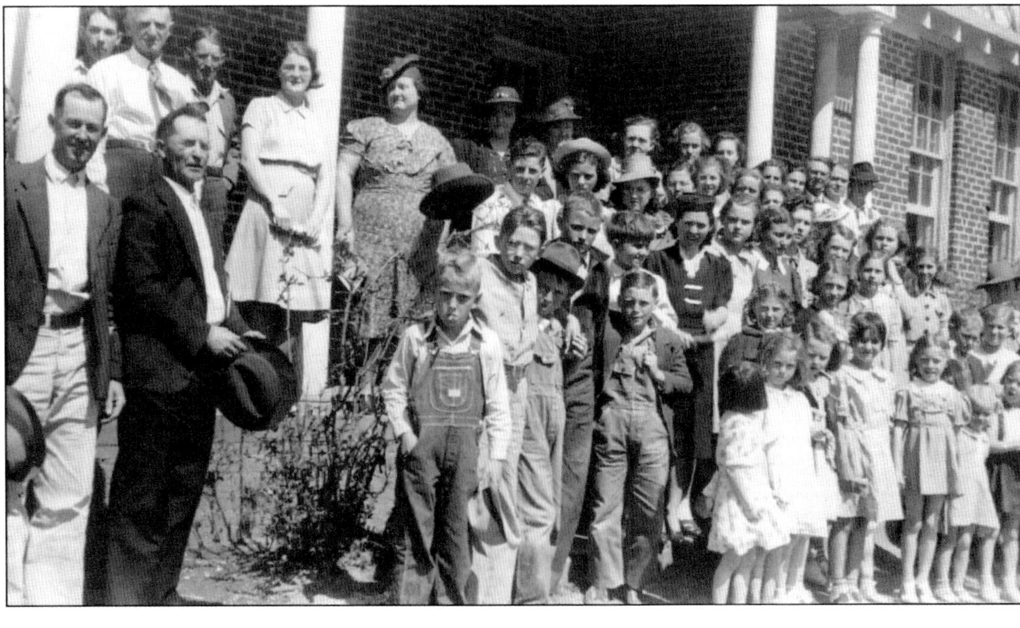

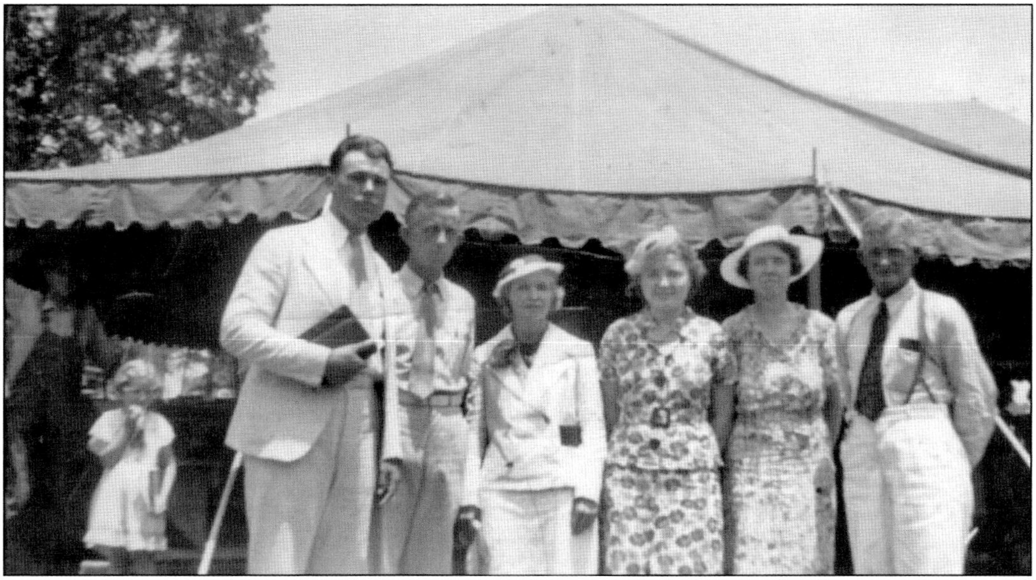

These photographs were taken on July 4, 1937, at a tent revival in Monroe. Pictured above from left to right are Pastor James Kelly, Charlie and Norma Sebastian, Louise and Virginia Meacham, and a man who is believed to be a Mr. Melton. The Baptists of Monroe held a series of religious meetings, known as revivals, in a tent provided by Ernest Loewer. The seating for the services was provided by Loewer and Presley Meacham. James Kelly, who led the revivals, later attended Ouachita College with Loewer's assistance and served as chaplain of the navy under Pres. Jimmy Carter. (Both courtesy of Wylie Meacham.)

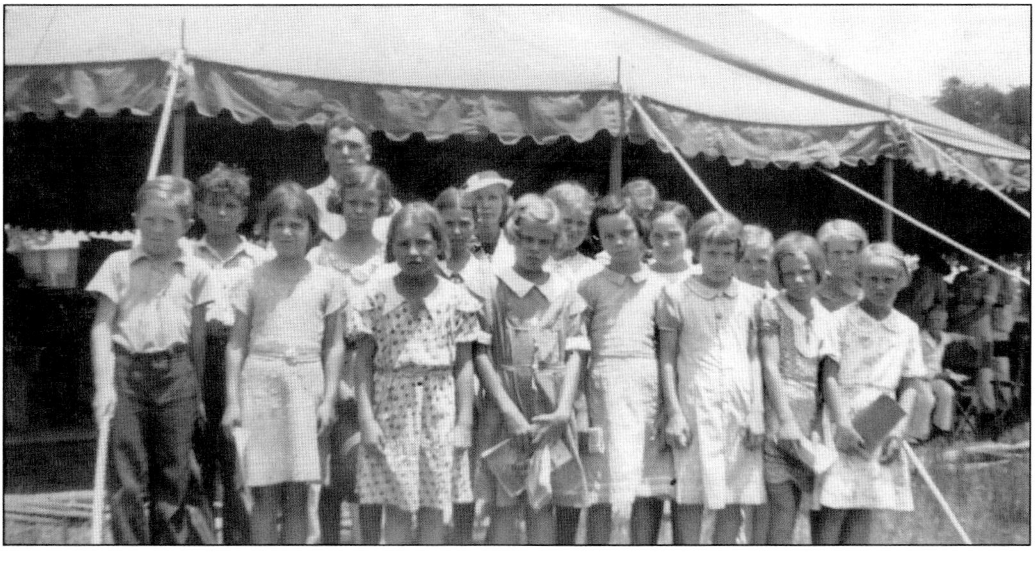

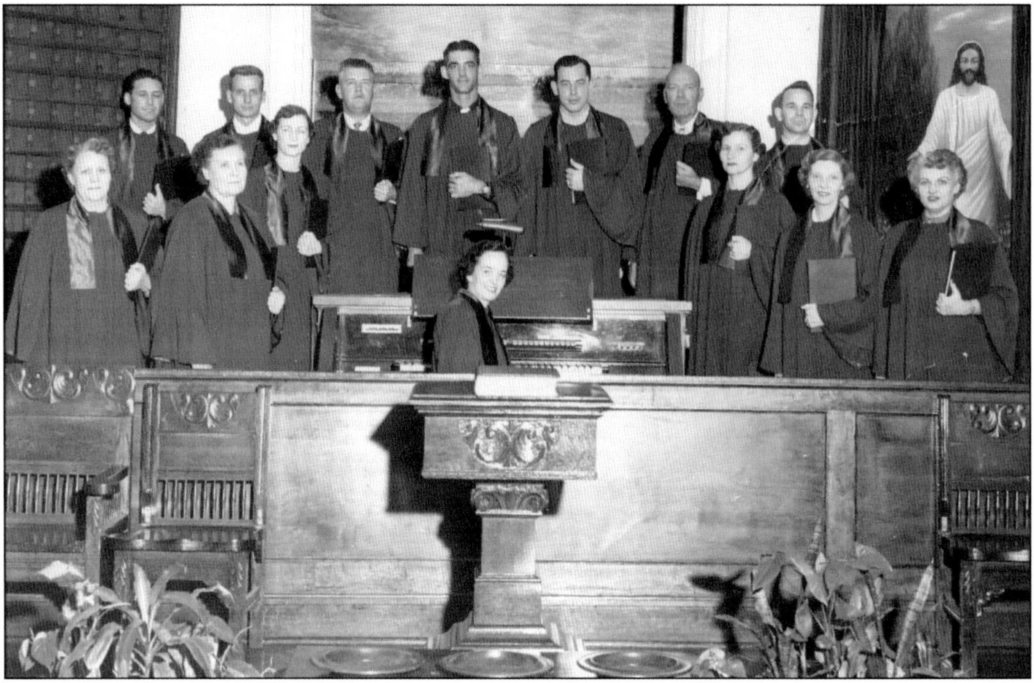

Dorcas Rusher, mother of Albert H. Rusher, (seated) smiles for the photographer in the choir loft of the First Baptist Church of Brinkley. She was devoted to the affairs of her church and directed the church choir for 50 years. (Courtesy of Albert H. Rusher.)

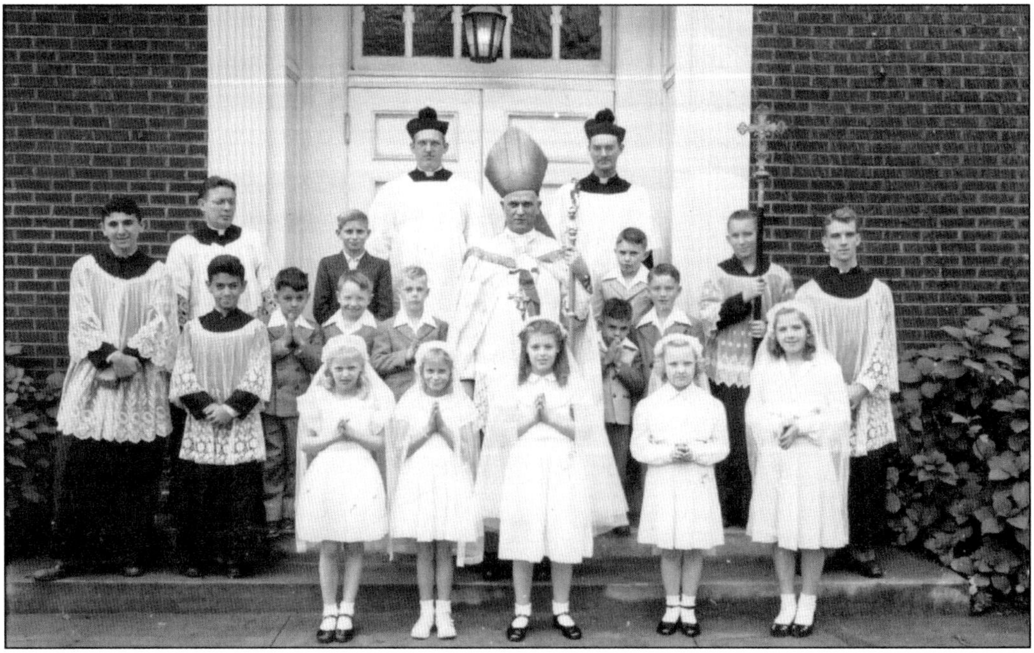

A confirmation class stands in front of St. John's Catholic Church in Brinkley in this undated photograph. Among those pictured are, from left to right, (first row) Helen Cooper, Mary Ann Wiesle, Mary Edna Cooper, Ann Warblow, and Jane Donovan; (second row) Charles B. Malham, Ronald Shaban, Donnie Shaban, Cary Warblow, and Jimmie Cooper.

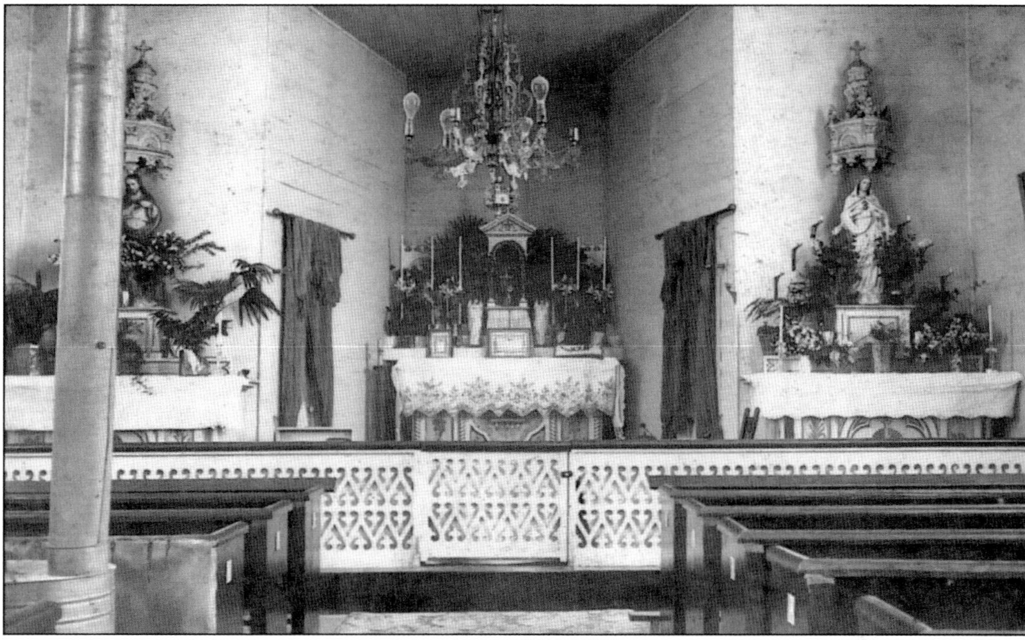

Catholics living in the Monroe County area were attended by missionary priests prior to 1870. Bishop Fitzgerald appointed Rev. D. A. Quinn to attend the spiritual needs of the Catholics living in eastern Arkansas in 1869. During his missionary travels, he discovered a dozen Catholic families living in Brinkley and decided to construct a church, which was completed in 1875. Through the years, the interior, as well as the exterior, has been extensively remodeled. The church still stands, and Mass is held there regularly. These undated photographs are of the sanctuary of St. John's Catholic Church in Brinkley. (Both courtesy of Billye Frein.)

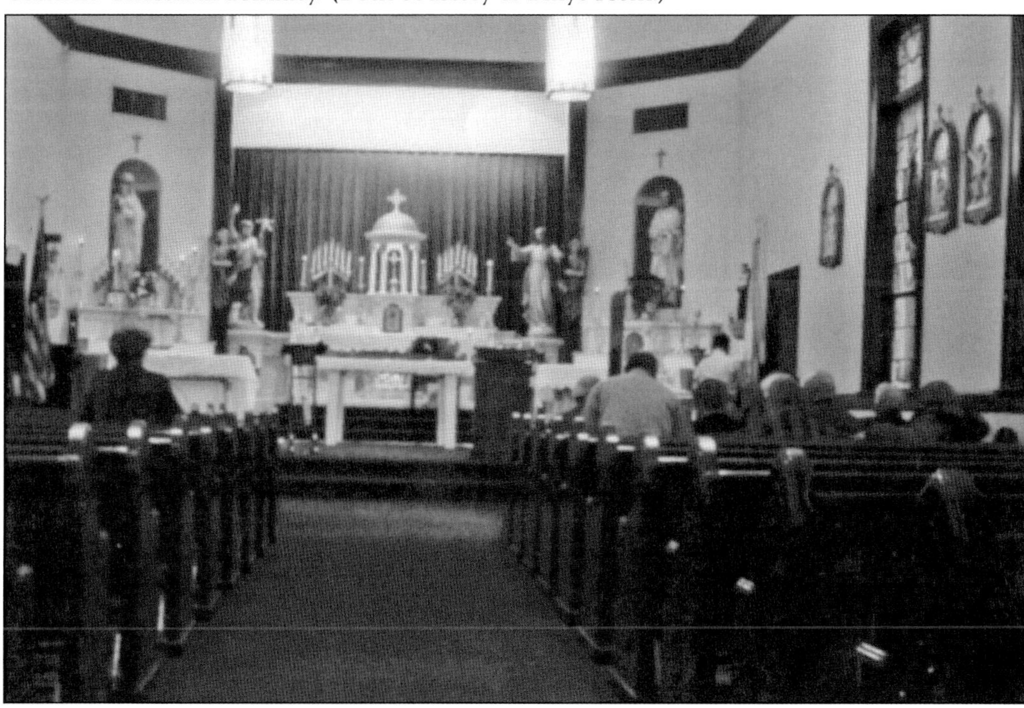

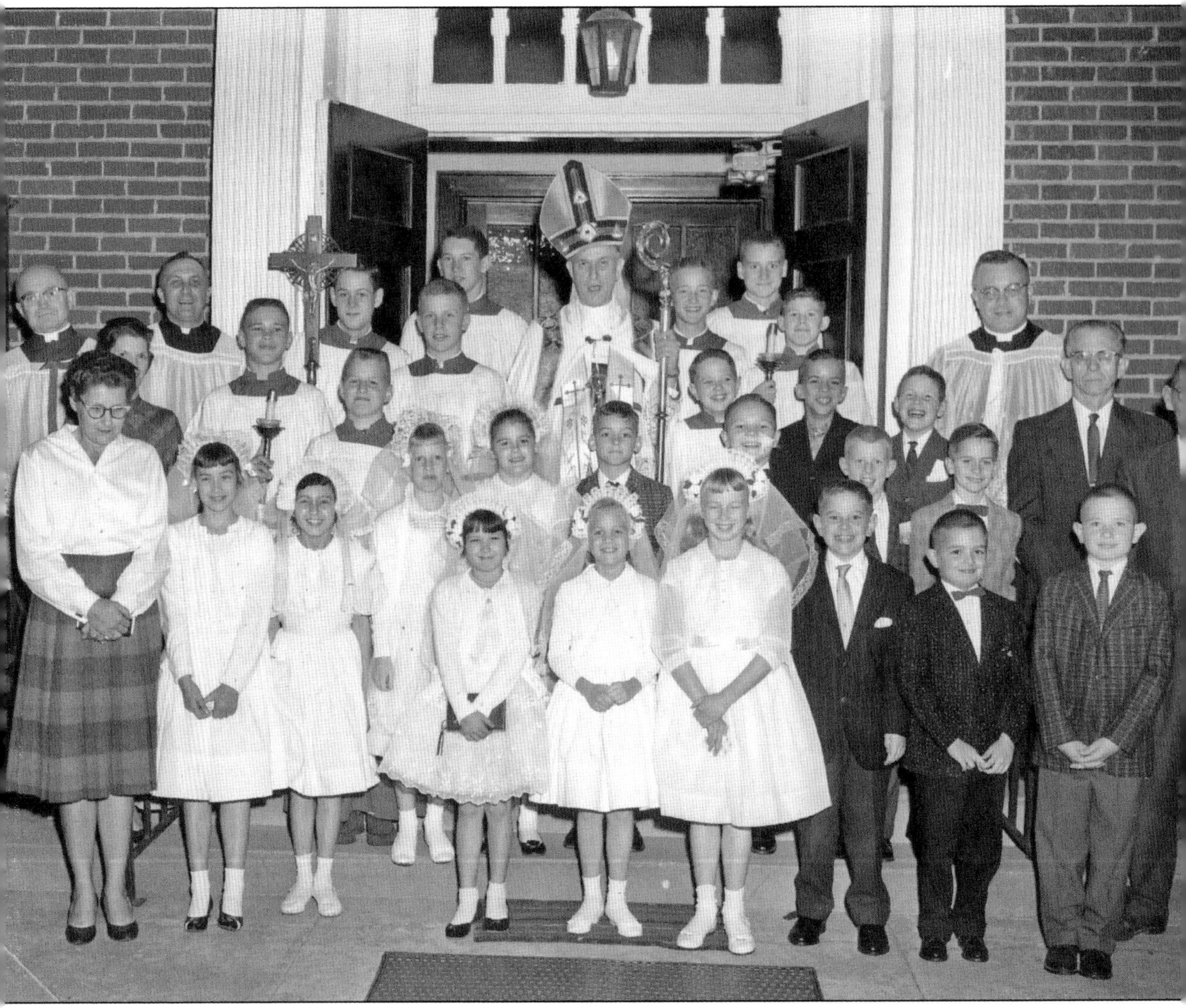

The Reverend Albert Fletcher, bishop of the Little Rock Diocese, administered the Sacrament of Confirmation on November 3, 1960. Pictured from left to right are (first row) Mrs. Hugh (Arta Lee) Webb, Jane Kenkel, Patricia Terrice, Felecia Sands, Becky Weis, Shirley Ann Donovan, Mike Farrell, Jimmy Mirabella, and Steve Smith; (second row) Genny Farrell, Vicki Bowles, William ?, Ronald Gilbrech, Bobby Cooper, Bruce Futrell, Garrett Warblow, and Hugh Webb; (third row) Mrs. Paul Kenkel, Jerry Smith, Ralph Clifton, Bill Cooper, Charles Farrell, Joe Clifton, and Jim Pat Farrell; (fourth row) Msgr. Edwin Hemmen, Rev. J. E. Barnes, Jodie Farrell, Danny Plafcan, Rev. Albert Fletcher, Lewis Blessing, Charles Holmun Jr., Fred Farrell, and Rev. William ?. (Courtesy of Felecia Sands.)

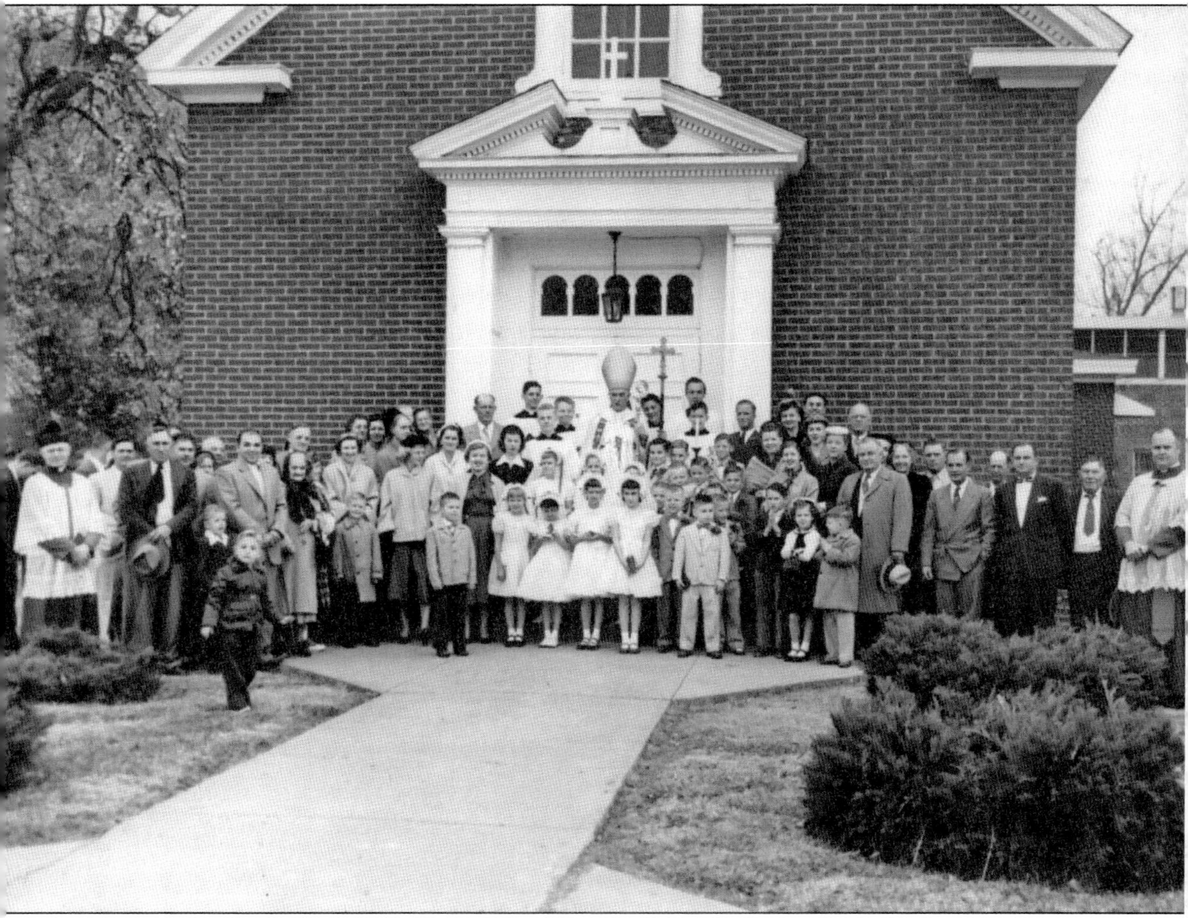

This photograph was taken on November 28, 1954, after the administration of the Sacrament of Confirmation to a class of 19 children and 3 adults. Among those pictured are the confirmation class, which included Hal Smith, Paul Farrell Jr., Lewis Blessing, Newton Kershaw, Michael Deuerling, Anthony Kenkel, Charles Holmun, Billy Cooper, Joseph Farrell, Patricia Clifton, Martha Blessing, Shelia Swearengin, Florence Sands, Virginia Kordsmeier, Susan Farrell, William Ehney, Mrs. Anthony (Billye) Frein, and Betty Plafcan. (Courtesy of Felecia Sands.)

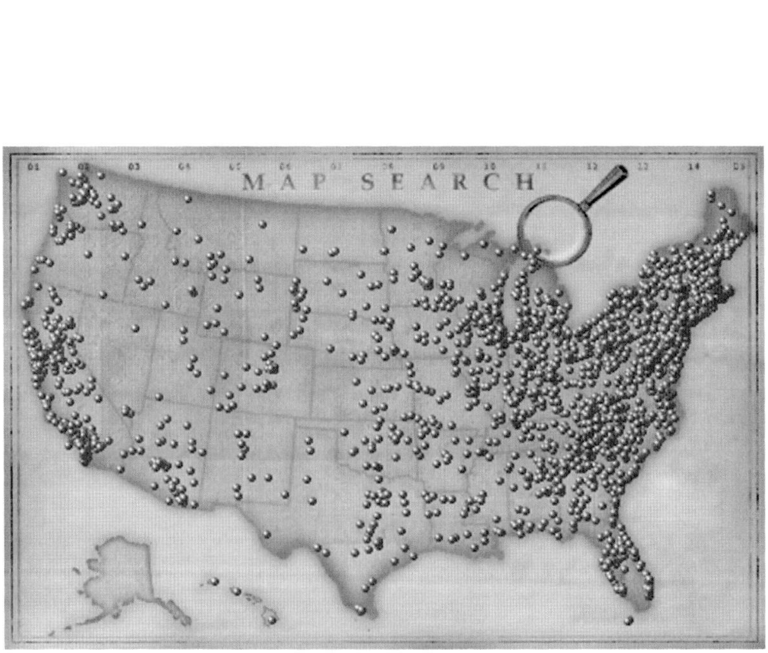
MAP SEARCH